D1696561

Small & Luxury Hotels *as a home*

First Published in Japan, July 1993

Copyright © 1993 Process Architecture Co., Ltd.
All right reserved. No part of the contents of this book may be reproduced by any means without the written permission of the publisher.

Publisher	Murotani Bunji
Author	Jiro Akiyama
Photographer	Shigeru Oki
Producer	Ortega Associates
Editorial Direction	Teruhisa Koida
Designer	Miki Nakamura
Editorial Management	Miwako Ito, Yumiko Fujimaki, Chiho Minamiguchi, Midori Mochizuki
Drawing	Arari Kashiwamura
Coordinators	Chris A. Carlson, Tomoko Yasuda
Translator	Lou Tingey
Special thanks	Tourism Australia
	New Zealand Tourism Board
	Tourism Development Corporation of Malaysia
	Coila Eade (Hana)

Process Architecture Co. Ltd.
1-47-2-418 Sasazuka Shibuya-ku, Tokyo 151 Japan
Phone 81-3-3468-0131 Fax 81-3-3468-0133

Separations	Toppan Printing Co., (S) Pte., Ltd.
Printed by	Isozaki Printing Co., Ltd. Tokyo

ISBN 4-89331-716-4

1993年7月15日第1版第1刷発行

発行人	室谷文治
編著	秋山寿郎
写真	大木　茂
プロデュース	オルテガアソシエイツ
企画構成	小井田光久
レイアウト	中村美樹
編集監理	伊藤美和子, 藤巻由美子, 南口千穂, 望月みどり
作図	柏村安良理
コーディネート	クリス・カールソン, 安田智子
翻訳	ルー・ティンギー
写植	協和クリエイト, ユニット, 大西写植
協力	オーストラリア政府観光局
	ニュージーランド政府観光局
	マレーシア観光開発公社
	コイラ・エアデ（ハナ）
発行所	株式会社プロセスアーキテクチュア
	東京都渋谷区笹塚1-47-2-418 〒151
	Tel 03-3468-0131 Fax 03-3468-0133
振替	東京 6-57446
製版	TOPPAN PRINTING CO., (S)PTE., LTD.
印刷	磯崎印刷株式会社

禁無断掲載

Small & Luxury Hotels *as a home*

Pacific Rim

Jiro Akiyama

珠玉のホテル
［環太平洋］編
秋山 寿郎

| Process Architecture |

- Tawaraya Inn
- Hotel Bela Vista

Pacific Ocean

- Carcosa Seri Negara
- The Duxton
- Amandari
- Tandjung Sari
- Amankila
- The Oberio Bali
- Sebel Town House
- Mount Lofty House
- Huka Lodge

- The Alexis
- Campton Place Hotel
- Post Ranch Inn
- San Ysidro Ranch
- Checkers Hotel Kempinski
- Hotel Hana Maui

Equator

- The Wakaya Club

CONTENTS

Introduction / Jiro Akiyama 8

US West Coast + Hawaii
Hotel Hana Maui / Maui, Hawaii 12
Checkers Hotel Kempinski / Los Angeles 26
San Ysidro Ranch / Santa Barbara 34
Campton Place Hotel / San Francisco 46
Post Ranch Inn / Big Sur 54
The Alexis / Seattle 66

Special Interview with Designers 74
Pamela Babey + David Moulton / San Francisco

Asia
Tawaraya Inn / Kyoto 84
Hotel Bela Vista / Macau 98
The Duxton / Singapore 110
Carcosa Seri Negara / Kuala Lumpur 116

Bali
Amandari / Ubud 130
Tandjung Sari / Sanur 142
Amankila / Manggis 150
The Oberoi Bali / Legian Beach 156

Oceania
Mount Lofty House / Adelaide 168
Sebel Town House / Sydney 178
Huka Lodge / Taupo, NZ 186
The Wakaya Club / Fiji 200

Information 214
Acknowledgments 232

目次

まえがき／秋山寿郎 …………………………………… 8

米国西海岸＋ハワイ
ホテル・ハナ・マウイ／マウイ島 ……………………… 12
チェッカーズ・ホテル・ケンピンスキー／ロサンゼルス … 26
サン・イシドロ・ランチ／サンタバーバラ …………… 34
キャンプトン・プレイス・ホテル／サンフランシスコ … 46
ポスト・ランチ・イン／ビッグ・サー ………………… 54
ジ・アレクシス／シアトル ……………………………… 66
スペシャル・インタビュー〈インテリア・デザイナー〉 … 74
パメラ・バビー＋デイビッド・モールトン／サンフランシスコ

アジア
俵屋旅館／京都 ………………………………………… 84
ホテル・ベラ・ヴィスタ／マカオ ……………………… 98
ザ・ダクストン／シンガポール ………………………… 110
カルコーサ・セリ・ネガラ／クアラルンプール ……… 116

バリ
アマンダリ／ウブドゥ ………………………………… 130
タンジュン・サリ／サヌール ………………………… 142
アマンキラ／マンギス ………………………………… 150
ジ・オベロイ・バリ／レギャン・ビーチ ……………… 156

オセアニア
マウント・ロフティー・ハウス／アデレード ………… 168
シーベル・タウン・ハウス／シドニー ………………… 178
フカ・ロッジ／ニュージーランド ……………………… 186
ザ・ワカヤ・クラブ／フィジー ………………………… 200

巻末資料 ………………………………………………… 214
あとがき ………………………………………………… 232

Introduction
Heaven in a Jar

Nowadays, in an age when people move freely around the world, cities are escalating towards uniformity and homogeneity. In other words, similar kinds of towns are springing up in every part of the globe and a loss of originality for the sake of convenience is happening again and again. A tendency for the people, who live in these urban settlements, to adapt their lives and customs accordingly is also arising and I feel that there is a danger that a shadow is being cast on culture itself. This kind of trend is probably inevitable, if considered from the point of view of internationalization of types, but it must be said that a great many things are obviously lost in the process.

The world environment, political and economic problems are undoubtedly connected and no effective action can be taken, if they are considered only within the society, which forms a nation, city or area, as they were before. People are at last beginning to act on a global scale, However, that does not mean that our ways of thinking and style of behavior are the same. We must follow the road that will lead to the coexistence of mutual cultures with an open mind, and be able to understand each other's different viewpoints.

When people come across homogeneity, they can look at themselves by observing other people's various different sense of values and are thus released from their own limitations by putting themselves in a homogeneous space, not normally found in every day life. Races in towns and cities around the world can obtain mutual stimulation by listening to other people's views. Encounters awake new excitement in people and it is here that a 'culture of encounter' is born.

I am personally very interested in hotels. That is to say, I enjoy staying in various kinds of hostelries especially those which have a strong flavor of the local atmosphere. In professional terms, too, hotels are also interesting from the architectural point of view because so many affairs are concentrated in one place. Work, life, and encounters are completely transposed into normal business there. It can be said that hotels are in some respects exactly like a city. However, uniformity is advancing into the hotel trade, too, and I am really concerned about the declining numbers of places where there is a sense of local originality.

I think there will probably be a much greater tendency to give serious consideration to the family and to individuals in the 21st century. Marketing with a large scale management will become less common than it has been up until now at some point in the future, and it is inevitable that an exact equivalent will be sought for individually run hotels.

In thinking about all this, I was reminded of a Chinese tale called 'Heaven in a Jar', which appears in *Gokanjo*, a historical record of the Later Han Period (A.D. 25-220). A pharmacist used to disappear into a jar, which hung in his shop, when he had finished his work for the day. The headman of the village, having seen this happen, asked if he might be allowed to enter, too. Having climbed into the pot together, they apparently found themselves in a completely different world full of wonderful seascapes and mountains, and a paradise of palaces and towers.

In Japan, attempts to create a "world apart" were different. It seems that the idea of introducing undulating landscapes to the city spread among exponents of the tea ceremony in the Muromachi Period. The sense of silence which was introduced into the urban clamor of the times was most unusual. The rustic, almost primitive *sukiya* building they constructed were like 'mountain retreats', hidden amongst the everyday urbanity of the main settlements. They were the original form of *hojo no ma*, or high priest quarters which still exist today. These were places where guests were received, tea was served and flower arrangements could be admired, and where a heterogeneous culture could sometimes be encountered.

During my recent travels, I found several hotels that had a feeling of self-respect about them. These were the small and luxury hotels, where the culture of the area and originality of both facilities and service were almost tangible. These places are on a human scale so consequently it is possible to get a real feeling of the richness of the community and their indigenous culture by encounters with really hospitable people.

Furthermore, great emphasis is being put on presentation at these hotels with a view to creating a welcome, homely environment, where guests can relax and, in essence, do nothing. What is extremely interesting to note is the fact that members of staff are building a far more secure relationship with their guests at such establishments, and are appealing to them in small ways, which ought perhaps to be a handicap. There are many different methods being deployed, but things such as local originality, unlimited comfort and personal service are common. Moreover, if the individuality of the hotel or the philosophy of its manager is not reflected there, then it will never become a small and luxury hotel. That is truly the thing that matters most.

It may perhaps have been more normal to start with Europe, the pioneer in this domain, but I rather daringly decided to look to the East and West nearer home in Asia and beyond, exploring the wide cultural sphere surrounding the Pacific. As the Mongoloid race spread throughout the Pacific area, it was probably only a matter of interpreting the influence of the special features of a specific area and moulding the various different cultures to be found in the Pacific area which makes up two thirds of the whole world.

This publication is a prejudiced selection of individuality and disparity, but if the selection has any disposition at all, then it must be due to my own personalized 'Heaven in a Jar'.

Jiro Akiyama

『壺中の天』

人の移動が地球規模で行なわれている昨今、世界の都市は、文字通り「点」となって存在し、均一化、もしくは均質化に拍車をかけている。すなわち、世界各地で同じような街が創生され、利便性と引き換えに、オリジナリティの喪失が繰り返されている。それにともない、そこに住む人々の生活や習慣にも同化する傾向が見られ、文化にまでその影を落とすようになってきていることに対して危機感を感じる。こういった傾向は、ある種の国際化にとってみれば、致し方ないことなのかも知れないが、当然のことながら、失うものも大きいといわねばならない。

確かに、世界の環境問題や政治・経済問題は相互に関連し合い、かつてのように国家や都市、地域といった完結した社会の中だけで考え、行動することはできない。人々は地球規模で考え、行動するようになってきている。しかしそれは、思考法や行動様式が同じであることを意味してはいない。真の国際化とは、互いの違いを認め合い、広い心で互いの文化を共存させる道を追求することだ。

異質なものと出会い、日常にはない異質な時空に身を置くことにより、人は自らの限定から解き放たれ、多様な価値観の中で相手を見、自分を見ることができる。世界の都市や街、民族もまた、それぞれが認め合い、互いに刺激を得ることができる。出会いは、人と環境に新しい興奮を呼び起こし、そこに「出会いの文化」が生まれる。

私は、一個人として「ホテル」に興味を持っている。というよりも、行く先々で色々なホテルに泊まることが好きなのだ。特にその土地の雰囲気を具に感じられるところが…。

一方、建築家という職業から見ても、「ホテル」は面白い。そこには、たくさんの事柄が凝縮されているからだ。仕事、生活、そして出会いなど、「普段の営み」がそっくりその中に置き換えられている。「街」そのものともいえる。ただここでも均一化は進み、その土地のオリジナリティを感じられるところが、少なくなってきているのが気掛かりだ。

21世紀には、「個人」もしくは「家庭」をより重視する傾向が強まるであろう。ホテルにおいても、今までのような、大きな括りでのマーケティングは早晩通用しなくなり、個々に対し、きめ細かな対応が求められるようになることは必至だ。

『壺中の天』とは、後漢書にみえる故事である。壺公という薬売りは、仕事を終えるといつも、店頭に掛けてある壺の中に姿を消した。それを見た市場役人の費長房は、ある日壺公に頼んで一緒に壺の中に入る。するとそこは、宮殿楼閣をなし、山海の珍味に溢れた別世界であったという。

一方、日本では室町時代に、数寄者の間に山里の景趣を、市中に取り込む様式が広まったという。雑踏の中に取り込まれた静寂、すなわち非日常。都の隠れ家ともいうべき『市中の山居』である。これが現在に受け継がれた「方丈の間」、あるいは「見立て」の原形ともなっている。そこは、主が客をもてなす場であり、茶や花のサロンであり、時に異質な文化が出会う場所であった。

近年旅を続ける中で、「気概」を感じさせてくれるホテルがいくつかあった。地域の文化やその「しつらい」、「もてなし」のオリジナリティを肌で感じることのできる、「スモール＆ラグジュアリー」タイプである。

ここでは、ヒューマンスケールであるがゆえに、もてなしの心を介した人と人との出会い、地域文化とコミュニティの豊かさを実感できる。また、基本的には「何もしない」ことや、自分の家のような「居心地の良さ」に的を絞って、密度の高いプレゼンテーションを行なっている。ハンディキャップである筈の、小さいことを逆に利用して顧客にアピールし、より強固な関係を築いていることは、とても興味深い。その展開方法はさまざまだが、「地域のオリジナリティ」、「快適さの限りない追求」、「パーソナル・サービス」などが共通している。その上で、ホテルの個性というか、経営者自身の「哲学」がそこに反映されていなければ、「スモール＆ラグジュアリー」は成り立たない。実は、それがここでの最も重要な『琴線』なのだ。

こういった領域では先駆的な欧州を、まず始めに取り上げることが普通かも知れない。しかし敢えて私は、自らの足元であるアジアから、環太平洋という広大な文化圏を巡り、そこにある東洋と西洋を見ることにした。地球上の3分の2を占める環太平洋地域では、モンゴロイドが太平洋を取り囲む形で、さまざまな文化を創り上げており、その地域独特の影響を読み取っていただけるのではないかと思う。個性や差異にこだわった選定であるが、ある種の性向があるとすれば、私の中の『壺中の天』がそうさせたようである。

秋山　寿郎

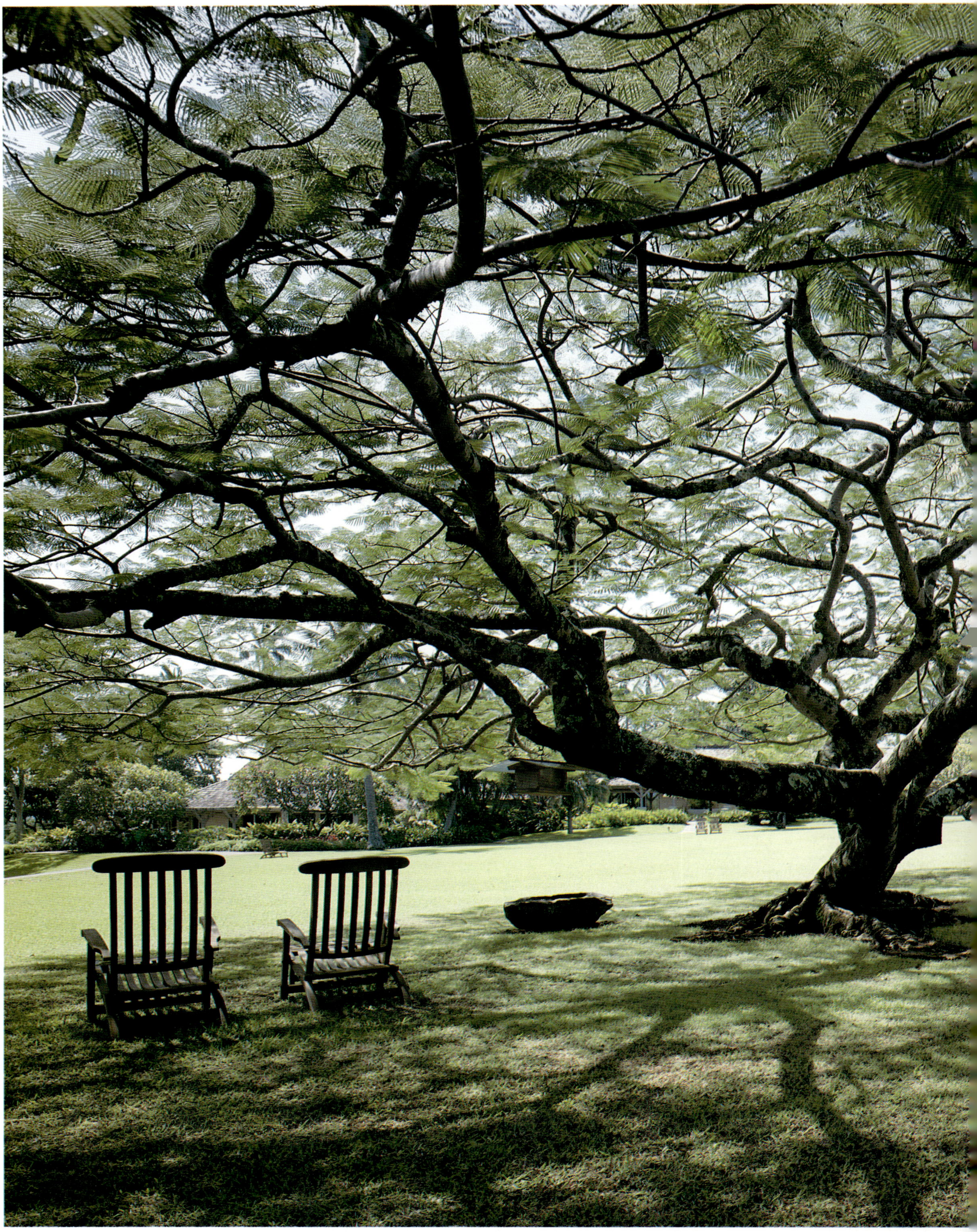

US West Coast & Hawaii

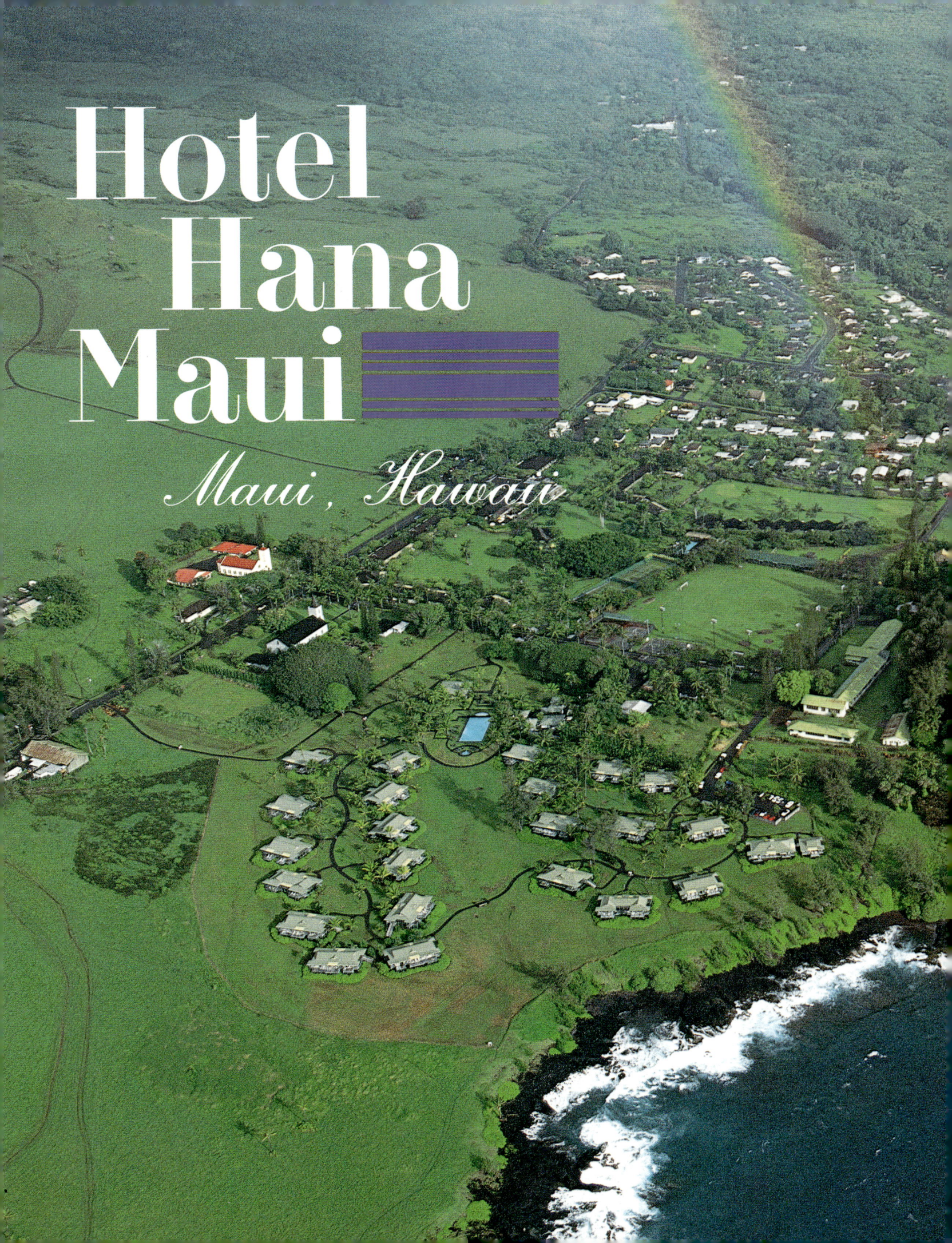

Hotel Hana Maui

Maui, Hawaii

ホテル・ハナ・マウイ／マウイ島（ハワイ）

Page 16 <From top to bottom> Terrace of Sea Ranch Cottages, Riding on the beach is enjoyed by guests, Hamoa Private Beach, Sea Ranch Cottage Pool
Page 17 Breakfast at The Dining Room

P.16　上から　海岸沿いの乗馬風景、プライベート・ビーチのハモア・ビーチ、シーランチ・コテージのプール
P.17　レストラン「ザ・ダイニング・ルーム」のテラスでの朝食

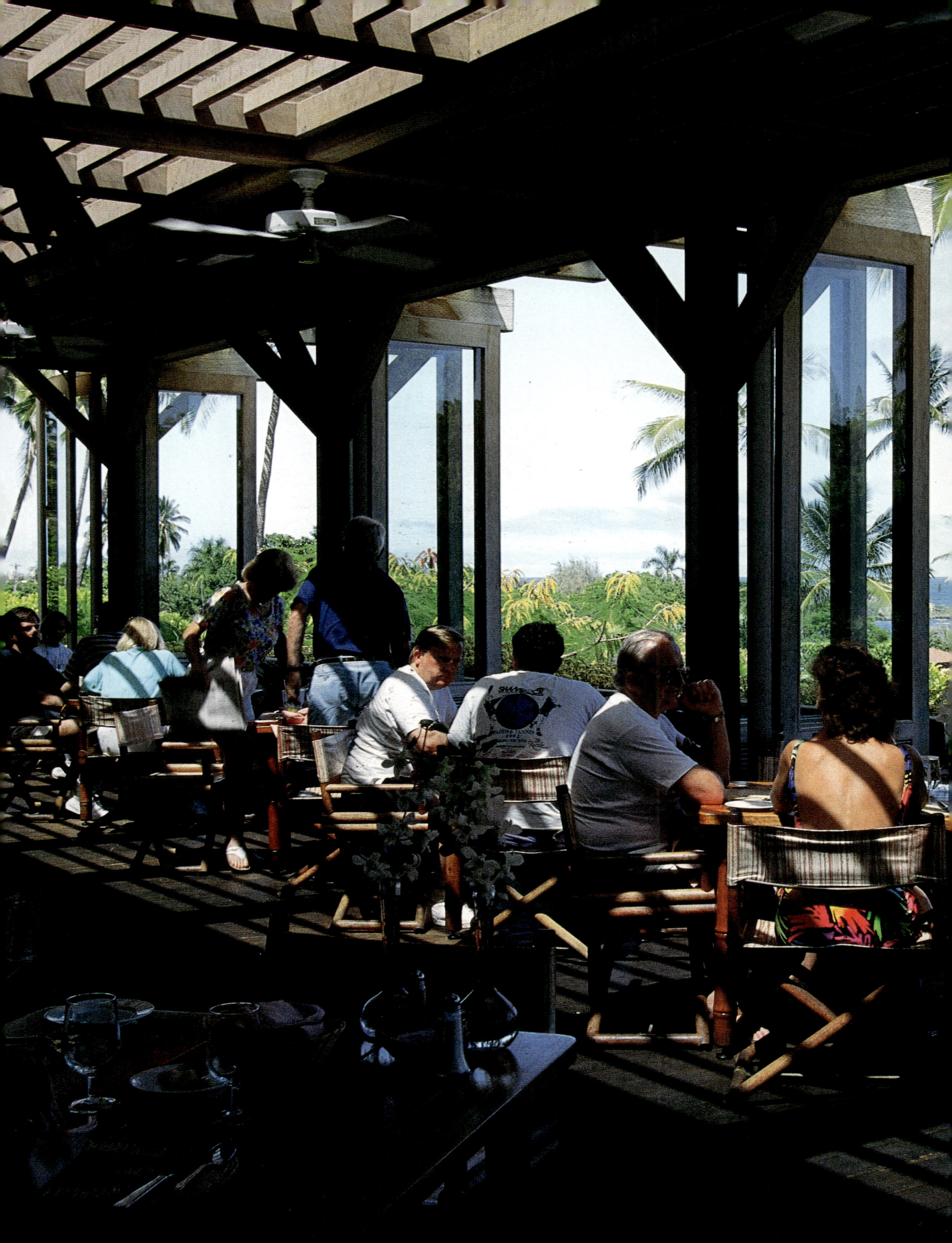

Page 18 <Top> Lobby lounge, <Bottom> Library, which boasts a first edition of Captain Cook's logbook
Page 19 Entrance hall

Page 20 <Top> Interior of a Sea Ranch Cottages, Page 21 <Top> Bathroom, <Bottom> Interior of Waikaloa Suite

P.18 上 ロビー・ラウンジ、下 クック船長の航海誌の初版本などがあるライブラリー
P.19 エントランス・ホール

P.20 上 「シーランチ・コテージ」のインテリア
P.21 上 同バスルーム、下 「ワイカロア・スイート」のインテリア

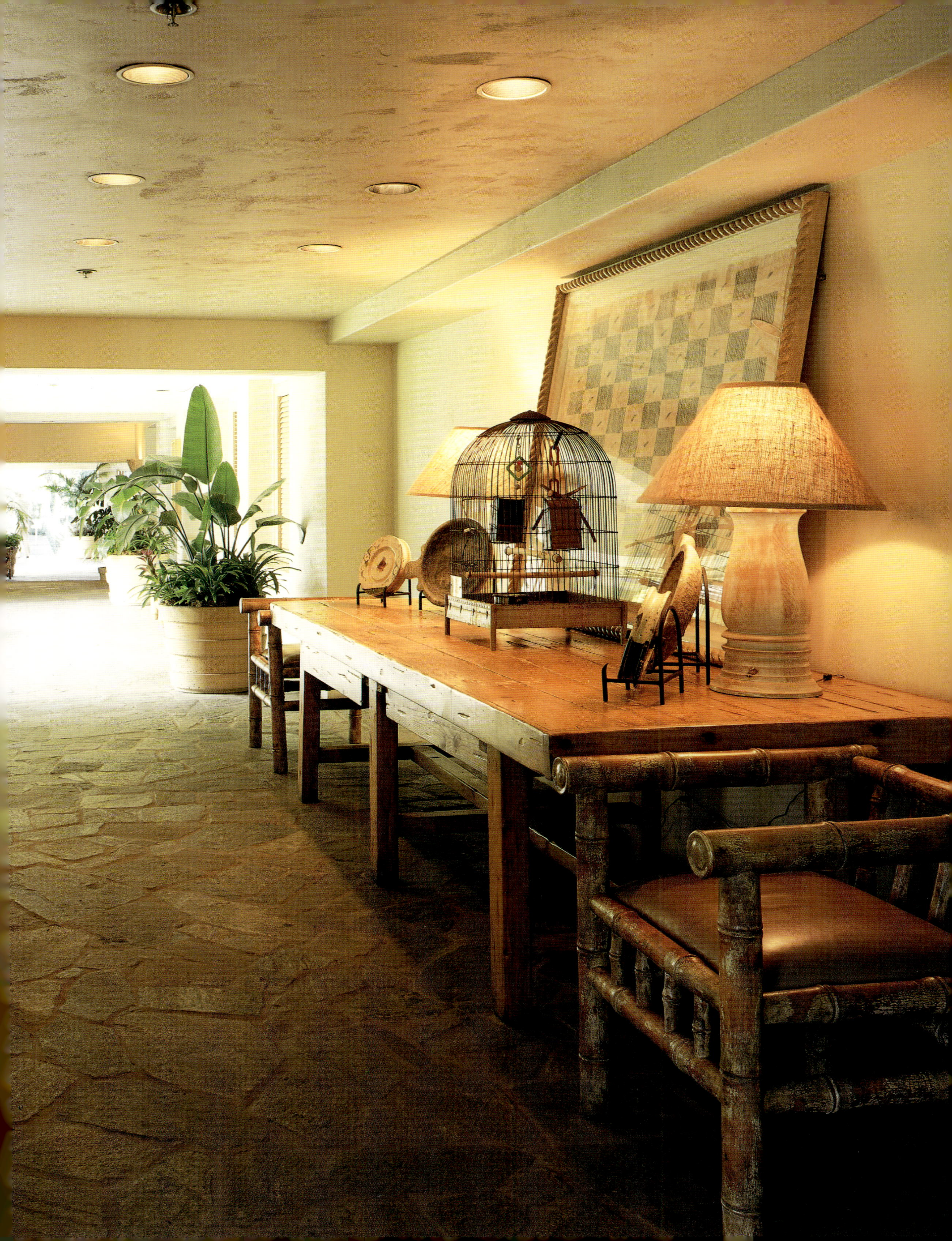

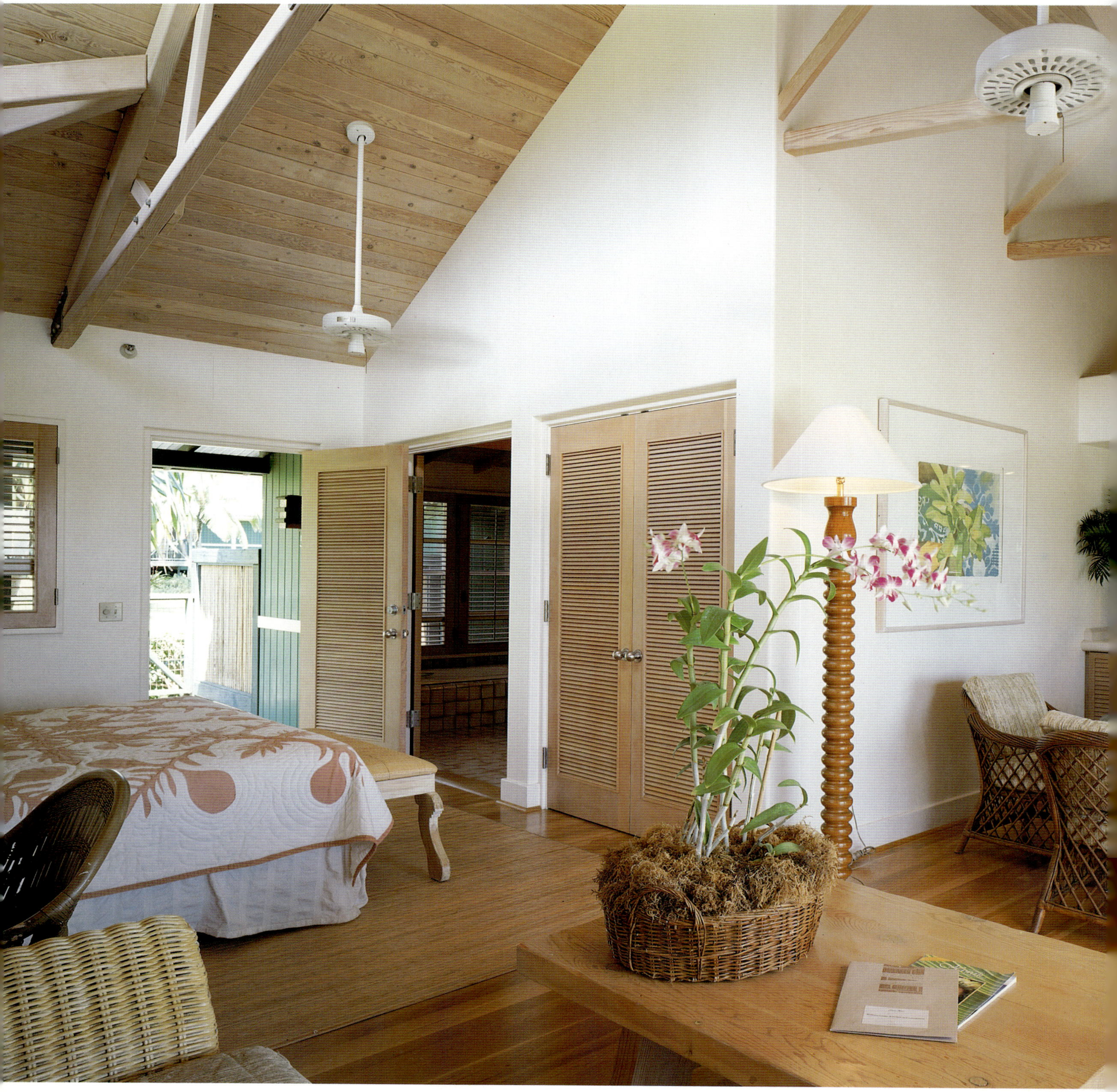

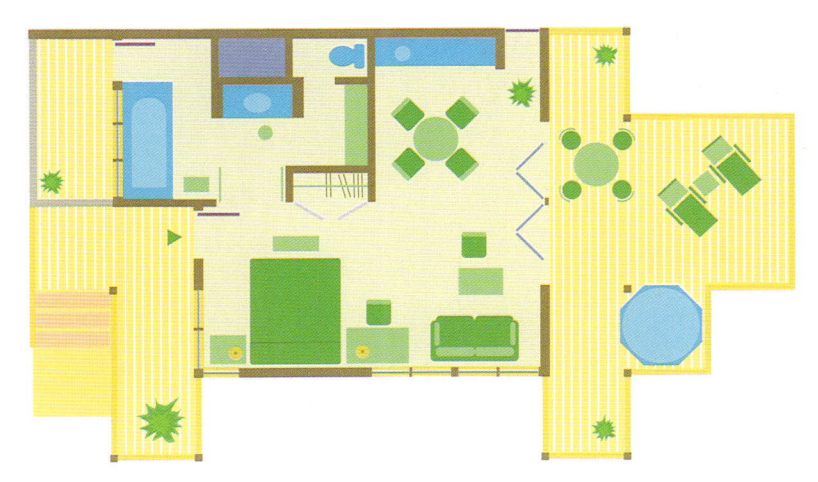

Sea Ranch Cottage

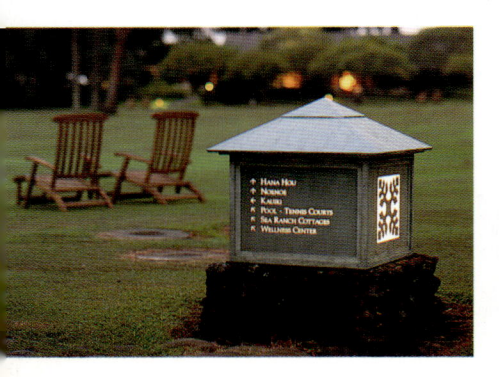

Page 22 <Top left> Sign, <Top right> Waitress, <Center> Interior of restaurant with skylight, <Bottom> Dinner on Hamoa Beach
Page 23 View of sea from terrace of Sea Ranch Cottages

P. 22 左上 案内サイン、右上 ウエイトレス、中 トップライトのあるレストラン内部、下 ハモア・ビーチでの「ルアウ」ディナー
P. 23 「シーランチ・コテージ」のテラスから海を見る

Hotel Hana Maui

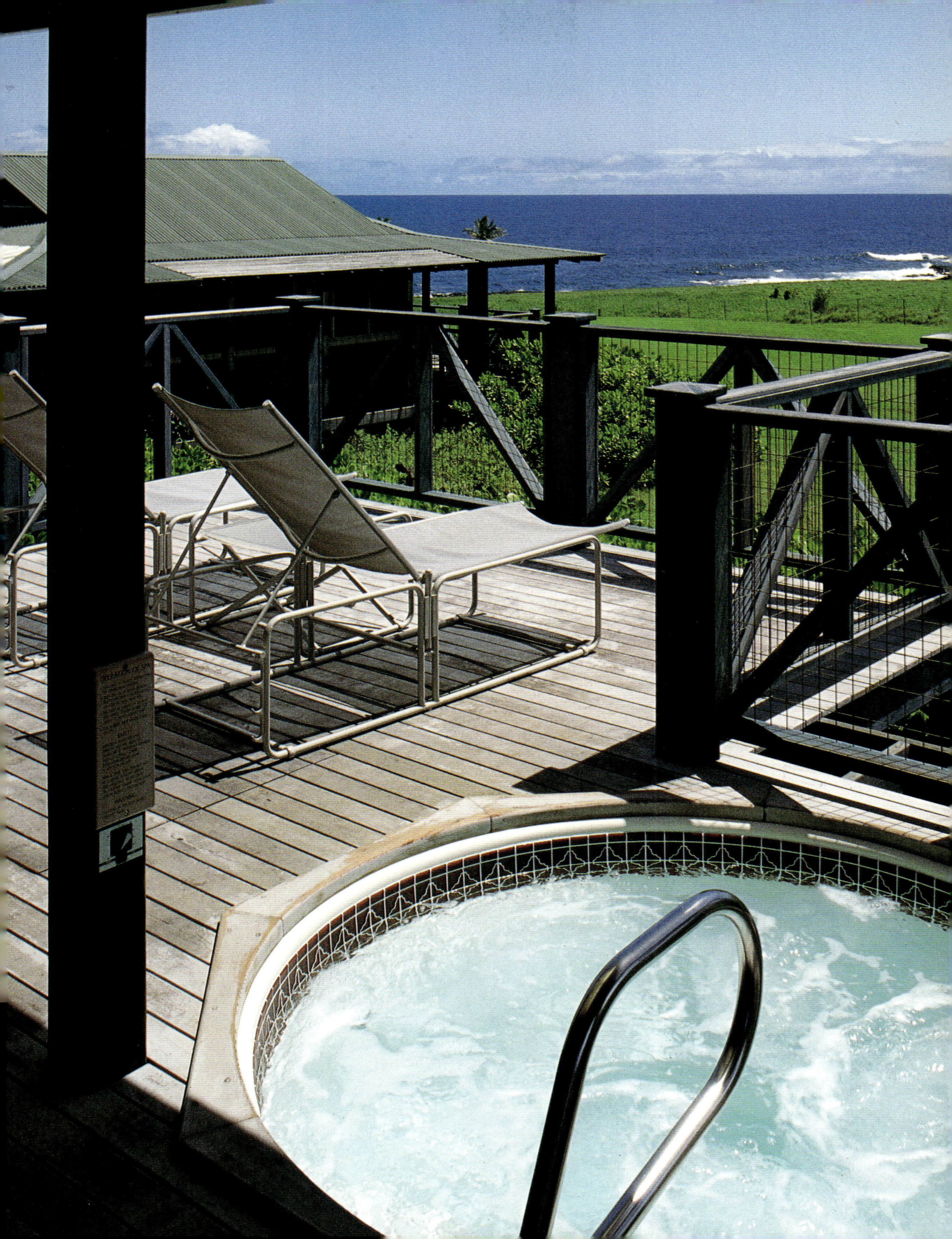

Interview

Hotel Hana Maui
General Manager: Mr. Frederik J. Orr
ホテル・ハナ・マウイ
総支配人　フレデリック・J・オア

What are the characteristics of your hotel?
First, this hotel is made unique by having the highest ratio of Hawaiian ancestry staff in the State of Hawaii. At least 80% of the people who work here grew up in the area. People who visit Hawaii want to meet and have an interchange with Hawaiian people. Second, what ties in with that is that almost everyone on the staff is related by marriage or blood; so there is a family feeling. There is a sence of being welcome to an estate with guest accommodations, the people here treat guests as though they are visitors to their own home. There is the true "sence of aloha". Also, no other hotel has the low density; we're spread out over 66 acres. There are finally appointed and large rooms; they range from 75–120 square meter (800–1,300 sqf).

What is the ratio of your guests, in state, out of state and out of country? What is the staying normal pattern?
60% of our guests probably come from South California; of the remainder, 35% come from the Midwest/ East Coast U.S. and 5% international. 20% are repeat guests, which can get as high as 60% like during Christmas time. The average length of stay is four nights. Recently, there have been more German, Italian and Japanese visitors.

What are the characteristics of your guests?
Guests here tend to be sophisticated, well traveled, discerning and usually affluent. They know they are coming to Hana Maui for a relaxed, serene and exclusive environment. The guests expect a high level of service and are willing to pay for it; they tend to be knowledgeable about out food and wine. They are friendly; they come looking for an interchange with the employees and the Hana community which grew up around the hotel.

Are there special characteristics of the local area which add to the business of the hotel?
The hotel has taken advantage of the natural surroundings; I like to think that we have a commune with nature; the gardens on the grounds, the mountains, the beach, the rain and the sunshine. This theme is carried out with the Wellness Center, the Wellness menu and the activities at the hotel.

What sorts of things are you focusing your attentions to everyday?
I focus my attention on personal contact with the guests experience, such as food and beverage, things that have a high priority and high visibility with the guests. There is more guest contact than at a 1,200 room hotel. As part of guest contact, my wife and I host a cocktail party at the Plantation House on Thursday nights.

With a limited number of guest rooms, how do you continue the success of the hotel?
Service standards, the quality of the food, and standards of materials; we need to make sure we make no compromises in these areas. Continue to hire local people. Also, the Sheraton

reservation system has helped with overseas marketing.

What are some of the more important aspects of a small & luxury hotel?

Personal contact with the guests and anticipating guest needs. We don't like to say "no"–we like the guests to have the freedom to do what they want and be flexible. If you need something, ask us and we'll try to get it.

What do you think about small & luxury hotels in the future?

I'm very encouraged about the future of Hana Maui; the mega–resorts in the islands have an immediate blush in the market, but their allure wears thin after a while. The Hana Maui represents the last of the truly Hawaiian experiences; this experience is why people want to come to Hawaii.

What were some of the specially surprising and unexpected things you came upon from your first day at the hotel?

I was surprised at the serenity and tranquility which overpower you; this astounded me. Go to the Sea Ranch cottages, they look like a plantation camp. This is the first hotel I've managed which has no carpet or drapes. Also, the friendliness of the people.

What are the future plans for the hotel?

We are going to develop a golf course that is not visible from the road. Other than this, there are no plans for new developments. Hana Maui is customer driven; and we pride ourselves on anticipating and responding to guest needs. The only changes we will make are those our guests want us to make.

If you were to start hotel of your own, were would you do it and what type of the hotel would it be?

I'm from Hawaii and zoning prohibits building another hotel in Hana, I would build a small type hotel like this in Hawaii; perhaps in Hanalei, Kauai Island.

──このホテルの特徴を教えて下さい。

まず最大の特徴は、ホテルの従業員に地元出身の正真正銘のハワイ人が数多くいることです。少なくとも従業員の80％はこの地域の出身です。ハワイを訪れる人たちは誰でも、ハワイ育ちの人々と交流したいと考えています。

　2番目は、彼らのほとんどすべてが何らかの血縁関係にあることからくる、家族のような親しさがあるということです。ここを訪れるお客様は誰でも、まるで我が家に迎えられたゲストのような歓待を受けます。これこそ、本当の「アロハの精神」です。

　もうひとつ大きな特徴は、客室が約26haという広大な敷地に低い密度で点在していることです。客室規模は73〜120㎡で、広くゆったりしています。

──ゲストの構成（どこから：州内、米国内、海外）と標準的な滞在パターンを教えて下さい。

お客様の60％は、南カリフォルニアからの方たちです。残る40％のうち、35％はカリフォルニア以外のアメリカ国内からで、5％が海外からの方たちです。

　お客様の20％はリピーターの方たちで、この数字は特にクリスマス時期には60％まで上がります。標準的な滞在パターンは4泊です。最近はドイツ人、イタリア人、そして日本人のお客様が増えています。

──ゲストの客層はどういう感じですか？

お客様の多くは、洗練され、旅慣れた裕福な方たちです。皆さん落ち着いた素晴らしい自然環境の中で、リラックスするためにハナ・マウイに来られるのです。お客様はレベルの高いサービスを求め、それに対しては充分にその代償を支払っていただいております。地元の食べ物に対しての知識も豊富です。また、ここを訪れる方たちは、好んで従業員や周辺住民と親しく交流します。

──周辺地域の特徴で、ホテルの運営上特に役立っていることは何ですか？

周辺の素晴らしい自然環境が最大の特徴です。私は常々、自然との共存ということに主眼をおいています。庭園、山や海、雨や太陽などです。このテーマは、ホテルのウェルネスセンターで、豊富なメニューや活動を通してさまざまに実施されます。

──毎日、どんな点に注意して運営されていますか？

何よりもまずお客様との細かい『ふれあい』を大切にします。お客様の飲食に対する意見など、直接の反応が聞こえるように努力し、運営に反映させています。客室数1,200室の大ホテルより密度の高いお客様とのふれあいが自慢です。こうしたふれあいのひとつに、私と妻は毎週木曜日夜に、プランテーションハウスでカクテルパーティを主催しています。

──限られた少ない客室数でホテルの運営をうまく行なうコツは何ですか。また季節による利用状況はいかがですか？

サービスの良さ、飲食の質、すぐれた素材という点では決して妥協しません。さらに地元の従業員を雇い続けます。海外からの利用客に関しては、シェラトンの予約システムが活躍してくれます。

──小規模なリゾートホテルとして重要なことは何ですか？

お客様とのふれあいとニーズの把握です。「ノー」ということのないように、お客様のさまざまな要望に応えられるようにしておくことが重要です。「何か必要なものがあれば、おっしゃっていただければすぐ準備いたします」という姿勢です。

──小規模なリゾートホテルの将来展望についてはどう思いますか？　ゲストのニーズは今後大きく変化すると思いますか？

将来については非常に楽観的です。なぜなら、ハワイにおける大規模なリゾート開発は一気に花開きましたが、その魅力が廃れるのも早いと思います。それに反してここは、ハワイならではの体験をもたらしてくれる最後の楽園です。これこそ人々がハワイに求めるものだからです。

──ここに来られて予期しなかった最も感動的なことは？

落ち着いたのどかさが、これほど素晴らしいことであるということです。シーランチのコテージを例にとると、まるでプランテーション・キャンプのようです。私の長年の経験でも、客室にカーテンもカーペットもないというのは初めてです。また友好的な人々も予想した以上です。

──今後の計画は？

目下、人々の目につかない場所でゴルフコースを造成中です。それ以外には新たな施設計画はありません。ハナ・マウイは顧客本位の運営です。私たちもまた顧客のニーズを予測し、それに応えていくことを喜びとしています。新たな変革があるとすればそれは、顧客のニーズによってです。

──もしご自分がオーナーのホテルを計画するとすれば、どんなタイプのホテルを考えられますか？

ハワイ出身ですから、やはりハワイの中で建てます。しかし、ハナは建築協定によって他のホテル建設は禁じられていますから、やはり小さな規模のホテルをカウワイ島のハナレイあたりに建てるでしょうね。

Page 26 Lobby lounge
Page 27 View of downtown L. A. can be seen from rooftop pool

P. 26　上　ロビー・ラウンジ
P. 27　屋上プールからのダウンタウン

Checkers Hotel Kempinski
Los Angeles

チェッカーズ・ホテル・ケンピンスキー／ロサンゼルス

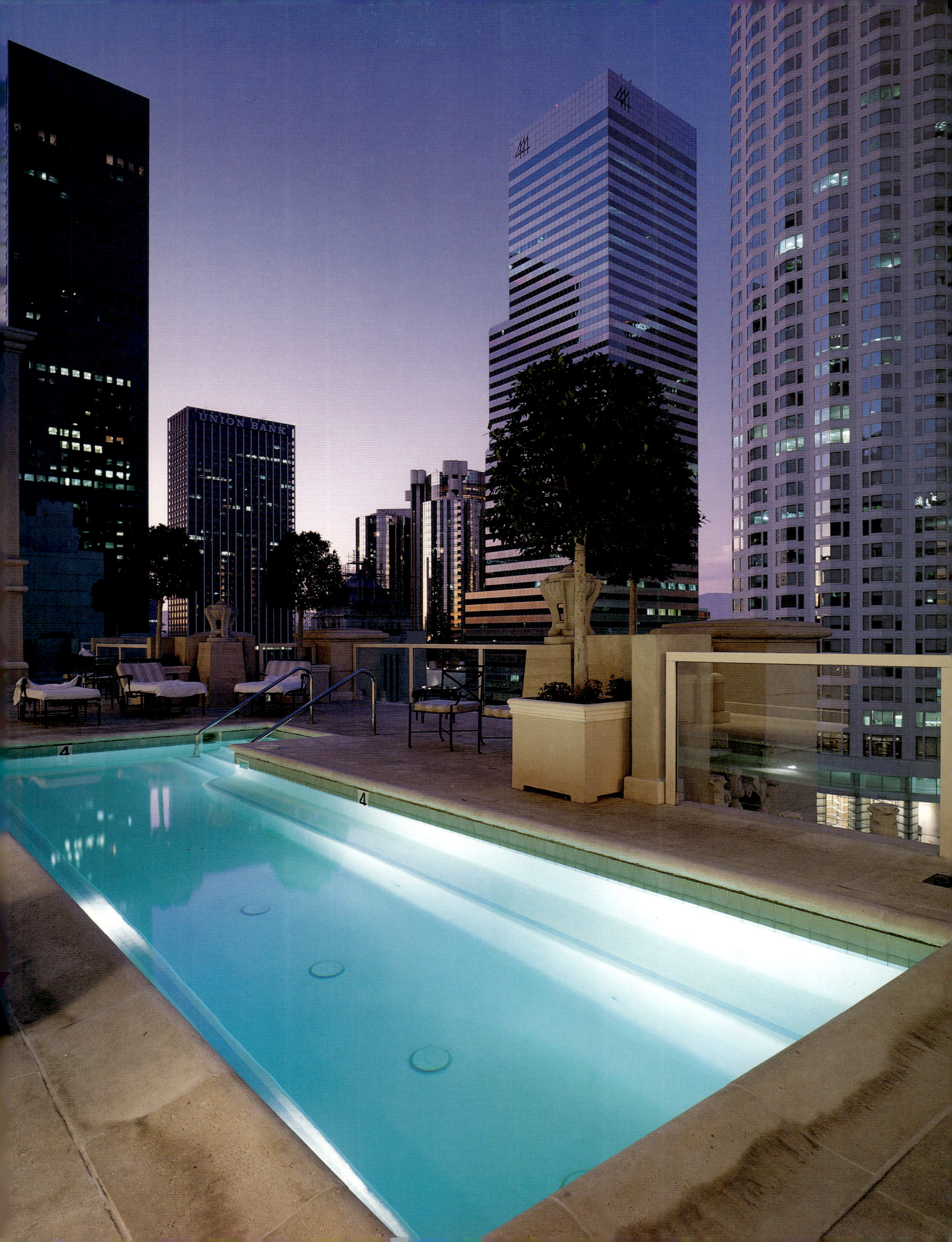
UNION BANK
4
4

Unprecedented Sophistication

インテリジェンス

In order to discuss the Checkers Hotel, we must first go back to its predecessor, the Mayflower. When the Mayflower Hotel was completed on 26th December 1927, it was the most beautiful and impressive building in downtown Los Angeles. The architect, Charles F. Whittlesey gained popularity generally and was also responsible for designing several buildings in San Francisco. Built in the Spanish style, the exterior was decorated with superb stone carvings especially on the lower three stories. The origin of the hotel's name, too, came from this special feature, the shape of the then contemporary passenger liner, the Mayflower, having been carved ?on? the entrance. The building, which was constructed for $1 million, just managed to keep within the downtown Los Angeles building regulations limit with its 12 stories. Each room had an adjoining bathroom, which was very rare at the time, and room charges were between $2.50 and $7 a night.

The hotel re-opened as the Checkers Hotel on the 1st July 1989, after extensive renovation work, costing $49 million, had been carried out. 190 out of the existing 348 rooms were refurbished in an effort to upgrade them significantly. Only the decoration on the exterior was left as a symbol of the building. Two years later, in July 1991, the hotel was taken over by the German company Kempinski and it is now known as the Checkers Hotel Kempinski Los Angeles. The sense of European luxury, which is the underlying concept of the Checkers, has increased still further under the German, Kempinski-style of management.

In a downtown area, there is an overwhelming need to meet the demands of the business community and this kind of small and luxurious style of development which differs so much from other hotels is well supported by executives not only in the United States, but also in Europe and in the Pacific, and the number of times people return to enjoy such facilities only serves to substantiate this fact. This is little wonder as these small hotels have so many advantages to offer the traveller. First of all, there is the aspect of safety. As there is only one entrance, a compulsory check can be kept on the comings and goings of patrons. Then there is the question of intimate service. As the number of staff usually exceeds that of the rooms, it is not surprising therefore that it is possible to provide a quick response to any request.

Then there is the other sales point, namely luxury. An elegant and restful atmosphere, which makes guests feel that they have been invited to stay at a tastefully decorated house rather that a hotel, is offered here. Nevertheless, everything is within easy reach. Unless the eye moves to the skyscrapers outside the window, it is possible to experience a tranquility not usually associated with Los Angeles. I know of no other hotel with such a feeling of unprecedented sophistication as this. Perhaps it would be possible to call it a "city resort" or an "oasis in the center of a huge city". Providing a relaxed sense of inhabitability combined with the convenience of being within easy access to anywhere in the downtown area, the Checkers Hotel could perhaps be called a model of the urban form of the "small and luxury".

チェッカーズを語るには、その前身メイフラワーホテルに話を戻さなければならない。1927年12月26日に完成したメイフラワーは、当時LAのダウンタウンの中で最も美しく、印象的な建物だったといわれる。建築は、チャールズ・ホワイトルセイが担当。彼は、サンフランシスコでいくつものビルを手掛けて、人気を博していた。外観は、スペインの様式を取り入れ、特に下部3層には、見事な石の装飾が施されていた。その特徴が顕著なエントランス部分には、ホテルの名前の由来である、当時の豪華客船「メイフラワー」号の船の形も彫り込まれている。建築コストは、100万ドル。建物の高さは、その時点のダウンタウン規制いっぱいの12階建。当時としては珍しく、全室バス付きで、宿泊費は一泊2.50～7ドルだったという。

1989年7月1日、4,900万ドル(約63億円)の一大リノベーションの結果、新生チェッカーズ・ホテルは誕生した。その時348室あった部屋は、実に190室にまでシェイプアップされ、格段に居住性の向上が図られた。そんな中にあって外部の装飾だけは、ビルの象徴としてそのまま残された。2年後の1991年7月、経営はドイツのケンピンスキー社が担当することとなり、正式名称Checkers Hotel Kempinski Los Angelesとして現在を迎えている。

チェッカーズのコンセプトである"ヨーロピアン・ラグジュアリー"は、やはりドイツのケンピンスキーの経営に移ってから、より一層磨きがかかったようだ。ダウンタウンという場所柄、ビジネス客の需要が圧倒的に高く、その中でもスモール＆ラグジュアリーという、他のホテルとは全く違う視点での展開は、米国人だけでなく、欧州や太平洋地域のエグゼクティブたちに支持され、リピーターという形となって実証されている。それもそのはずで、小さいということは、旅行者にとって多くのメリットを生む。まず、安全。エントランスはひとつで、人の出入りが否応無しにチェックされる。そして濃やかなサービス。スタッフの数が部屋数を上回り、当然のことながら素早い対応が可能となる。

そしてここのもうひとつのセールスポイント、"ラグジュアリー"。ホテルにいるというよりは、趣味の良い家に招かれたような、上品で落ち着いた雰囲気。それでいて、すべてに手が届く身近さがある。窓の外に広がる高層ビル群に目を移さない限り、LAのダウンタウンにいるとは思えないやすらぎを覚えることができる。これほど「インテリジェンス」を感じさせてくれるホテルを、私は知らない。それは大都会の中のオアシス、シティ・リゾートといってもよいかも知れない。ダウンタウンのどこにでもすぐアクセスできる利便性と、落ち着いた居住性を併せ持つ、ここチェッカーズは、都市型スモール＆ラグジュアリーのひとつの規範といえるだろう。

Page 28 Penthouse Suite favored by Gorbachev, Thatcher and others
Page 29 Living room

P. 28 ゴルバチョフやサッチャーも愛用する「ペントハウス・スイート」
P. 29 同リビング・ルーム

CHECKERS

535

CHECKERS
HOTEL
KEMPINSKI

Page 30   Ornamented entrance
Page 31   <Top> Executive Suite enhanced with some of the old decoration, <Bottom> Views of downtown L. A. can be had from the guest room
Page 32   <Top> Main dining room, <Bottom> Library
Page 33   Lobby

P. 30　昔の装飾を生かしているホテル外観
P. 31　上　室内にも装飾が残されている「エグゼクティブ・スイート」、下　部屋の窓からのダウンタウン
P. 32　上　メイン・ダイニング「チェッカーズ・レストラン」、下　ライブラリー
P. 33　ロビーホール

Executive Suite

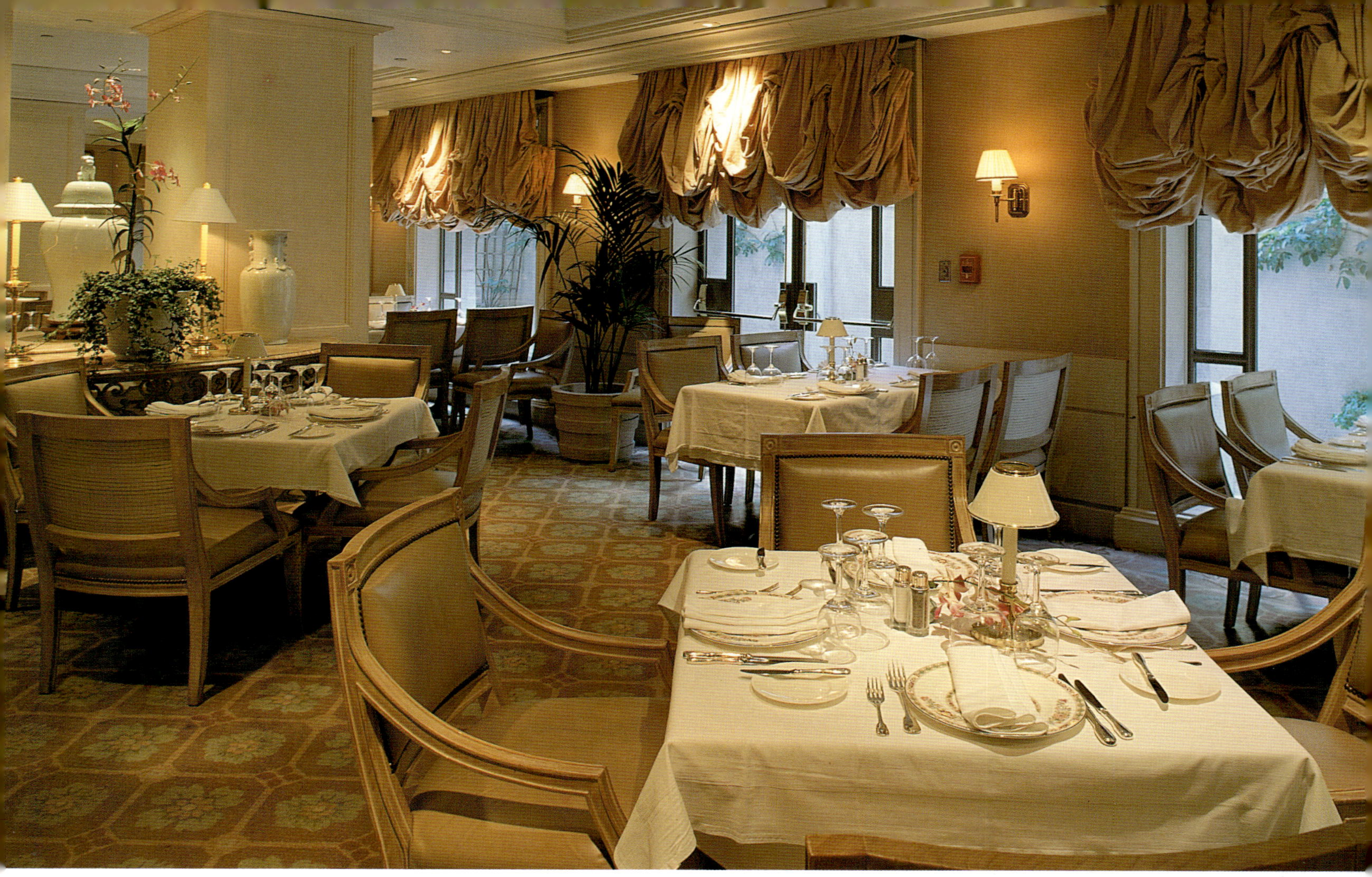

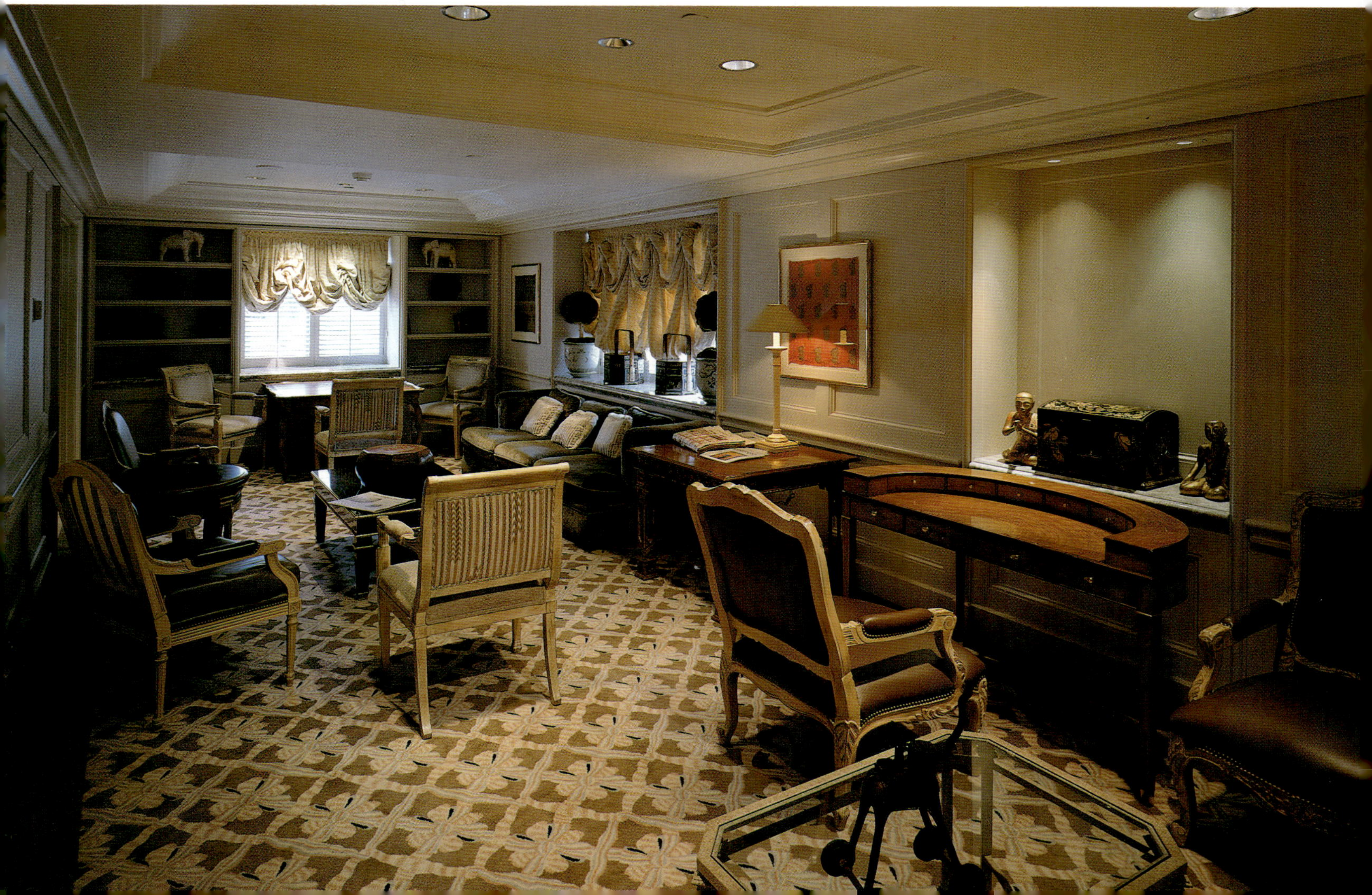

General Manager Mr. Volker Ulrich

総支配人　ヴォルカー・ウルリッヒ

Checkers Hotel Kempinski

in MEMORY of
RUTH JOHNSTON HOLBROOK
Her husband, Wales and daughters, Susan and Charis, present
to the Ranch this copy of Galsworthy's
"ODE" to San Ysidro
How beautiful! When the wood smoke goes up straight, and the pepper trees stand unstirring, and behind the screen of the tall eucalyptus trees the fallen sun glows, a long slow fire over the sea, and the lavender color-mists rises between.
How beautiful, the mountains, behind us, remote in that late light, a little unearthly!
The loveliness of these evenings moves the heart; and of the mornings, shining, cool, fragrant.
There is something in it all of that dream, as of Paradise, which stirred the Italian painters in old days.
Well may it be sainted – San Ysidro, Santa Barbara!
New Year 1926.
John Galsworthy
Historical Note: RUTH was born in old CREEK Cottage; she managed the Ranch in the 30's, up to the time of its sale, forty years ago this May 1975.

San Ysidro Ranch
Santa Barbara

サン・イシドロ・ランチ／サンタバーバラ

Page 34 Pictures of guests who have stayed at this hotel
Page 35 Scattered cottages
Page 36 Overall view of garden

P. 34 フロントに飾られたゲストの写真の数々
P. 35 点在するコテージ
P. 36 庭園全景

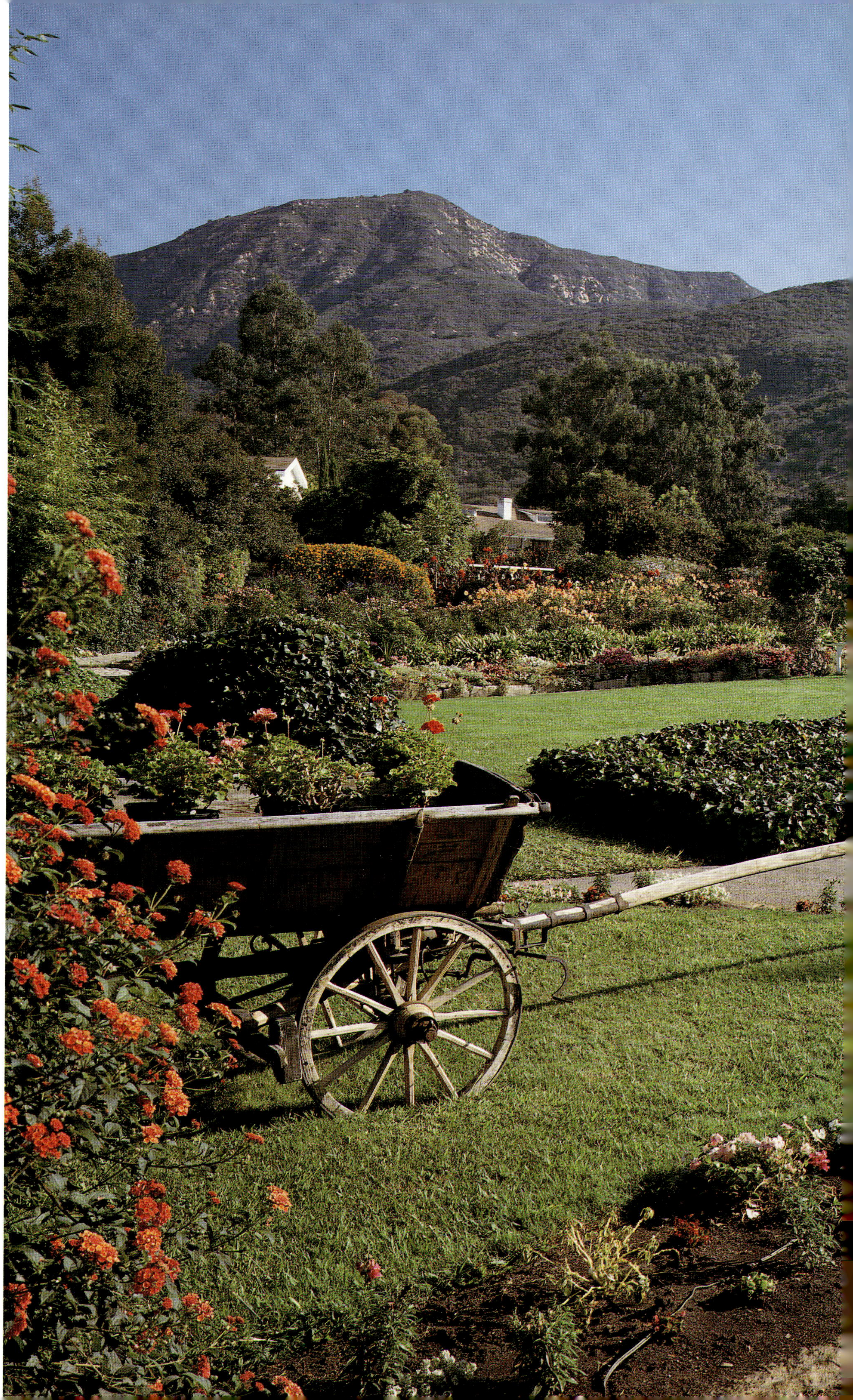

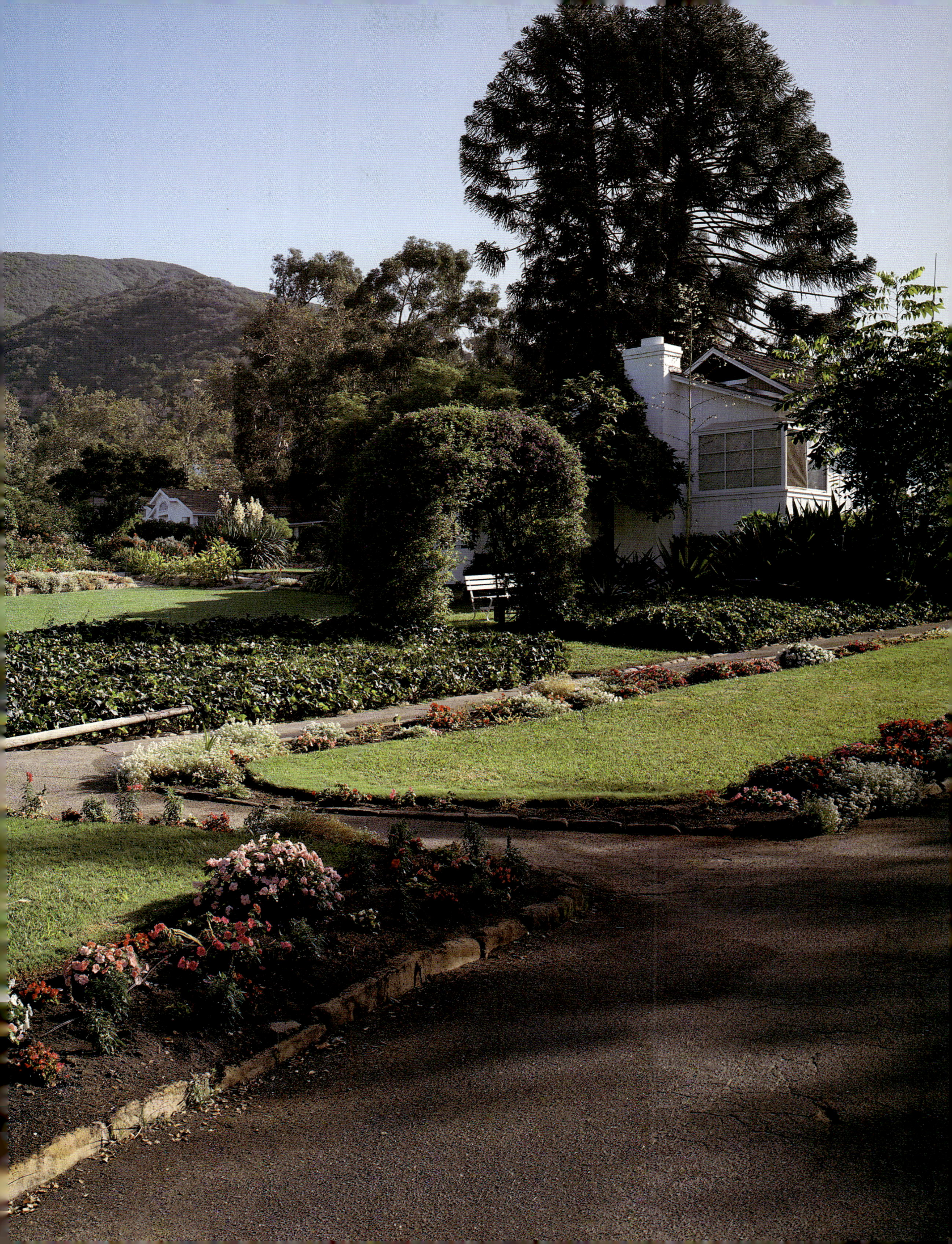

A Century in the Making
100年の重み

Located some 90 minutes by car from Los Angeles, Montecito is a quiet town with a population of some 9,000 people adjoining Santa Barbara, a city where anyone would contemplate retirement.

The San Ysidro Ranch itself stands quietly in a location midway up a mountainside here. To call it a hotel would certainly be inappropriate and it is far too simple a word to describe the impression created by the scattered cottages in particular. It is like wandering through a completely different world with seasonal flowers blooming in wild profusion, extensive woodland and a river flowing through the 216 ha (540 acres) site. The very atmospheric and tastefully appointed cottages, the scrupulously kept gardens, the herb garden where herbs are grown for use in the kitchens, and the fireplaces in each room, all these things have come together to create a wonderful atmosphere. In a gracious attempt to make guests feel at home, a name plate is hung at the door of each cottage throughout their stay.

Nearly a century has passed since San Ysidro Ranch was opened. Harleigh Johnston, who was himself from the East, built this small resort on his cattle ranch with the wealthy from the East in mind, in 1893. It stayed in the Johnston family until 1935 when it was bought by the popular Hollywood actor Ronald Coleman. Everything changed under Coleman because it became sought after as an exclusive Hollywood retreat rather than a resort for people who had stayed before from the East Coast.

The hotel register at the time was like a record of Hollywood celebrities. Bing Crosby, Audrey Hepburn and Gloria Swanson all stayed at the ranch and Laurence Olivier married Vivien Leigh in the gardens. In fact there are no end of anecdotes for John F. Kennedy also chose to spend some days at the ranch during his honeymoon.

The year 1987 deserves a special mention as it marked the second big turning point for the San Ysidro Ranch. This was when Claude Rouas took over the management. Having gathered his experience in the restaurant business in Europe, he crossed over to America where he set up a restaurant in San Francisco followed by the Auberge du Soleil, a hotel with a restaurant in Napa Valley on the outskirts of San Francisco. He immediately added his special Rouas touch to turn this historical facility into a luxury resort both in name and reality. First of all, he renovated 21 of the cottages, replacing the wooden floors and making comfortable additions such as bathrooms with skylights and Jacuzzi. At the same time he made various improvements in the restaurant department which for him is his pride and joy. The outcome of these improvements became evident in a very short space of time and the main dining room called the Stonehouse, has now become known as one of the most outstanding restaurants in California. The Adobe, which is next door to this restaurant, was built as a ranch house in 1825 and is still being used nearly 170 years later as a private dining room. Much of "Good Old America" has been carefully preserved here and guests can experience things that they cannot usually enjoy such as an open hearth in the cottages or a pleasant ride on horseback along bridle paths in the grounds. And for those who are not content with just these pleasures, there are tennis courts and a pool, too. But in addition to all of this, there is, of course, the service.

LAから車で90分余り、「リタイアしたら」と誰もが思うサンタバーバラ市に隣接する静かな街、モンテシト(人口約9,000人)。この街の山の中腹にひっそりと佇むサン・イシドロ・ランチ。ここはホテルと呼ぶにはあまりにも繊細で、また点在するそのコテージ群のイメージからも似つかわしくない。66万坪の敷地には、川が流れ、森が広がり、四季折々の草花が咲き乱れ、まるで別世界に迷い込んでしまったよう。年輪を感じさせる味わい深いコテージ、手入れの行き届いた庭園、自家用としてのハーブを育てているハーブ・ガーデン、各部屋に備え付けられた暖炉、それらすべてがひとつにまとまって、ここの雰囲気をうまく構成している。コテージの玄関には、滞在中ずっと「表札」が掛けられ、我が家としての心憎い演出も図られる。ここがオープン以来、既に1世紀を迎えていることに驚く。

サン・イシドロ・ランチ100年に亘る歴史は、1893年ハーリー・ジョンストンが、東部のお金持ち(彼自身も東部出身)を対象に、自らの牧場の中に開いた小さなリゾートとして幕を開ける。ジョンストン家による経営は、1935年まで続いた。が、その後ハリウッドの人気俳優ロナルド・コールマンに買い取られることになった。コールマンたちの代になってから、すべてが一変した。それまでの東海岸の人向けのリゾートから、「ハリウッドの隠れ家」として、もてはやされることになったからである。当時の宿泊名簿は、まるでハリウッドの名士録のようだった、といわれている。ビング・クロスビー、オードリー・ヘップバーン、グロリア・スワンソン等々。ヴィヴィアン・リーとローレンス・オ

リヴィエが、ここの庭園で結婚式を挙げたこともよく知られている。1953年にはジョン・F.ケネディが新婚旅行先のひとつにここを選び、何日間か過ごしていることなど、逸話には事欠かない。

1987年に、特筆すべき2度目の大きな転機を迎えた。それは経営者として、クロード・ロアスを迎えたことだ。彼はヨーロッパでレストラン・ビジネスの経験を積んだ後、アメリカに渡り、サンフランシスコでレストランを、その郊外ナパ・ヴァレーで"オーベルジュ・ドゥ・ソレイユ"というレストランつきのホテルを次々に成功させている、名うての経営者だ。彼は早速、この歴史あるリゾートを名実ともにラグジュアリー・リゾートに変えるべく、彼独自の方法"ロアス・スタイル"で手を加えていった。まず手始めに、21のコテージでリニューアルが行なわれ、木の床が張り換えられ、天窓付きのバスルームやジャクージといった快適な装備が加えられた。同時に彼の最も得意とするレストラン部門においても、さまざまな改良が行なわれていった。その成果は驚くほど早く表われ、メインダイニングの"ストーンハウス"は、既にカリフォルニアでも指折り数えられるレストランとして知られている。レストランの隣にある"アドベ"は、1825年に牧場の家として建てられたもので、160年以上たった現在もプライベート・ダイニングとして立派に活躍している。

ここにはまだ、「古き良きアメリカ」がたっぷりと、大切に残されている。暖炉付きのコテージ、庭園散歩に乗馬で、普段では味わえないゆったりとした時を過ごすことができる。それでも物足りない人には、プールとテニスコートも待っている。勿論とっておきのサービスと設備を添えて…。

Upper Hillside East/West

Page 39 <Top left> Upper Hillside where John F. Kennedy stayed <Center left> Leather key ring, <Bottom left> Bathroom amenities, <Bottom right> Bathroom of Upper Hillside

P.39 左上 ジョン・F.ケネディも泊まったコテージ「アッパー・ヒルサイド」、左中 革製のキーホルダー、左下 バス・アメニティー、右下 「アッパー・ヒルサイド」のバスルーム

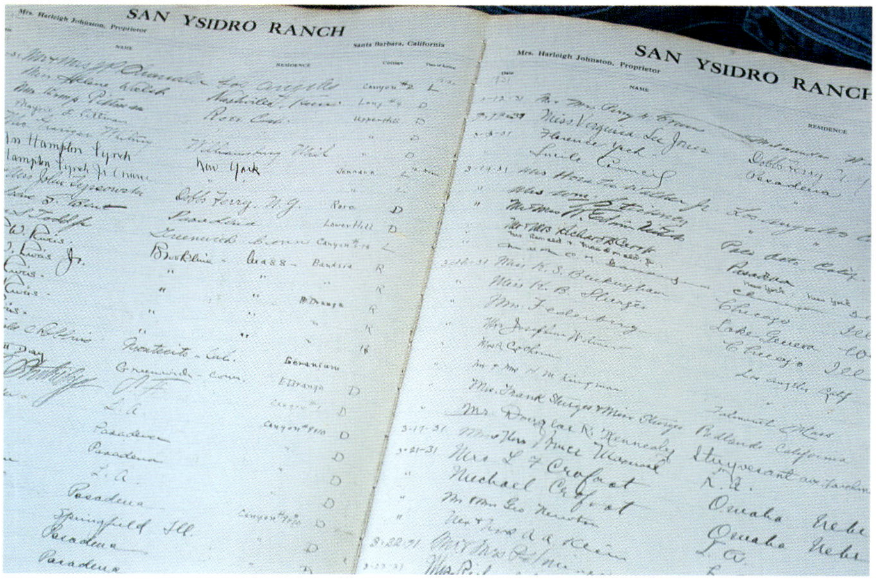
SAN YSIDRO RANCH
Santa Barbara, California
SAN YSIDRO RANCH
Mrs. Harleigh Johnson, Proprietor

HACIENDA
REGISTRATION

General Manager Ms. Janis Clapoff

総支配人　ジャニス・クラポフ

Page 40 <Top> Stonehouse restaurant, <Bottom left> 1930s hotel register, <Bottom right> Entrance to Hacienda, the office building
Page 41 <Top> Gate sign to the resort, <Center> Guests on horseback, <Bottom> Pool

P.40　上　レストラン「ストーンハウス」、左下　1930年代のゲストブック、右下　オフィス棟「ハシエンダ」の入口
P.41　上　リゾートのゲートサイン、中　ゲストに人気のアクティビティ、乗馬で丘の上まで、下　プール

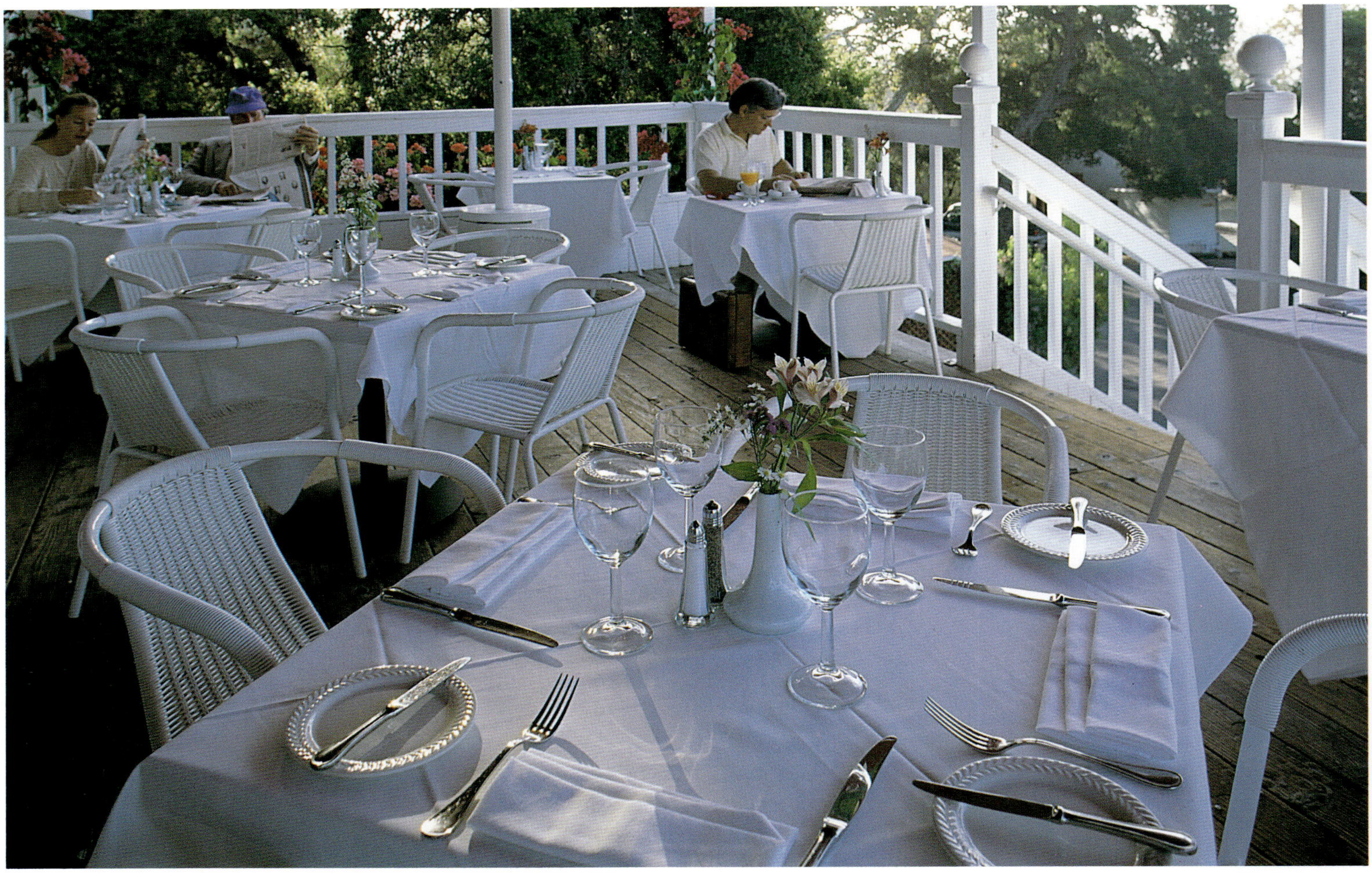

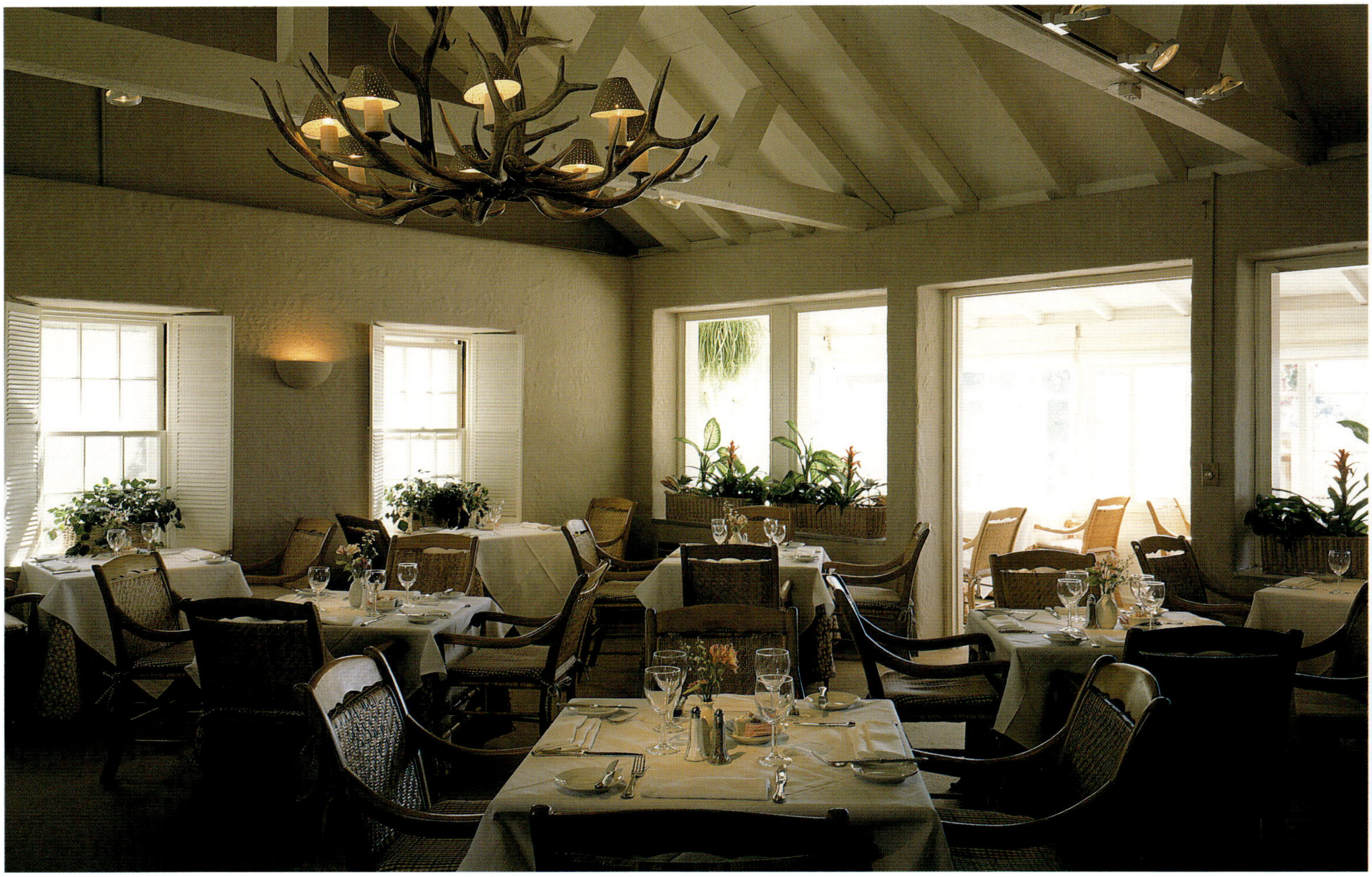

Page 42 <Top> Breakfast on the terrace of this restaurant is a must, <Bottom> Interior of the restaurant
Page 43 <Bottom> This 150 year old building is used as a private dining room called Adobe

P. 42 上 朝食に最適なレストランのテラス、下 レストランのインテリア
P. 43 下 150年以上たった今もプライベート・ダイニングとして活躍する「アドベ」

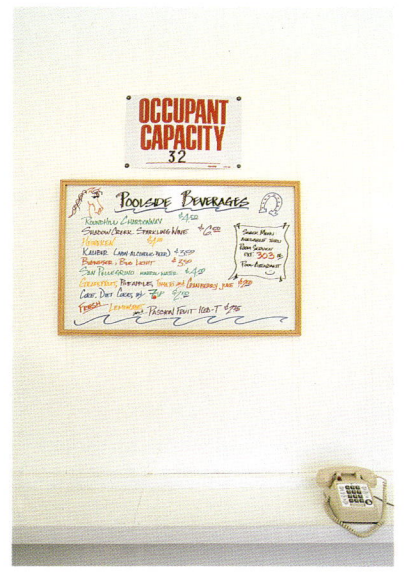

BVLGARI
SUITE
211 & 212

Campton Place Hotel
San Francisco

キャンプトン・プレイス・ホテル／サンフランシスコ

Good Neighbor

ゲストとホテルのいい関係

The name Campton Place first appeared as a street name on a 1909/10 map of San Francisco. That street was originally known by its present name, Stockton Place but, after the great San Francisco earthquake of 1906, the name was changed to Campton Place as a symbol of the newly regenerated town.

What later became a means of expansion, a seven storey stone structure called Wilson Building was erected on a street corner in the north east of the city in 1910. A 12 storey hotel had been built on the adjacent site the previous year and this was the predecessor to the present hotel. Its name was the Drake Wilshire Hotel. Built in the Spanish colonial style of old, the hotel became widely known by the people of San Francisco for its geniality and the beautiful lines of its exterior. In fact it became so popular that it was necessary to increase the number of stories by three floors in 1916. As its popularity continued to grow so the the two buildings were eventually connected in a very interesting experiment to make a much larger hotel, upon which the present one is founded.

Situated half a block from Union Square in the center of San Francisco, Campton Place Hotel is prized by tourists and business people alike. Since it opened as a new hotel ten years ago, it has become familiar to the people of San Francisco and has gathered many fans as a small and luxurious hotel. It is in an ideal situation, playing host to local business men and women during the week and tourists who take advantage of the area at the weekends. It is also able to offer a high degree of safety because of its size and has a quiet and welcoming lobby. The Campton Place Restaurant ranks amongst the top 25 restaurants in the United States and many local people come here to enjoy a meal.

The superb balance between east and west displayed in the bright and tastefully furnished rooms has created composed spaces in which guests may relax. With between four and eight rooms per floor, the question of guaranteed privacy has not been overlooked either. Another face-lift is planned in ten years and it will be interesting to see in what way it will change.

The average guest here is probably in a different class compared to those in other hotels, but this does not have anything to do with age. All guests, whether they are business people or tourists, are all individuals who have an air of affluence about them. This too contributes to the high

Page 48 <Top> The bar which is never without guests
Page 49 Exterior of the hotel and the street from which it got its name

P.48 上 一日中人の絶えることのないバー
P.49 名前の由来となった通りとホテル外観

General Manager
Mr. Peter Koehler

総支配人
ピーター・クーラー

quality image of this hotel. Being one of the most prominent tourist spots in the world, San Francisco has a constant stream of visitors throughout the year. Moreover, being in the center of this city, guests enjoy looking round the shops or eating their fill before returning to the hotel in two's or three's just as if it were their own home. The amazing thing about Campton Place Hotel is that it accepts this as being natural and does not make it an attitude. No special devices are used, however, but it is, nevertheless, a really superb hotel in which travellers can stop over for a while. It is truly a place of refuge in the middle of the metropolis.

キャンプトン・プレイスの名は、1909/10年版のサンフランシスコの地図に、「通り」の名前として掲載されたことに始まる。元々は、現在の通り名にもあるストックトン・プレイスとして知られていたが、1906年のサンフランシスコ大震災の後、新しく生まれ変わった街の象徴として、キャプトン・プレイスと名付け換えられたというエピソードを持つ。

1910年北東に位置する通りの角に、石積みの7階建のビルが建てられた。ビルの名は、ウィルソンビル。その前年には既に、隣接する土地に12階建のホテルが建てられていた。そのホテルが、現在の前身であるドレイク・ウィルシャー・ホテル。昔のスペイン植民地時代の様式を取り入れたこのホテルは、その美しい外観やホテルという親しみやすい機能も手伝って、市民の間にも広く知られることとなった。その甲斐あってか1916年には、3層分を増築しなければならない程だったといわれている。その後もその勢いは止まらず、後にこの2つの建物は「繋げる」という面白い試みによって、より大きなホテルとして、現在の礎を築いている。

サンフランシスコの中心、ユニオン・スクエアから半ブロック程にある、ここキャンプトン・プレイス・ホテルは、ビジネスに、観光にとても貴重な存在。新しいホテルとしてオープンして10年の時が流れ、スモール&ラグジュアリー・ホテルとして多くのファンを生み、サンフランシスコの人たちに親しまれてきた。土地柄平日はビジネス客、週末は地の利を生かし観光客にと、まさに理想的なコンビネーション。落ち着きあるロビー、適度な規模で安全性も抜群。レストラン"キャンプトン・プレイス"は、全米25のベスト・レストランのひとつに数えられている程で、ここでの食事を楽しみに来る地元の人も多い。

一方、明るい中間色でまとめられた客室は、東洋と西洋が絶妙に組み合わされた効果的な演出で、ゆったりと寛げる空間をつくりだしている。各フロアは4〜8室程度で、プライバシーの確保も怠ってはいない。10年を機にリニューアルも計画されているという。どのような変身を見せてくれるか、それもまた楽しみだ。

ここのゲストの平均は、他のホテルに比べ高いかも知れない。しかし、その「高さ」とは決して年令を指すのではない。ビジネス、観光、そのどちらのゲストも、豊かさを感じさせる個人客ばかりで、それがまた、このホテルの高質なイメージをつくりだすことに貢献している。世界でも有数の観光名所で、一年中人の絶えることのないサンフランシスコ。その中心のそのまたひとつで、ゲストたちが気軽にショッピングを楽しみ、おいしい食事を堪能して、三々五々ホテルに戻ってくる様は、まるで「我が家」の感覚。また、それを受け入れるホテルとの関係が自然で、構えのない、そんなところが魅力のキャンプトン・プレイス。特別な仕掛けは何もないけれど、旅人としてひととき立ち寄るのにとても素敵な宿。正に、都会の隠れ家だ。

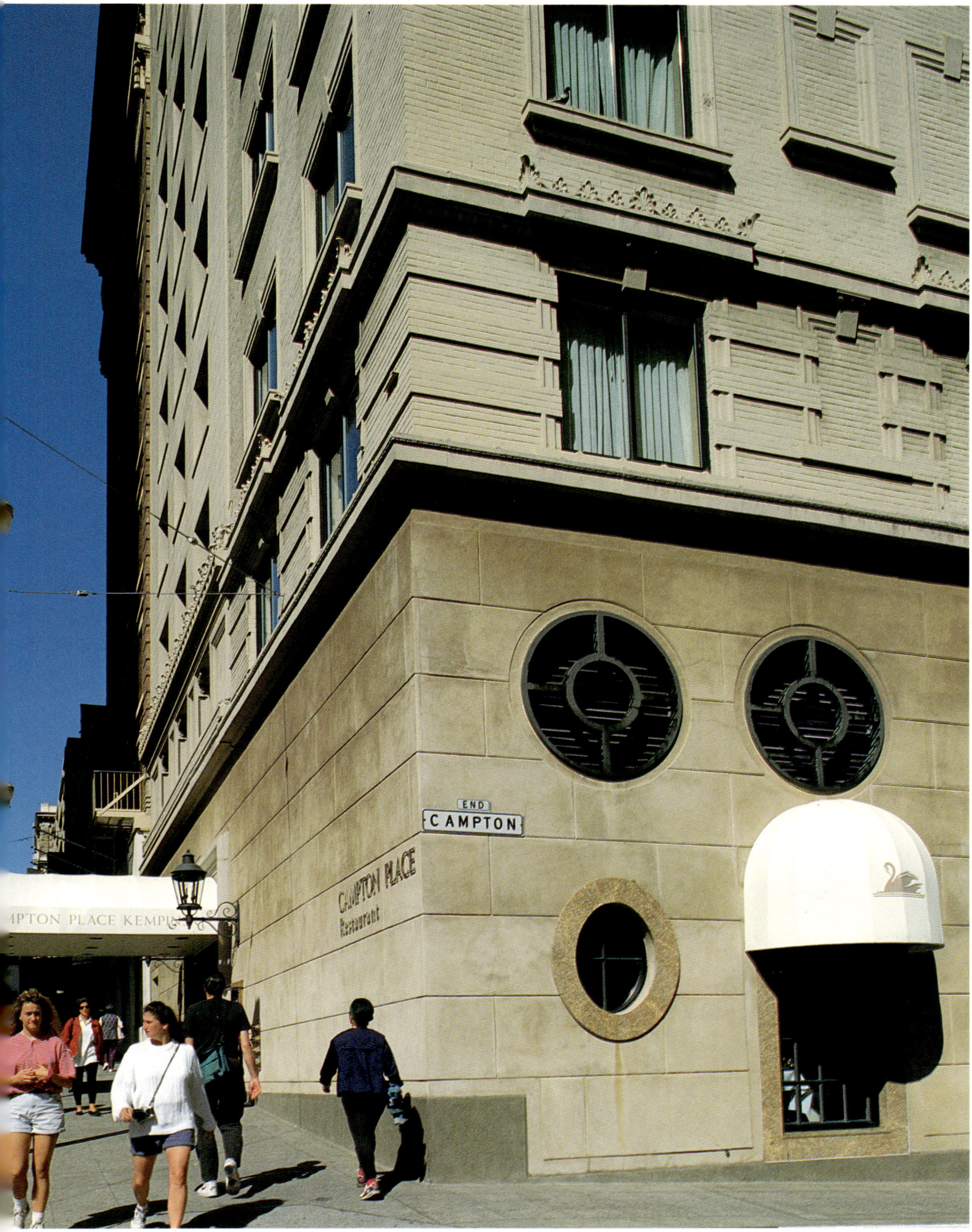
END
CAMPTON
CAMPTON PLACE
Restaurant
MPTON PLACE KEMPI

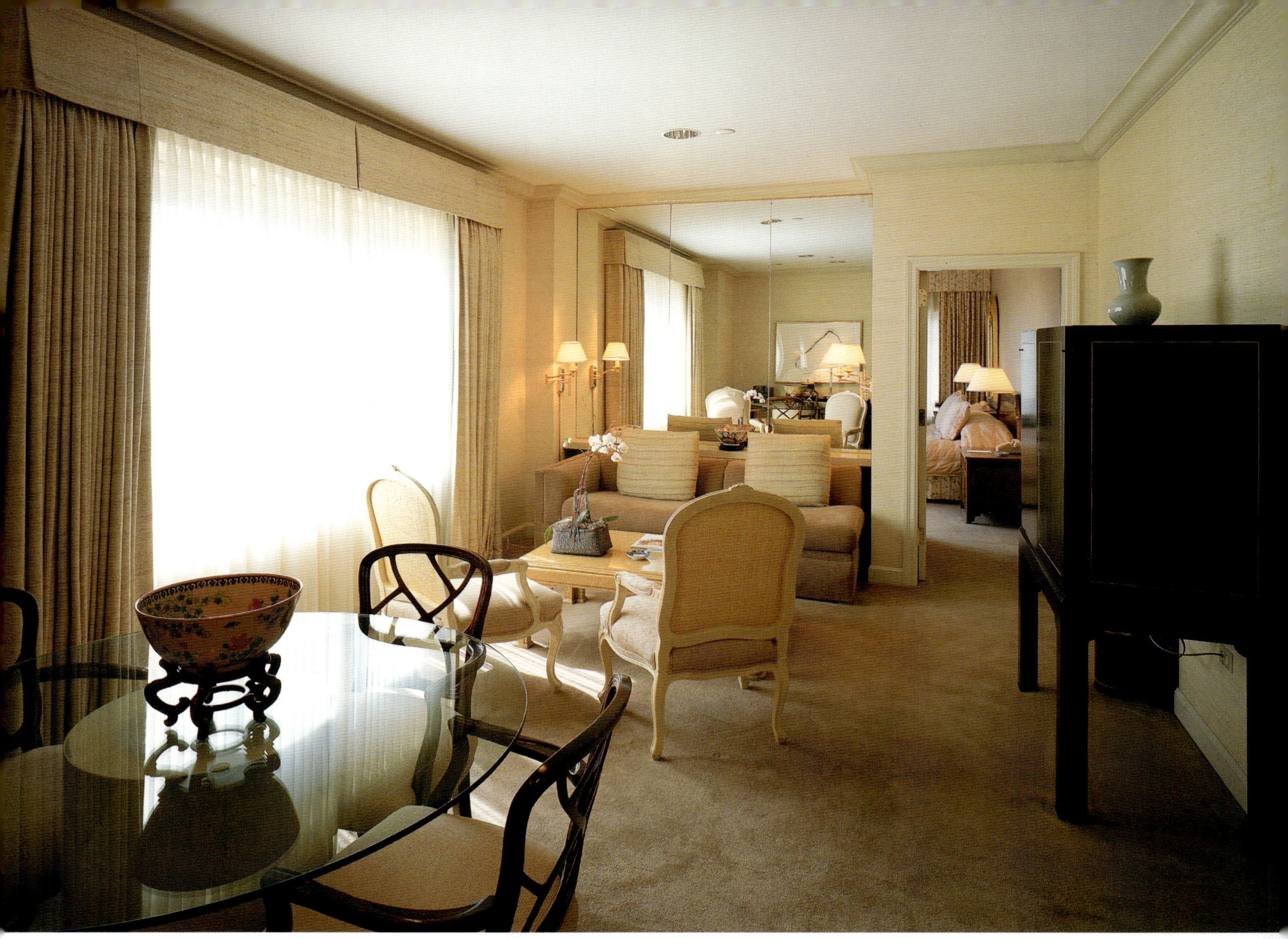

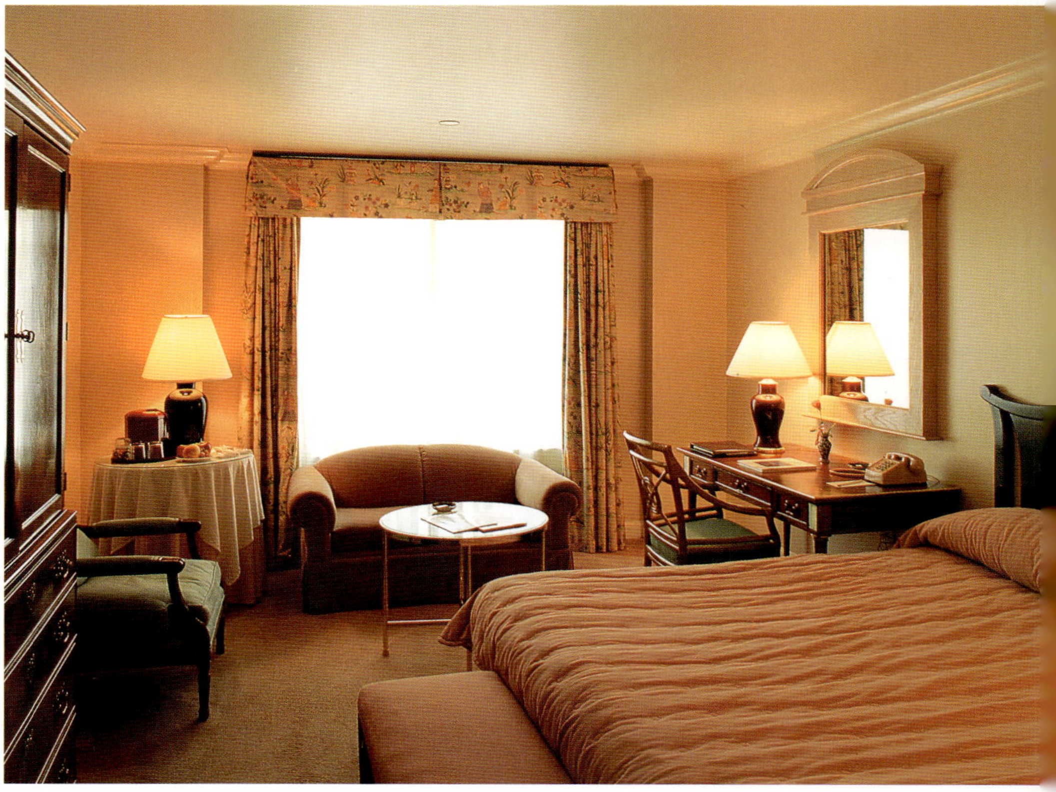

Page 50 <Top> Living room of suite, <Bottom> Deluxe double room
Page 51 <Top left> Elevator hall, <Top Right> Writing desk of guest room
Page 52 <Top> Campton Place restau-rant, <Bottom left> Door to hotel entrance, <Bottom right> Entrance to restaurant
Page 53 <Top right> Lobby seen from the lounge, <Bottom left> Touch of verdure in the lobby, <Botto right> Stone figure by the entrance

P.50 上 スイートルームのリビングルーム、下 「デラックス・ダブルルーム」
P.51 左上 エレベーター・ホール、右上 部屋のライティング・デスク
P.52 上 レストラン「キャンプトン・プレイス」、左下 ホテル入口のドア、右下 レストラン入口
P.53 右上 ラウンジからロビーを見る、左下 ロビーの植栽、右下 玄関脇に飾られた石像

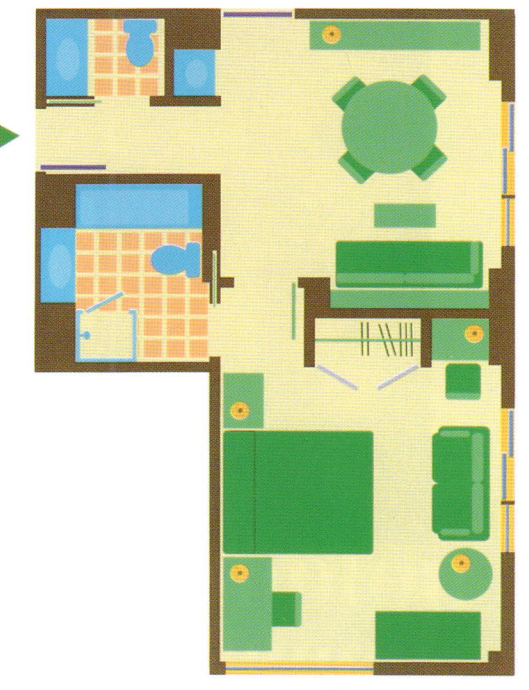

Campton Suite

Post Ranch Inn
Big Sur, California

ポスト・ランチ・イン／ビッグ・サー（カリフォルニア）

Page 54 Pool overlooking the Pacific Ocean with the Siera Mar restaurant beyond　　P.54　太平洋を望むプール、奥にはレストラン「シェラ・マー」

Big Sur, Eight Years, Thirty Rooms
ビッグ・サー、8年、30室

This small resort, the first such facility to be built in Big Sur since 1973, made its debut in May 1992. Despite the fact that there are only 30 cottages on the 39.2 ha (98 acres) site, it actually took eight years to complete. This can be attributed to the natural environment in which the buildings stand.

Even though it is situated in California, which itself abounds with natural beauty, some 240 km (150 miles) to the south of San Francisco, Big Sur is famous for its unique views. The wild untouched natural environment and the 144 km (90 mile) deeply indented coastline, running from north to south charms all who visit there. It is not just the tenacious power of life within the majestic natural surroundings, which have rejected penetration for so long from the outside, for there is a mystical sense of power besides. Having chosen to build the hotel on a site such as this, utmost care was given to environmental consciousness and in fact only one tree was felled in the process. All the buildings have been constructed in such a way as to be completely hidden from the road. This concept is reflected in everything.

The hotel project was prompted by a gathering of people, none of whom was a so called specialist in the hotel business. The owner of the land, Bill Post, who is the grandson of William Brainard Post, the pioneer, first put forward the proposal to construct a hotel. His partners were attorney, Michael Freed, who was his consultant in the matter, and Myles Williams who was attached to the musical group, The New Christy Minstrels, were also involved. All of them live in the area and have a simple and elegant life style which has become associated with Big Sur. It is probably true to say that the hotel was planned so that guests could have a chance to experience this lifestyle in the proper manner.

A wealth of devices have been amassed so that guests can make the most of their time at this hotel in an environment so rich in natural beauty that it is doubtful whether a similar place could be constructed even in Big Sur. Each room is furnished with an open fire, a CD player instead of a television, a coffee maker instead of room service and what is more, all the nonalcoholic beverages are on the house. The fixtures are all handmade originals made by various artists. Not only that, the most up to date systems whereby guests can make direct calls overseas or have a jet bath have also been installed. These are superb in the fact that they are all so unobtrusive.

1992年5月、ビッグ・サーに久々の(1973年以来19年振り)、新しくてそれは小さなリゾートが誕生した。約12万坪の敷地に、僅か30室という規模ながら、実に完成まで8年という歳月を費やしている。それは、この土地の自然環境に起因する。

サンフランシスコから南へ240km、豊かな自然を誇るカリフォルニアにあってもここビッグ・サーは、その特異な景観で知られている。南北144kmにわたる複雑に入り組んだ海岸線、手付かずに残された荒々しい自然環境は、訪れた人々を唯々魅了する。長い間外部の進入を拒んできた雄大な自然には、強靭な生命力だけでなく、神秘的な力さえ感じる。そんな土地柄だけに、ホテル建設にあたっては「環境を意識すること」に最大の注意が払われ、木を切ったのは後にも先にも1本だけ。そしてすべての建物は、道路から完全に隠れるように造られている。この思想は、あらゆることに反映されている。

このホテル・プロジェクトは、いわゆるホテルの専門家ではない人々の集まりによって進められていった。土地のオーナーであり、ホテル建設の発案者ビル・ポスト(この土地の開拓者ウィリアム・B・ポストの孫)、その相談を受けたパートナーの弁護士マイケル・フリード、元"ニュー・クリスティ・ミンストレルズ"という音楽グループに所属していたミルス・ウィリアムズ。いずれも皆このエリアに住み、「シンプル&エレガンス」というビッグ・サー独特のライフスタイルを実践している。ホテルはゲストに、正しくこのライフスタイルを味わってもらうために計画された、といってもよい。

ビッグ・サーの中でも、もう二度とこんなホテルはできないだろうといわれる自然環境の中で、このインには、豊かな時を過ごしてもらう為の工夫が豊富に揃っている。各部屋に設けられた暖炉、TVではなくCDプレイヤー、ルームサービス代わりに部屋にあるコーヒーメーカー、すべて無料のノンアルコール飲料。そしてアーティストたちによる、オリジナル・ハンドメイドの備品の数々。それだけではと、ジェットバスやダイレクトで国際電話がかけられる最新のシステムも備えられている。それでいてすべてが、人間を邪魔しないところがまた素晴らしい。

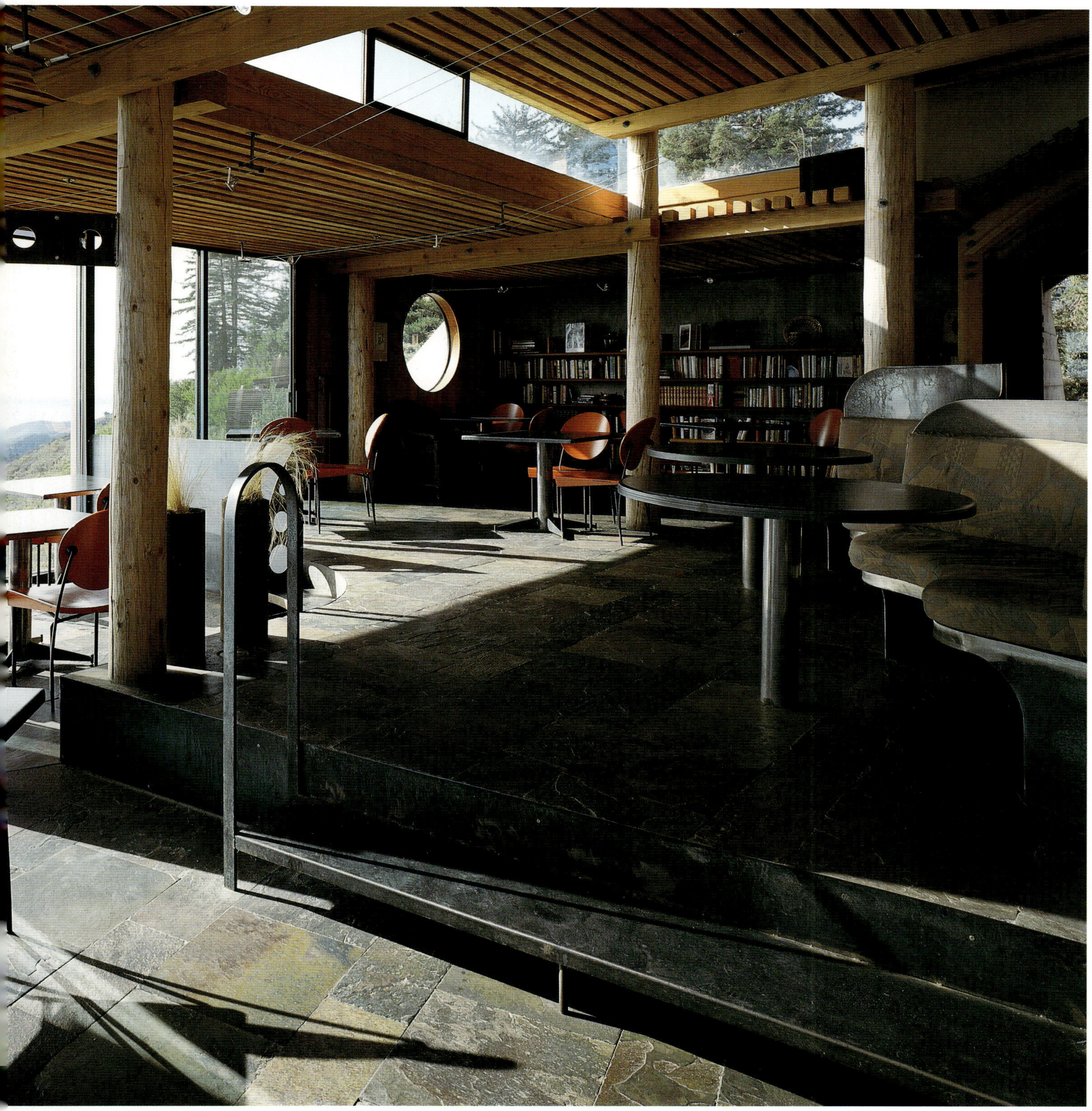

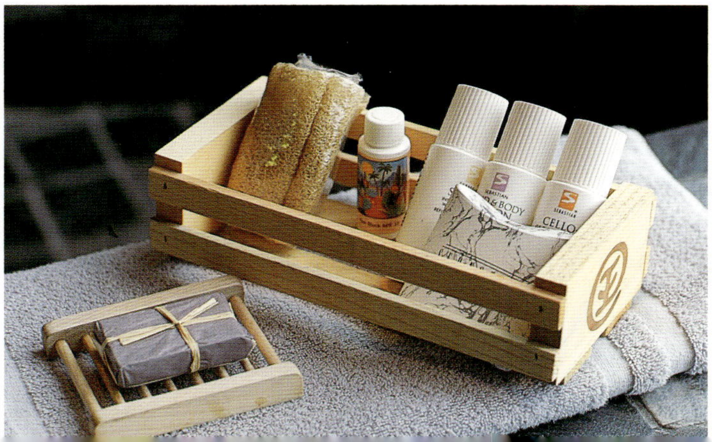

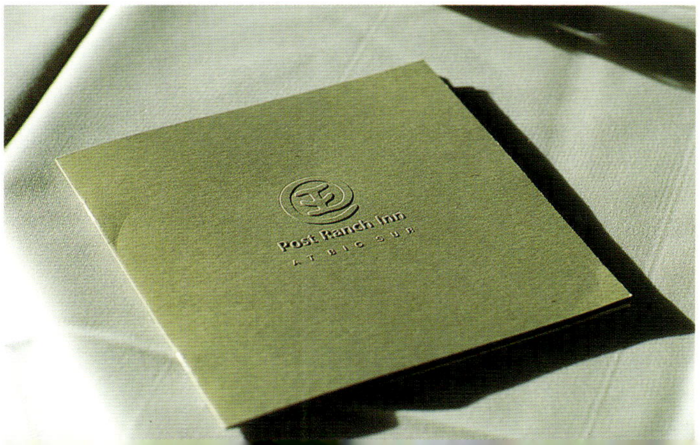
Post Ranch Inn
AT BIG SUR

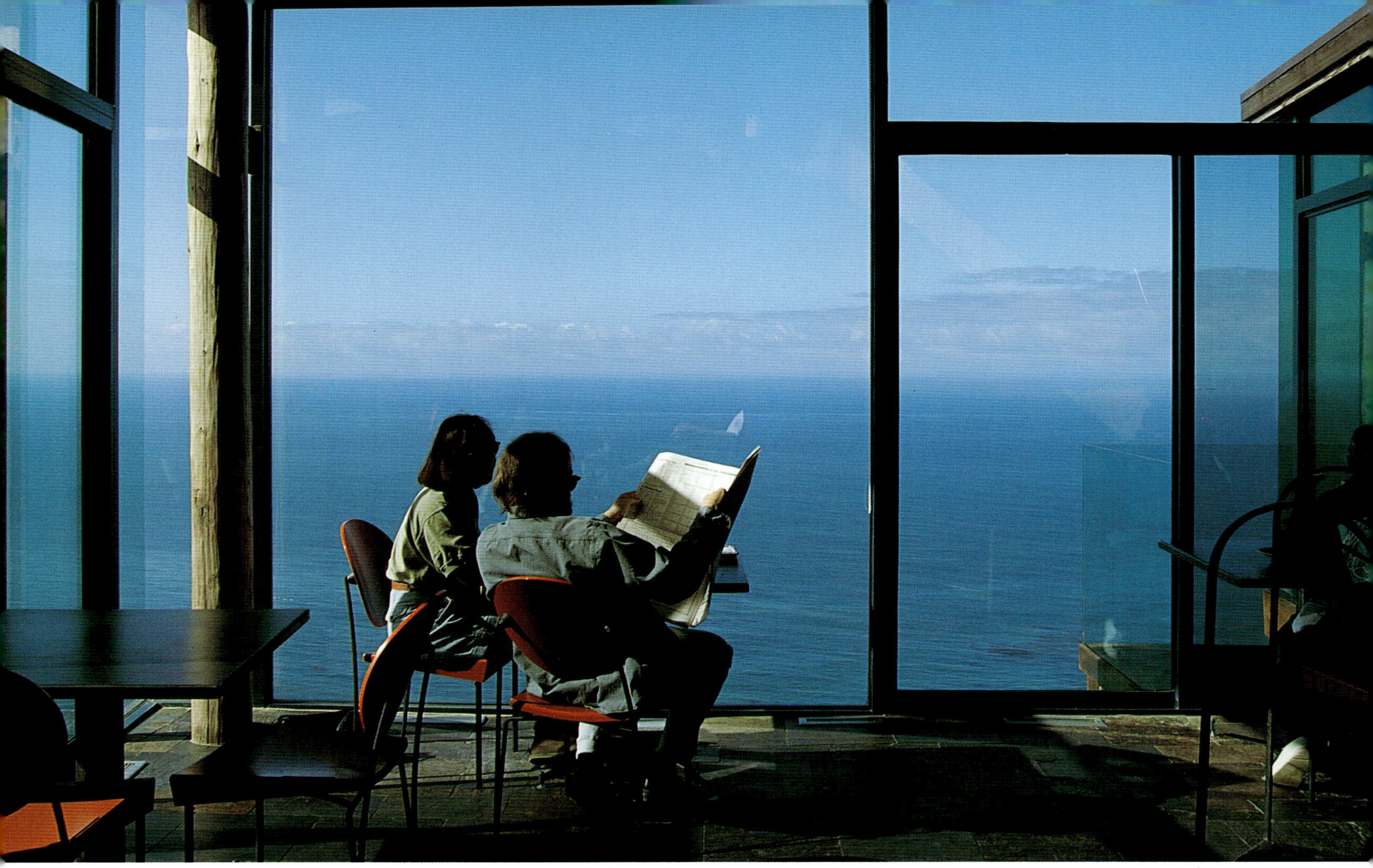

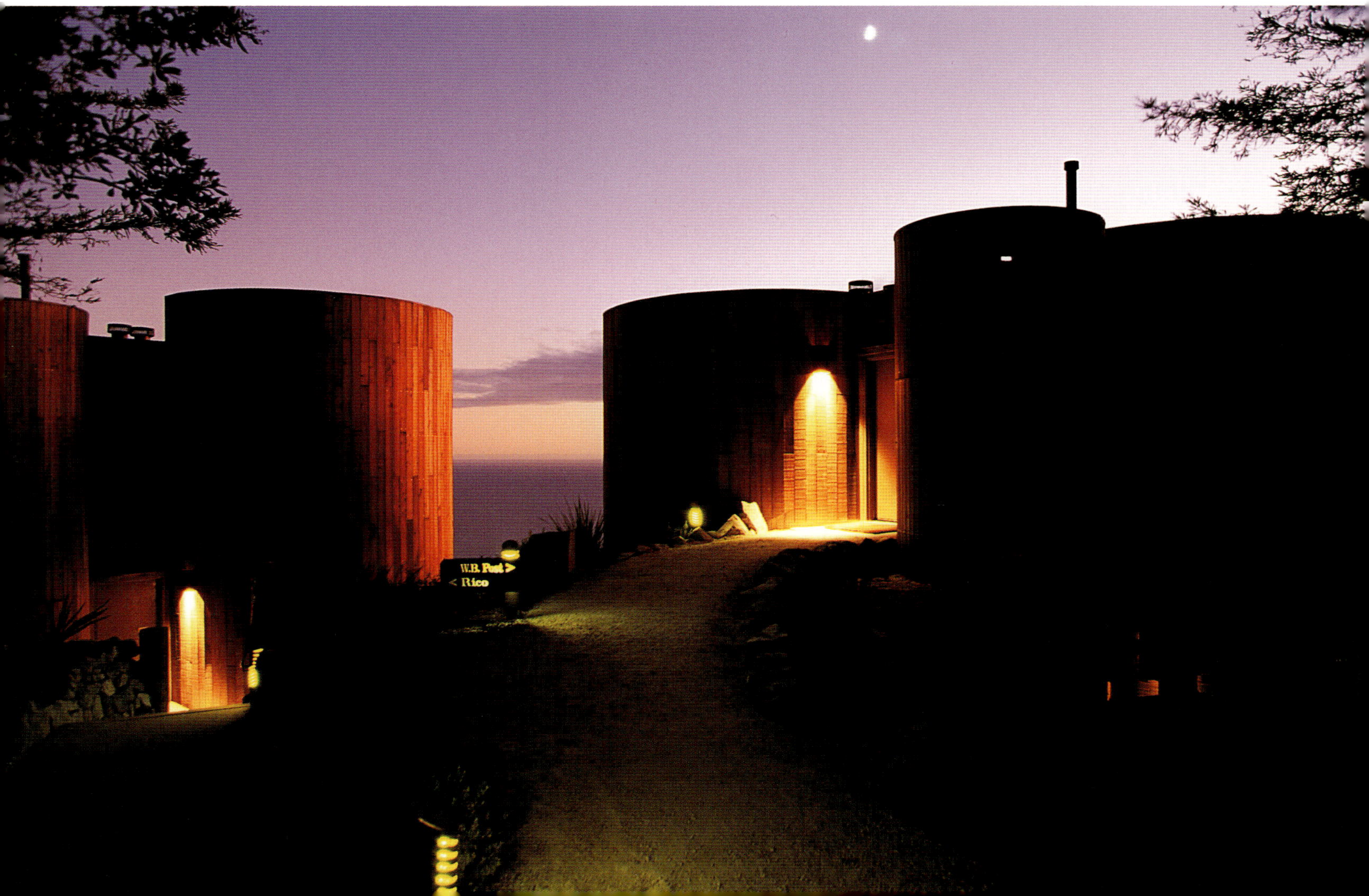
< Rico

Page 57 <Top> Restaurant with library beyond, <Bottom left> Bathroom amenities tastefully set out in a natural way, <Bottom right> Hotel leaflet made from recycled paper
Page 58 <Top> Restaurant overlooking the Pacific Ocean, <Bottom> Ocean House
Page 59 <From top right> Steel door with magnetic Plate, A walk in the ground, Pfeiffer Beach near the hotel
Page 60 Ocean House with wonderful views of the ocean
Page 61 A nest box-like Tree House

P.57 上 レストランと奥に見えるライブラリー、下左 ナチュラル・テイストのバスルームのアメニティ・グッズ、下右 再生紙で作られたホテル・リーフレット
P.58 上 レストランで太平洋と向かい合う、下 海に面した「オーシャン・ハウス」の外観
P.59 右上から 鉄製のドアとマグネット・プレート、敷地内での散歩、ホテル近くのファイファー・ビーチ
P.60 上 海を眺めるための「オーシャン・ハウス」
P.61 上 巣箱のような「ツリー・ハウス」

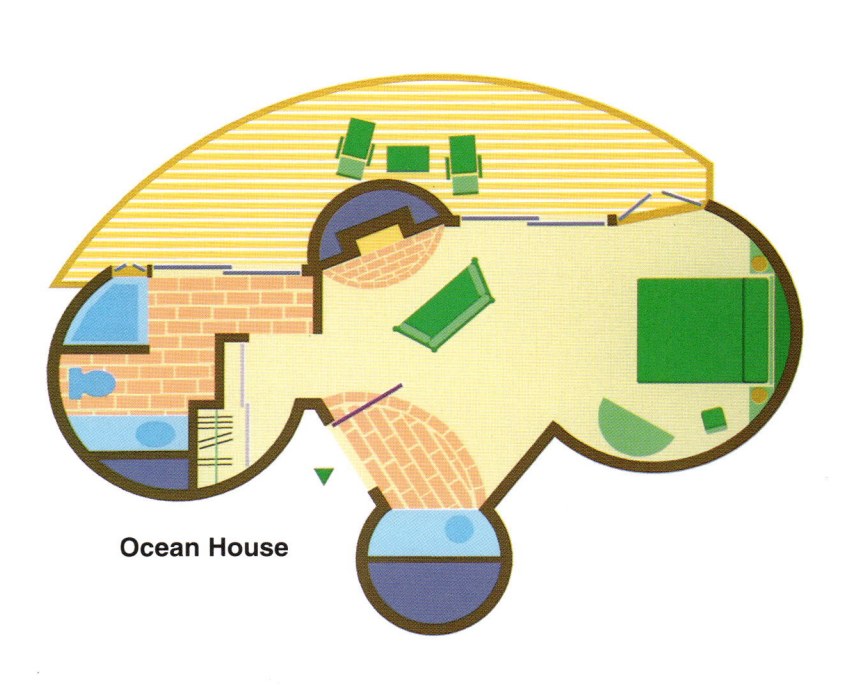

Ocean House

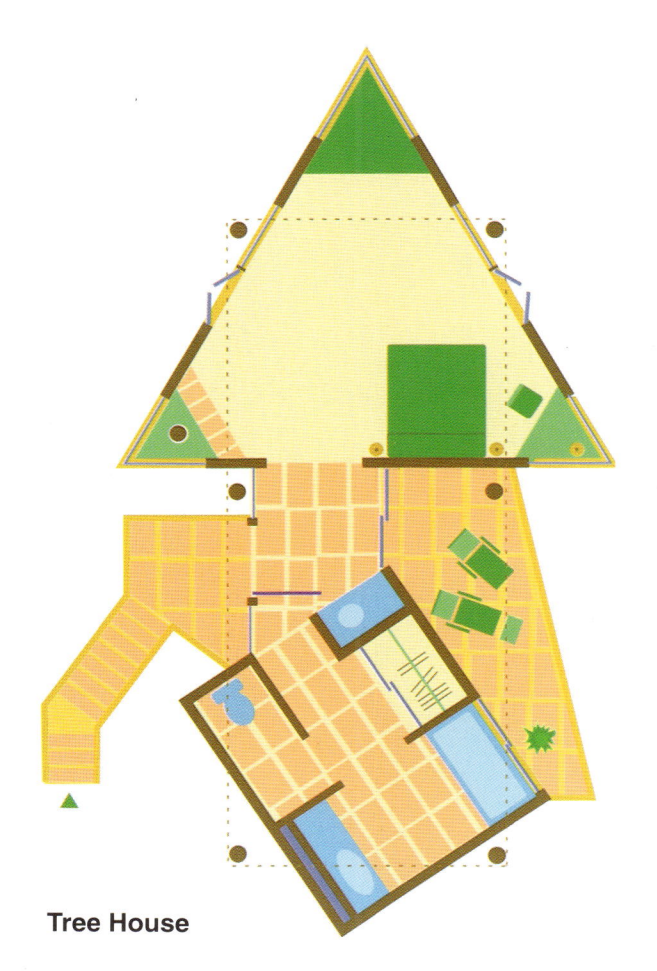

Tree House

61

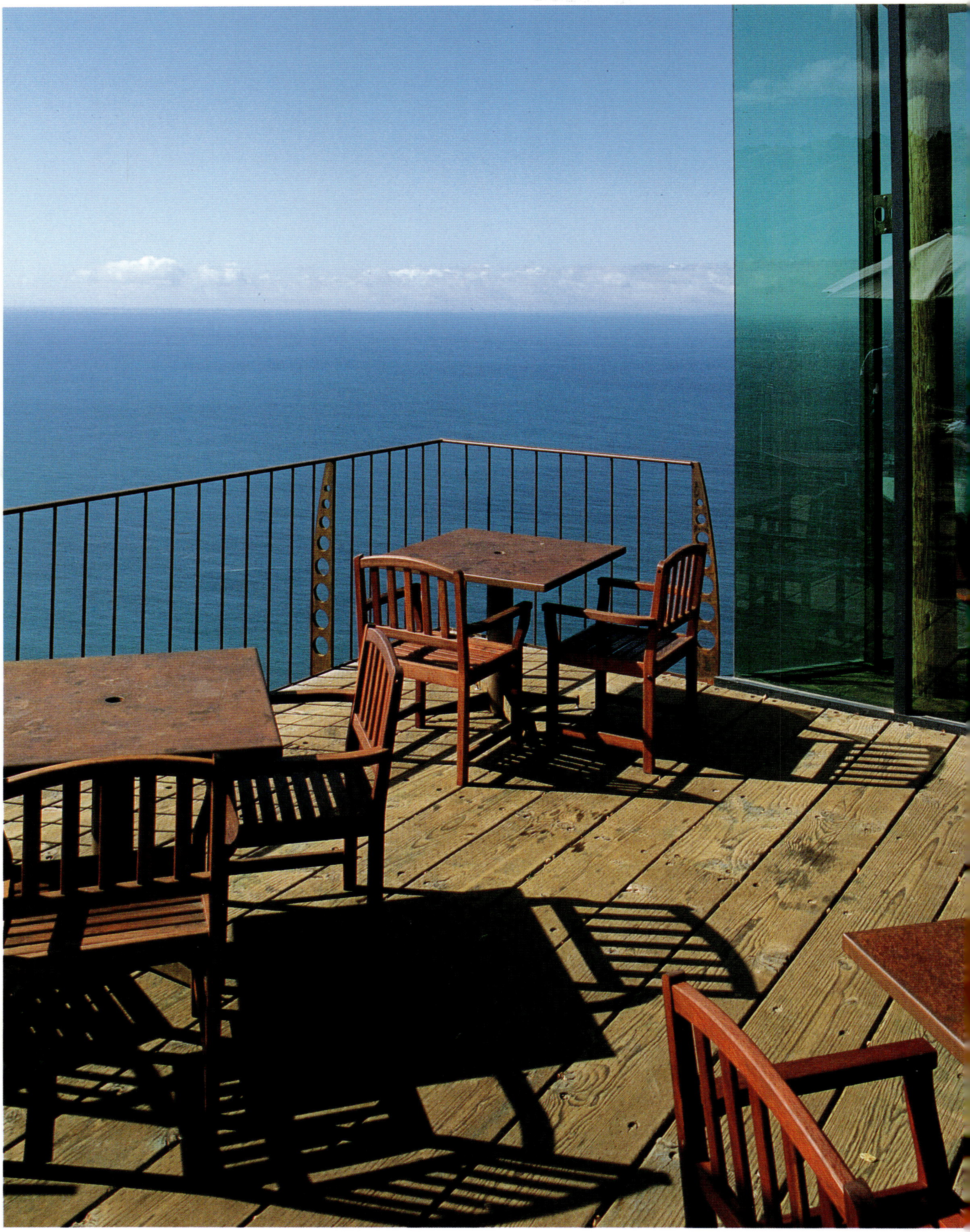

Mickey Muening, the local architect in charge of the construction of this hotel was well known for his house design but had no previous experience in designing a hotel resort. As a result, he was able to come up with a design which was completely unfettered by the conventions of existing hotels. Using very simple materials such as wood, steel and glass, he thought only of bringing these textures to life and set about putting his idea into action. The results can be seen in the cylindrical Ocean House, the "nest box" like Tree House and the Sierra Mar restaurant with its panoramic views. He may also have chosen this method, of course, so that the buildings do not interfere with the superb location. The fact that local artists were involved in the planning of everything from the interior design and fabrics down to the china in the restaurants is evident in the completed project.

One other thing that deserves a special mention is the fact that the hotel and restaurant are run by different management. For this reason, the hotel itself can be run with only 40 members of staff. In the three hours between checkout time at 1pm and check in time at four, the rooms are rapidly cleaned by staff working in pairs. It is astounding that it is possible to provide such an impeccable service with such a small staff. New California cuisine, which mainly concentrates on the fruits of the sea can be enjoyed in the Sierra Mar restaurant. Priority is given to guests staying at the hotel at dinner but visitors can also try the food, if there is room in the dining room.

Being blessed with such a splendid location at Big Sur, the Post Ranch Inn is augmented by the 30 rooms which took a total of eight years to complete.

建築を担当した地元の建築家ミッキー・ミューニングは、住宅設計ではその名を知られているものの、ホテル・リゾートの設計は経験がなかった。しかし結果的には、既存のホテルの常識に捉われることのない、自由な発想でこの設計を進めることに成功した。彼は、木、鉄、ガラスなど素材としては極めてシンプルなものを用いて、そのテクスチュアを忠実に生かすことだけを考え、それを実行に移した。ガラス張りの展望レストラン"シエラ・マー"、巣箱のようなツリー・ハウス、シリンダー状のオーシャン・ハウス等に、その魅力的な特徴を見ることができる。逆の見方をすれば、素晴しいロケーションをできるだけ邪魔しない為に、こういった方法がとられたのかも知れない。その他、インテリアデザインからファブリック、レストランの皿に至るまで、地元のアーティストの参画により、プロジェクトの完成を見ることになる。

もうひとつここでの特筆すべきことは、レストランがホテルとは別経営であるということ。そのことは、ホテル自体を極めて少ない人数の従業員で運営することを可能にしている。「ダブル・アップ」という2人一組の方法にて、チェックアウトの午後1時からチェックインの4時までの3時間の間に、素早く各部屋のクリンアップを行なう。こういったことにより、ホテルは従業員何とたった40人。それでいて、申し分のないサービスを提供できるのだから、これは感動に価する。一方レストラン"シエラ・マー"では、海の幸をメインにした、新カリフォルニア料理を存分に味わうことができる。ディナーは、ホテルゲストを優先に、余裕のある場合に限り、ビジターでもその定評ある味を試すことができる。

ポスト・ランチ・インは、ビッグ・サーという絶好のロケーションを得て、8年の歳月をかけ、そうしてできあがった30室という部屋、それらの中にすべてが集約されている。

General Manager Ms. Janis Donald
総支配人　ジャニス・ドナルド

Page 62 Simple materials have created this charming terrace to the restaurant
Page 64 <Center> Office building, <Bottom> Impressive entrance sign to the resort
Page 65 Interior of office building

P. 62　荒々しい素材感が魅力のレストラン・テラス
P. 64　中　オフィス棟外観、下　印象的なリゾート入口のサイン
P. 65　オフィス棟内部

Post Ranch Inn

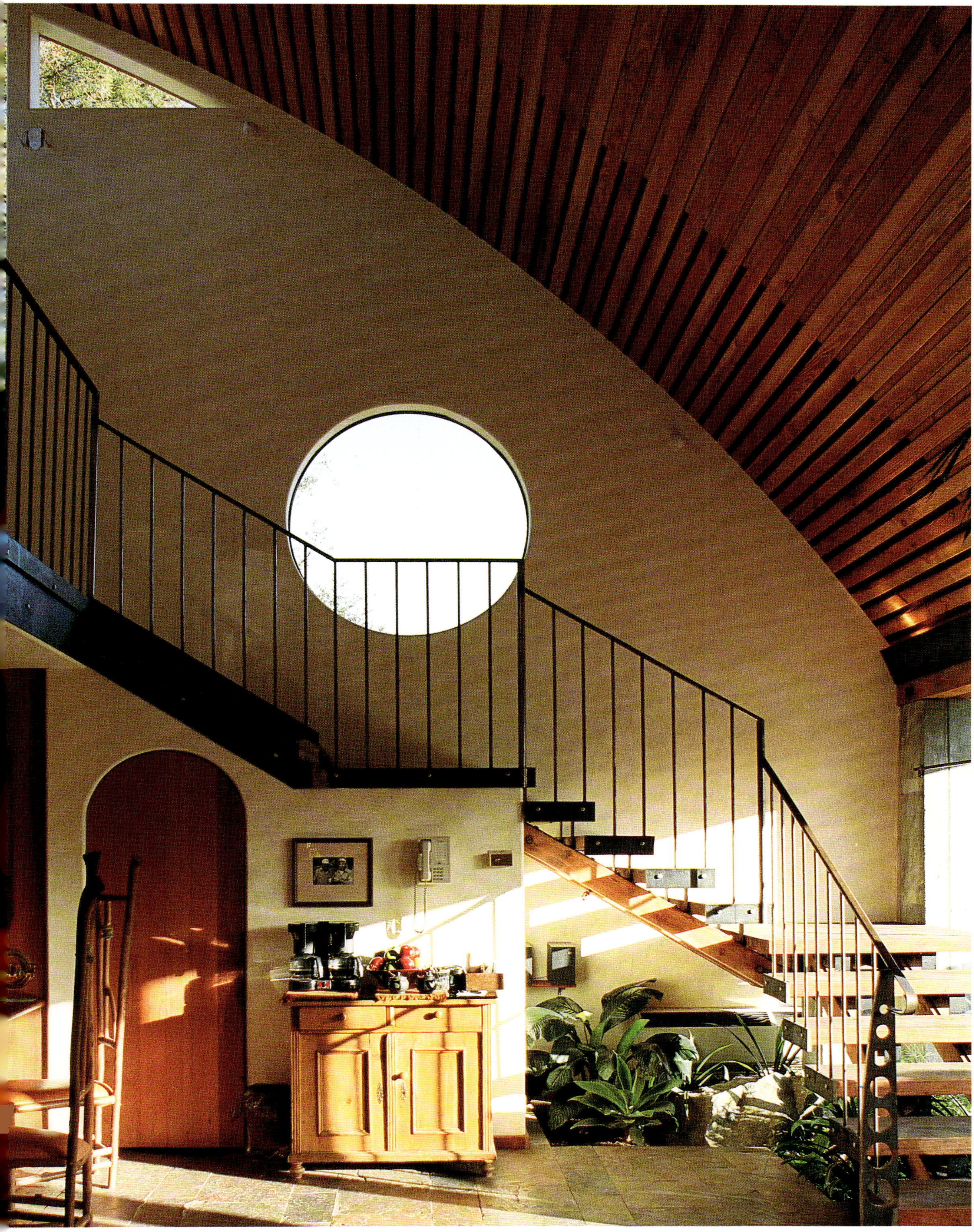

The Alexis
Seattle

ジ・アレクシス／シアトル

Secret of Seattle's Popularity
シアトルの人気の秘密

Situated in the extreme northwest of the United States, Seattle always appears in a list of the top five cities in which Americans would like to live. In addition to this, it has recently gained the number one spot in America for being the most appropriate city in which to do business.

This city, which is affectionately referred to as the "Emerald City" because of the abundance of greenery and water, is splendidly located facing the sea with the Olympic Mountains to the west, and the Cascade Mountains to the east. People living in the city have an enviable life style in which they skillfully combine both business and pleasure, using the natural environment to the fullest. That is why people are obsessed with this city. Obviously, the fact that it is blessed with both the fruits of the neighboring mountains and the sea means that it is also one step ahead of other cities from the point of view of cuisine. No wonder Seattle ranks as one of the most liveable cities in the country.

The Alexis, which is situated in the center of the city, opened in September 1982 after renovations were made to an 80 year old building. It was built in 1901 as an office building but was turned into a multi-storey parking building called the Arlington Garage in the 1930s. Work to transform it into a hotel began in the early eighties and everything was refurbished except the inner courtyard and external walls. The building next door, which was built in the same year as the hotel, is now called the Alexis Hotel Arlington Suite and consists of condominium-type suites with a kitchenette. Here too, it is possible to take advantage of the same services as are available in the hotel. Both buildings are registered as national historic buildings.

The pride of the hotel must be its restaurant and bar. Delicious Pacific North West *haute cuisine*, served nowhere else, can be savoured in the Painted Table, a new top-class restaurant, thanks to the chef, Emily Moore. The various paintings on the walls are loaned by a local gallery for exhibition purposes which means that the hotel is always embellished by new art works. What a brilliant idea on the part of the gallery to increase sales and introduce new artists! The Bookstore Bar on the other hand is loved not only by the guests themselves but also by the residents of the city and is included in the list of the ten best hotel bars in America. At one time, the number of books on the shelves out numbered the bottles so it was more like a book shop or library than a bar. But recently the numbers have unfortunately been reversed. I have never seen such a mellow place in which to have a drink. A classical atmosphere usually springs to mind when thinking about hotel bars. In which case, why was it not left out of the listing for the ten best bars in America?

The unaffected, understated design for this luxury hotel, together with a graceful bar, no tip system and just the right amount of service, all overlap somehow with the image of the city. Is it perhaps not possible that the secret of Seattle's popularity lies unexpectedly hidden here?

Page 67 European style courtyard seen from a hotel room　　P. 67　部屋からヨーロッパを感じさせる中庭を見る

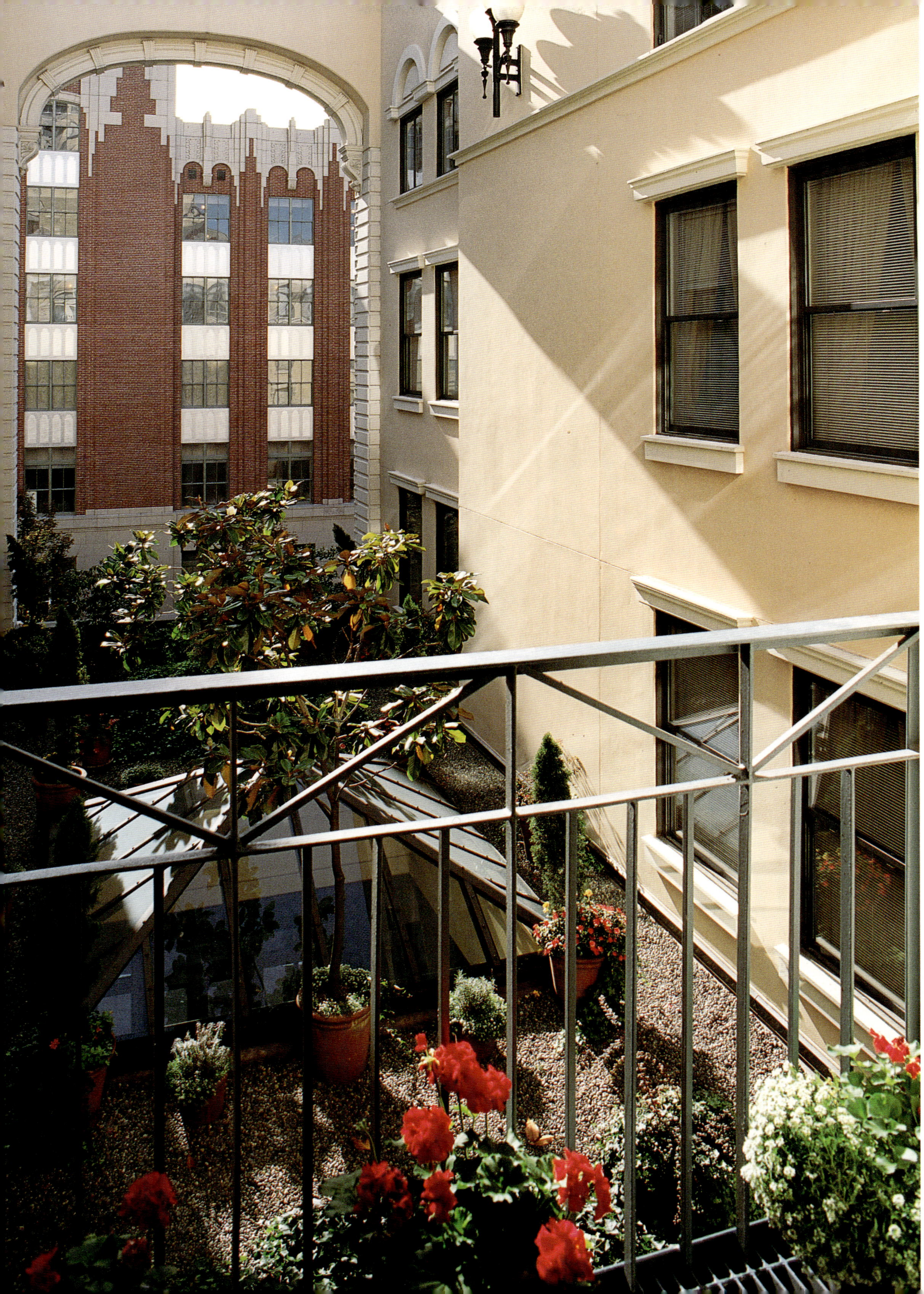

アメリカの最も北西部に位置する都市、シアトル。アメリカ人の「住みたい街」の投票では、いつもベスト5に顔を出す。それに加えて最近では、「ビジネスに最も適した都市」の全米第1位を獲得してしまった。

"エメラルド・シティ"の愛称を持つ、水と緑あふれるこの街は、正面に海を見据え、東にキャスケード山脈、西にオリンピック山脈が連なる、絶好のロケーション。その自然環境を最大限に活用して、仕事と遊びが上手にとけあったライフスタイルを送れる。そういったところが、この街に人々が憑かれる所以。当然のことながら、それらの背景を生かした海の幸、山の幸に恵まれ、食べることにおいても他の街を一歩も二歩もリードしている。なるほど、「住みたい街」の上位にランクされるということにも納得できる。ジ・アレクシスは、そんなシアトルの街の中にある。

オープンは、1982年9月。それは築後80年は越そうかという、古いビルをリニューアルしてのことだった。最初に建てられたのは、1901年でオフィスとして。1930年代に入り、駐車場ビルとして改修され、"アーリントン・ガレージ"となった。1980年代初めにホテルとしてへのリニューアルが始まり、外壁と中庭を除いてすべてが新しく生まれ変わった。ホテルに隣接するアーリントン・ビルも同じ年に建てられたもので、現在は"アレクシス・ホテル・アーリントン・スイート"という名の、キッチンネットを備えたコンドミニアム・スイートとして利用されている。こちらでも、ホテルと同様のサービスを受けることが可能だ。どちらの建物も現在、国の「歴史的建造物」として登録されている。

ホテルの自慢は、レストランとバー。シェフにエミリー・ムーアを迎え、その名も"ザ・ペインテッド・テーブル"とした新星レストランでは、ここでしか食べられない、おいしいパシフィック・ノースウエスト料理が味わえる。その壁面を飾るアートの数々は、地元の画廊と協力して、ギャラリーとして活用している。これによりホテルは、いつでも新鮮なアートに囲まれ、画廊の方はアーティストの紹介やセールスに繋げられるという、よくできたアイデアだ。

一方、バー"ザ・ブックストア"は全米のホテルのバー・ベスト10に数えられるほどの知名度で、ホテルのゲストだけでなく、「街の顔」として人々に愛されている。本棚にはたくさんの本が並び、酒瓶より多い位だったが、残念なことに最近はそれが逆転してしまった。一見バーというよりは、本屋か図書館といった雰囲気。こんなやわらかな酒場を見たことがない。ホテルのバーといえば、お堅い雰囲気がまず頭に浮かぶが、こんなところをベスト10に選ぶなんて、なかなかどうして捨てたものではない。

General Manager Mr. David Morgan
総支配人　デイビッド・モーガン

ラグジュアリー・ホテルとしては飾らない控えめなデザイン、ノー・チップ制を取りながらも過不足ない的確なサービス、「しなやか」なバー、それらは街のイメージとどこかで重なる。それはまるで、シアトルの街とひとつになって息づいているようだ。シアトルの人気の秘密は、意外とこんなところに隠されているのかも知れない。

Deluxe Double Room

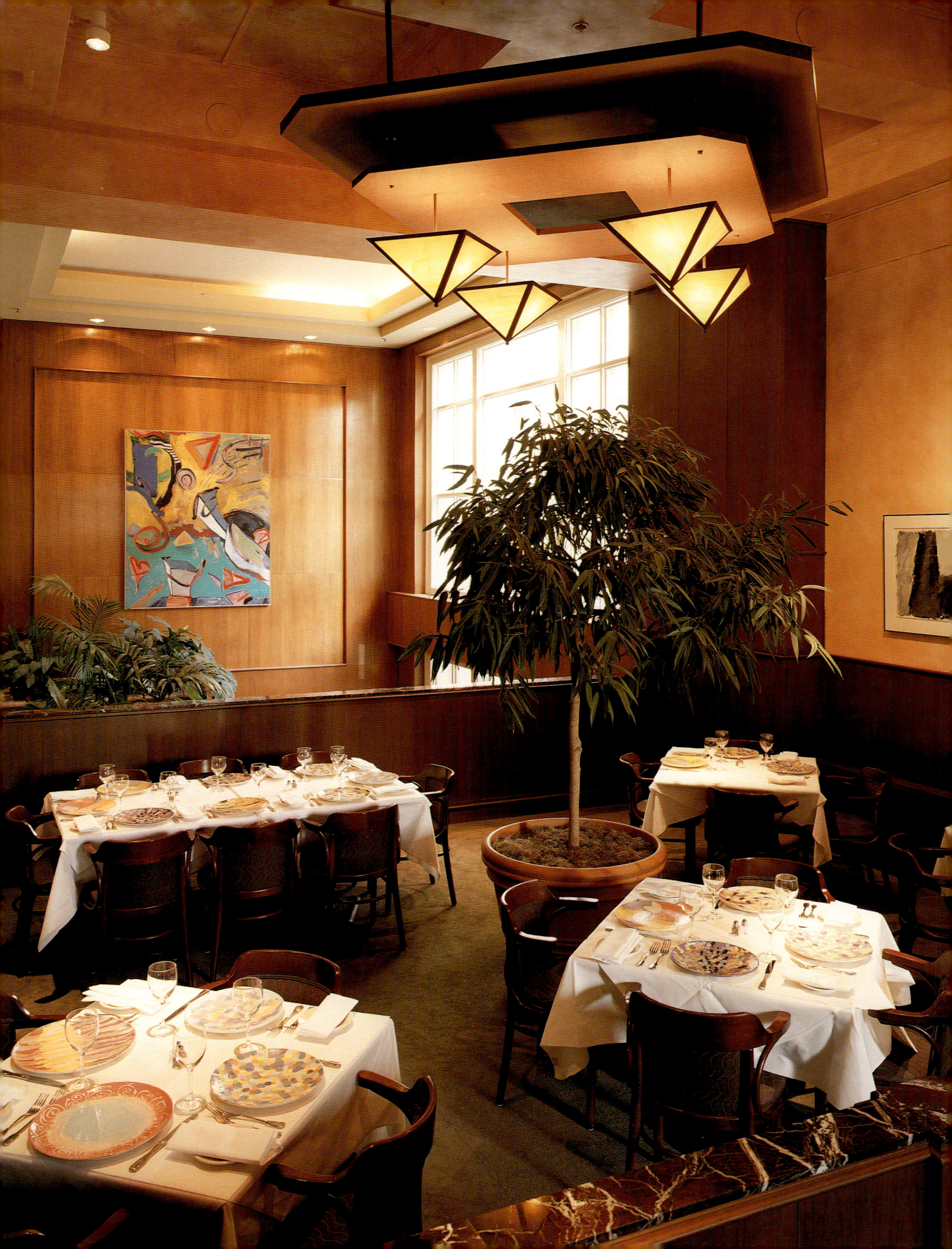

Page 68 Lobby lounge
Page 69 <Top> Deluxe double room, <Bottom> Arlington Suite which is next to the hotel
Page 70 The Painted Table restaurant
Page 71 <From top to bottom> The restaurant's logo, The walls of the restaurant are used as a gallery, Tables set for dinner
Page 72 Interior of The Bookstore bar

P. 68　ロビー・ラウンジ
P. 69　上「デラックス・ダブルルーム」のインテリア、下　隣接する「アーリントン・スイート」のインテリア
P. 70　レストラン「ザ・ペインティッド・テーブル」のインテリア

P. 71　上から　レストランのロゴ、ギャラリーとして利用されているレストランの壁面、ディナー・セッティング
P. 72　バー「ザ・ブックストア」のインテリア

The Alexis

TODAY'S BLENDS
YUKON BLEND
VIENNESE DECAF
HENRY'S BLEND
PERUGIA MEDIUM ROAST

Special Interview with Designers

Special Interview with Designers

Pamela Babey + David Moulton
Babey・Moulton, Inc. / San Francisco

パメラ・バビー＋デイビッド・モールトン
バビー・モールトン社／サンフランシスコ

What influences your design philosophy? For example, is it a person, place or thing?
Babey: Your education and architectural background, the approach to the project, the hotel operator, the environment and place are all things which influence your design.

1) Proportions, scale (Classical references)
2) Spatial sequence
3) Visual order
4) Functional organization
5) Simplicity
6) Some Contrast/Contradiction for interest

When I reject an architectural principle such as 'symmetry' because it is not appropriate in a given design situation, I do it with the understanding that I have not replaced it with chaos. Being disappointed in the effects of the 'Americanization' of the hotel industry, where all the hotel rooms look the same, we would like a chance to try and make them different. However, this is getting harder to do as more and more companies want their 'look.' People aren't happy with hotel chains all looking the same as in Hawaii; that is an aspect of hotel design that has changed.

The design approach also depends on what a hotel is to be used for. Is it a resort or is it for business? A hotel should respond to a sense of place and locale. We try and deliver something which responds to the forces of the project, including the philosophy of the operator and management regarding service. It is really important that all these elements are there.

Are there any past projects that are really special to you and why?
Babey: The Four Seasons Hotel in Milan, which has now finally opened and the Plaza Las Fuentes Hotel in Pasadena. Both were a challenge because the clients wanted unique hotels which reflected the locations. As both clients recognized the designers as professionals, they didn't question everything we did. A project is memorable when there is trust, on the part of the owner, in the designer's talent and experience, and an understanding on our part to respond to the owner's requirements for service and maintenance.

Also, the project for the Royal Dutch Shell's headquarters in the Hague is memorable because of client participation in the project. The Mandarin Oriental was interesting in the fact that we were doing an Asian Hotel in California. Obviously, because it is a Hong Kong based company, we were able to bring in the British and Asian influences and still be fresh way.

You can't design down to a client, especially in the upper end of the market,. you can't assume that the client doesn't know or doesn't understand and isn't chic. You have to design up instead.
What are the biggest differences in designing a hotel as opposed to a restaurant or office building?
Moulton: One big difference is that you have many clients; there are a tremendous number of consultants, the operator, the owner and finally the guests. You have the guest rooms, the kitchen and the bathroom. Because there are public functions pertaining to the guests staying there and functions pertaining to staff hotel projects are just much more complicated. Also, a hotel has to be completed and finished before the users arrive, whereas when an office is completed, it it usually has. The people who move in bring their personal touches with them.
Babey: A hotel is very much like a home and that makes it much more time intensive and dependent on the designer to do the last things well, particularly the small things like sheets and pillow cases. These kinds of things are a shared responsibility between the designer, the owner and the operator. In fact a hotel can be more closely compared to a residential project than a commercial one. As in a home, there are rooms of different scale; large 'public' rooms in which to watch the 'action', small intimate rooms in which to play card or read a book or talk intimately with a friend. There should be small distractions such as a flower shop or a jewelry shop, pleasant places to explore and wonder. This is especially important in the resort or the hotel, where guests tend to stay longer.

What must you pay particular attention to in hotel design?
Babey: I like to feel comfortable in a hotel; I need to know the way in, through and back out. The organization of major architectural elements should be clear and the interior design should

photo by Aldo Ballo

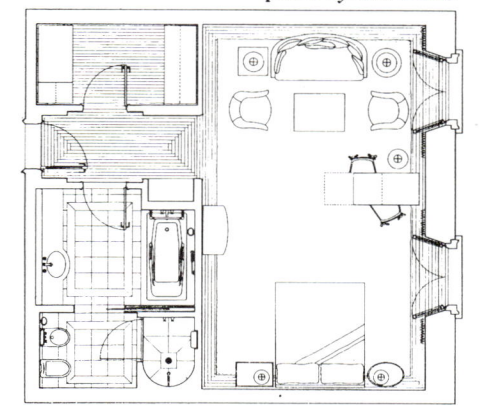

photo by Aldo Ballo

Pamela Babey

President of Babey・Moulton, Inc.

BA of UC California at Berkeley (1968)

SOM New York as Interior Designer
SOM San Francisco as Interior Designer
The Pfister Partnership as Principal (1981〜91)
Babey・Moulton,Inc. (1991)

* Project Experience:
Empress Place Museum, Singapore
Four Seasons (Regent) Hotel, Milan
Shell Central Headquaters, Netherland
Knoll International Showroom, Paris
Plaza Las Fuentes Hotel, Pasadena, CA
Polo Ralph Lauren, Palo Alto, CA

パメラ・バビー
バビー・モールトン社代表取締役社長

1968　カリフォルニア大学バークレー校建築学科卒業
　　　インテリア・デザイナーとして、SOMニューヨーク事務所、
　　　サンフランシスコ事務所勤務
1981　チャールズ・フィスター事務所設立に参画
1991　バビー・モールトン社設立、現在に至る

主なプロジェクト／
・シンガポール王立博物館
・フォーシーズンズ・ホテル（ミラノ）
・シェル石油本社（オランダ）
・ノル・インターナショナル・ショールーム（パリ）
・プラザ・ラスフェンテス・ホテル（カリフォルニア）
・ポロ・ラルフローレン、パロ・アルト店（カリフォルニア）

David Moulton

Senior Principal of Babey・Moulton, Inc.
Architect (AIA)

BA of UC California at Berkeley (1971)

SOM San Francisco as Architect
The Pfister Partnership as Director of London Office (1987〜91)
Babey・Moulton, Inc (1991〜)

* Project Experence:
The Northern Trust Company, London
Next Inc, Redwood City, CA
UC Berkeley Main Library, CA
Kapalua Bay Hotel, Maui, Hawaii
Boeing Corp. Headquaters, Tacoma, WA

デイビッド・モールトン
バビー・モールトン社代表取締役
建築家

1971　カリフォルニア大学バークレー校建築学科卒業

　　　建築家として、SOMサンフランシスコ事務所勤務
1987　チャールズ・フィスター事務所ロンドン所長として入所
1991　バビー・モールトン社設立、現在に至る

主なプロジェクト／
・ノーザン・トラスト社（ロンドン）
・ネクスト社オフィスデザイン（カリフォルニア）
・UCバークレー校図書館（カリフォルニア）
・カパルアベイ・ホテル（ハワイ）
・ボーイング本社（ワシントン州）

support that. But that is not to say there shouldn't be something left to be explored and discovered; some pleasant surprises as you get to know the hotel.

When a design respects its environment and its requirements, then, I feel that you reach a unique solution and there can be no other hotel like it. I like an orientation to the outside from within, a design to notify you of where you are. This surely does not mean 'corny' local references. It may mean the use of old indigenous material in new fresh relationships. One can never assume that the guest is not sophisticated, knowledgeable or chic.

Moulton: You have to work as a team with the owner and operator, but design can't be driven by operations. That would be a terrible mistake as more often than not, there are two clients, a developer or owner, and the operator. Sometimes the hotel's owner and operators are different and may not agree. Decision making can be difficult and unclear. Aside from design, there is a lot of paper work, documents, technical operations and program items.

What we try to do with a hotel design is to 'paint the picture' for our clients in order to help them to envisage the hotel and experience what it would be like to be a guest staying there. We try to design what the client wants and something which will also please the guests. In fact, we have to wade through all the dreams of the people involved and find a solution that is pleasing to everyone.

When you travel, how do you choose a hotel and what are some of your favorites?

Babey: If I'm traveling, I'm on business so I usually look for a hotel which is centrally located and has good service. I like a hotel to be pretty and I want to know what has been newly done; something that is not too simple and doesn't have too many amenities such as shops or conference rooms. I almost always look for an intimate hotel that is small in size. I also try to find out if I know the manager,

One of my favorites is the Carlyle in New York, because all of the rooms are different; some are big, some are small but all have been personally designed. I also like the Mark in New York because the manager used to be at the Regent and he is so good. I've come in late, when the restaurant was closed and the staff has asked me it there was anything they could get for me to eat. I like to go to a hotel that is an experience, a place to explore. Other hotels which I like are the Manzone in Milan, not because of an overwhelming service or style, but it is a block from our construction site; and the Shangri-La in Singapore, where I always choose a room in the garden wing with a view of the pool.

What are some of the new directions in hotel design?

Moulton: There are many new problems which force new directions. For example, there are so many difficulties with time constraints on construction, the cost of construction, manufacturing internationally, especially with furnishings and quality control of materials. Also every kind of natural material is becoming precious. All these problems force you to re-think design.

As far as hotels that get published and are recognized are concerned, it is a very small percentage. There is the Phillipe Stark new direction of almost the 'anti-hotel', which is not designed for comfort but for interest. Then there is Michael Graves and the 'theme hotel' approach.

The direction now tends less towards the anonymous chain hotel and more towards the personalized and the individualized hotel at the upper end of the market. The competition among hotel operators is stiff and the question is how they will answer that competition in the future? If you have a small hotel with a fabulous location like Campton Place here in San Francisco, you will always have people staying there but, if you build a big hotel up a hill, like a Ritz-Carlton with all those rooms to keep occupied, how do you do it? I think it is a difficult assignment and I don't know how hotel people will be able to keep on building and building.

Babey: These small hotels and small resorts seem to have a panache and style about them that can attract enough guests. If you look at the whole spectrum, the competition is fierce on every level as there are so many hotels. At the lower end of the market, however, there is a strong trend to franchises like Day's Inn, Ramada and Motel Six do. There are a lot of choices and guest expectations all have to be met or they will go elsewhere. Hotels can't just depend upon location and being associated with some known product; they have to be good. This will have positive and negative effects and bring new challenges in design.

If you could build your own hotel, what type of hotel would it be, what kind of design would you choose and where would it be?

Moulton: There is a little town in Italy, a hill town half way between Rome and Florence called Spelio; and there is a restaurant there. I thought it would be wonderful to buy the stone houses on either side of the restaurant and turn them into two or three rooms each.

Babey: Mine would be on a boat which had sails and a motor with 15 or so rooms. It would service two cities, Istanbul and Venice and would always be moored away from the pier with a view of the cities so the guests would be able to see the historic perspective of the cities. It would have lots of white materials and fabrics so that when people came, there would be no question that it was clean; there would always be a clean, fresh look to it; lots of stripes and button tufted closets wall.

If you hadn't chosen this profession, what would you like to have done?

Babey: I would have been a rock-'n'-roll star; a female Mick Jagger.

Moulton: And I would have been a Grand Prix racing driver.

——ホテルのデザインに影響を与える主たる要素は、人々、場所、それともその他の事柄ですか？

（P）自分が学んだ建築的背景、プロジェクトへのアプローチ、ホテルの経営者、環境、場所などがデザインに影響します。

例えば、① プロポーション、スケール（古典の参照・引用）
② 空間の連続性
③ 視覚的なオーダー
④ 機能的な構成
⑤ シンプリシティ
⑥ コントラストや矛盾への関心

私がシンメトリーといった建築的な原則を拒否するときは、そのデザインの環境にふさわしくないからです。決してカオスと置き換えるようなことはしません。

どのホテルも同じデザインを指向するというホテル業界のアメリカ化に失望し、何か違ったものをつくりたいと常に考えています。ところが経営者は「顔」を要求しますから、個性のあるホテルをデザインすることはますます難しくなっているのです。

ハワイのホテルのように、どこに行っても同じというホテルチェーンに人々は失望しています。だからこそ、ホテルのデザインはいま大きく変わるべきなのです。

また、そのホテルがリゾートかビジネスホテルかでも異なります。場所やその地方に合ったデザインで、かつホテルの性格に呼応していなければなりません。プロジェクトにふさわしい何かを付加する努力が必要です。さらに、経営者のフィロソフィー、サービスに対するマネージメントの方法も反映されなければなりません。これらすべての要素が一緒になってデザインすることが重要です。

——これまでの実績の中で、あなたにとって特別な意味を持つプロジェクトは何ですか。またその理由は何ですか。

（P）まだオープン前で現在工事中（注：1993年4月オープン）のものですが、ミラノのフォーシーズンズホテルと、パサデナ（注：LA近郊）のプラザ・ラス・フェンテスです。これらはロケーションを考慮して、クライアントがユニークなホテルを望んだので、デザイナーとしていかなる問題もないように完全に対処するという意味で大きなチャレンジでした。オーナーがデザイナーの才能や経験を信頼してくれ、デザイナーの側にもホテルのサービスやメンテナンスに理解が持てるとき、そのプロジェクトは特別な意味のあるものになり得ます。

また、オランダ・ハーグのロイヤル・ダッチ・シェル本社プロジェクトは、クライアント自らが計画に参画したという意味で忘れられない仕事です。マンダリン・オリエンタルはアジア風のホテルをカリフォルニアに建てるという意味で思い出深いものです。オーナーは香港を拠点とする企業で、そこに私たちはイギリス風とアジア風を採り入れ、新鮮なデザインが生まれました。クライアントはきっと知らないだろう、わかってくれないだろう、シックじゃないと思い込んで、デザインの質を落としてはいけません。上を見てデザインするべきです。

——レストランやオフィスビルのデザインとホテル・デザインの根本的な違いは？

（D）レストランやオフィスとホテルが大きく異なる点は、ホテルには非常に多くのクライアントがいるということです。コンサルタント、実際に運営する人たち、オーナー、そしてゲストです。ホテルには客室をはじめ、厨房、宴会場といったそれぞれ規模の大きな異なる施設が存在します。滞在客を満足させ、働く人たちを満足させ、なおかつその仕事は複雑そのものです。オフィスでいえば、建物本体が完成すれば、後は使う人たちが家具等を運び込んで完成させてくれますが、ホテルは使用開始前にすべて完成していなければなりません。

（P）ホテルはちょうど住宅と同じです。シーツから枕カバーのような細かいものにいたるまで、ホテル・デザイナーの仕事になるのです。すべてがデザイナーとオーナーと運営する人の責任となる事柄なんです。ですから、ホテルはオフィスなどと比較できるものではなく、住宅に近いものです。

住宅では、大きなパブリックな部屋、カードをしたり本を読んだりする小さく親密な部屋といった具合に、スケールがさまざまな部屋があります。どこにいても花屋とか宝石店とか、散策したりおしゃべりするに適した楽しい場所といった、ちょっとした気晴らしが大事なんです。リゾート地や長期滞在客の多いホテルでは特にこうした配慮が重要です。

photo by Aldo Ballo

photo by Aldo Ballo

――ホテルのデザインで特に配慮すべきことは何ですか？
（P）ホテルは快適でなければなりません。つまり出入りがしやすいことです。建物が明快で、インテリア・デザインもそれを支えるようなものが必要です。かといって、そこに思わぬ発見や驚き、喜びといった要素がなくていいことにはなりません。

　まわりの環境やホテル独自の要望に応えてデザインすることで、他のどこにもないユニークな解決に到達します。私は、ゲストがどこにいても自分のいる場所がわかる、インテリアと外部空間が一体となったデザインが好きです。これは、単にその地方の田舎風の踏襲という意味ではありません。伝統的なその地方独自の素材を新しい関係において使うということです。ゲストは何も理解できない人種であると考えてはいけません。

（D）オーナーや経営者と一緒になって考えることは、いままで述べてきた通りです。しかし、デザインは経営とは異なり、同じと考えるのは大きな間違いです。大抵の場合、クライアントのディベッロパーあるいはオーナーと、実際の経営者は異なります。ときとして、ホテルのオーナーと経営者の考えは相違し、合意に達せず、決定を見ないことがあります。デザインの面でいえば、多くの図面上の問題、書類、技術的な問題そしてプログラム上の問題などがあります。

　そこで私たちが採用する方法は、ホテルのデザインをまるで「絵を描く」ように、どのようにゲストがこの施設を使うかをクライアントに示すことです。クライアントが喜び、ゲストが楽しむことは何かを明示することです。すべての人々の夢が盛り込まれていれば、結果としてすべての人々を楽しませることになります。

――あなたご自身が旅行されたときは、どんなホテルに泊まりますか？　お好きなホテルはどんなホテルですか？
（P）私が旅行するのは、大抵ビジネスです。したがって都心の交通の便のいい、サービスのいいホテルを探します。洒落たホテル、そしてシンプル過ぎず、かつあまり便利な施設が多過ぎない新しいホテルで、どちらかというと小さな規模の親しみの持てるホテルがいいです。またマネージャーを知っていることも選ぶ要因の一つです。

　私の好きなホテルのひとつに、ニューヨークのカーライルホテルがあります。ここはすべての部屋のインテリアが異なり、規模も大小さまざまで、個性があります。ニューヨークのザ・マークも好きなホテルです。ここはマネージャーがリージェントホテルにいた人で非常に優秀です。例えば、私が夜遅くに、スタッフを連れてどこかで食事にありつきたいと考えているときなどは、やはり知っているホテルに直行します。他にもミラノのマンゾーニなどは、ただサービスやスタイルがいいというだけでなく、私の目下の現場から近いということも馴染みになる要素です。シンガポールのシャングリラは、プールを眺められるガーデン・ウイングがいいですね。

――ホテルの新しい潮流に何かありますか？
（D）新しい方向を指向するためには解決すべき大きな問題があります。つまり、建築工期、建築コスト、国際的な建築水準、特に仕上げや材料の品質管理が大きな問題です。あらゆる自然素材が少なくなっています。新たなデザインがその面からも要求されます。

　ホテルの新しい潮流ということでいえば、フィリップ・スタルクが「ホテルらしくないホテル」という新しい方向を打ち出しています。しかし、彼のデザインは快適というより興味本位で、主流とはいえません。また、マイケル・グレイブズの「テーマホテル」という方向もあります。

　しかし、全体としては新しい潮流はホテルチェーンやアノニマスといった方向に向かわず、もっと上流指向で個性化の方向に向かっています。ホテルの経営者間の競争は激しく、問題は将来への読み

photo by Aldo Ballo

にかかっています。サンフランシスコでいえば、キャンプトン・プレイスのような恵まれた場所に位置する小さなホテルであれば、いつでもゲストは来てくれるでしょう。しかし、丘の上にリッツ・カールトンのようなホテルを建て、その客室をいつも満室にしておくためには、どうすればいいのか？　それは不可能に近いことであると思います。次から次へと新しいホテルを建設して維持できるとは考えられません。

（P）小さなホテルやリゾートはそれ自身の中にゲストを引きつける魅力を持っています。しかし全体を見ると、ホテルの数はあまりにも多く、どの規模においても競争は熾烈です。底流では、デイズインやラマダ、モーテル・シックス（注：アメリカの低価格モーテル・チェーン）などに見られるように、フランチャイズ化の大きな流れがあります。選択肢は多く、希望が合えばいつでもゲストは鞍替えできます。ホテルはロケーションやそれまでの名声だけに頼ってはいられません。良くなければならないのです。これはポジティブにもネガティブにも働き、デザインに新たなチャレンジを求めてきています。

――もし、ご自分のホテルを建てるとしたら、どんなタイプ、デザイン、そして場所はどこに？
（D）イタリアのローマとフィレンツェの中間にスペリオという小さな丘の上の街があって、1軒のレストランがあります。そのレストランと両隣の石造の建物を買い取り、小さなホテルにしたら素晴しいだろうと考えています。

（P）私の夢は帆とモーターのついた15室ぐらい客室のある船です。そしてイスタンブールとヴェニスの間を航行します。それらの街の沖合いに停泊し、ゲストはいつも遠くから歴史的な街を眺めます。建材もファブリックもすべて真っ白な素材を使います。人々は問題なくそこに清潔さを感じ取ることでしょう。本当の清々しさが充満しています。ストライプや房飾りのついたクローゼットもあります。

――この職業でなければ何になっていたと思われますか？
（P）私はロックンロール・スターで女流のミック・ジャガー。
（D）僕はグランプリのレースのドライバー。

photo by Phil Toy

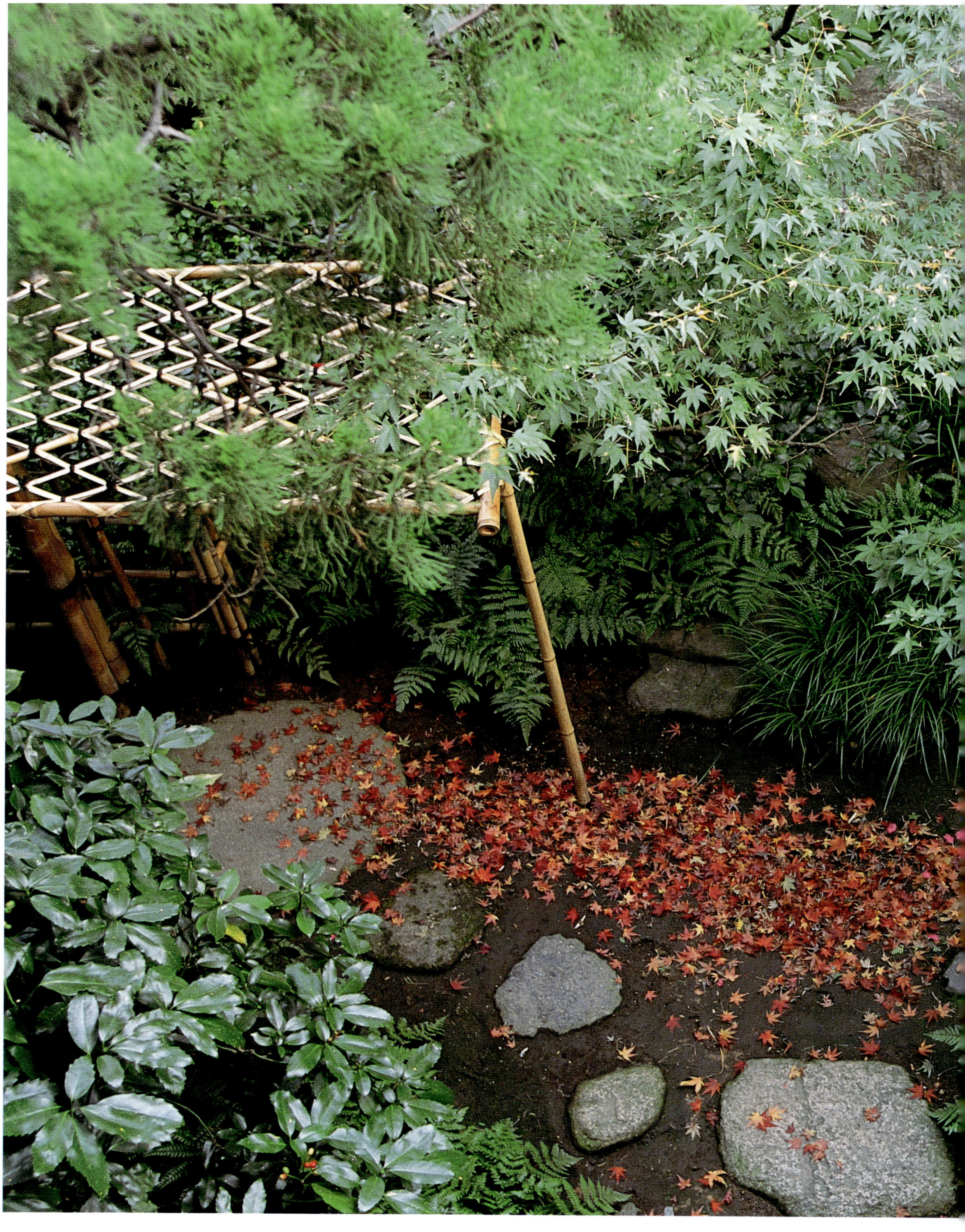

Asia

Tawaraya Inn
Kyoto, Japan

俵屋旅館／京都

Page 84 Cigarette tray
Page 85 Courtyard and Tsukubai

P. 84 煙草盆
P. 85 中庭の蹲

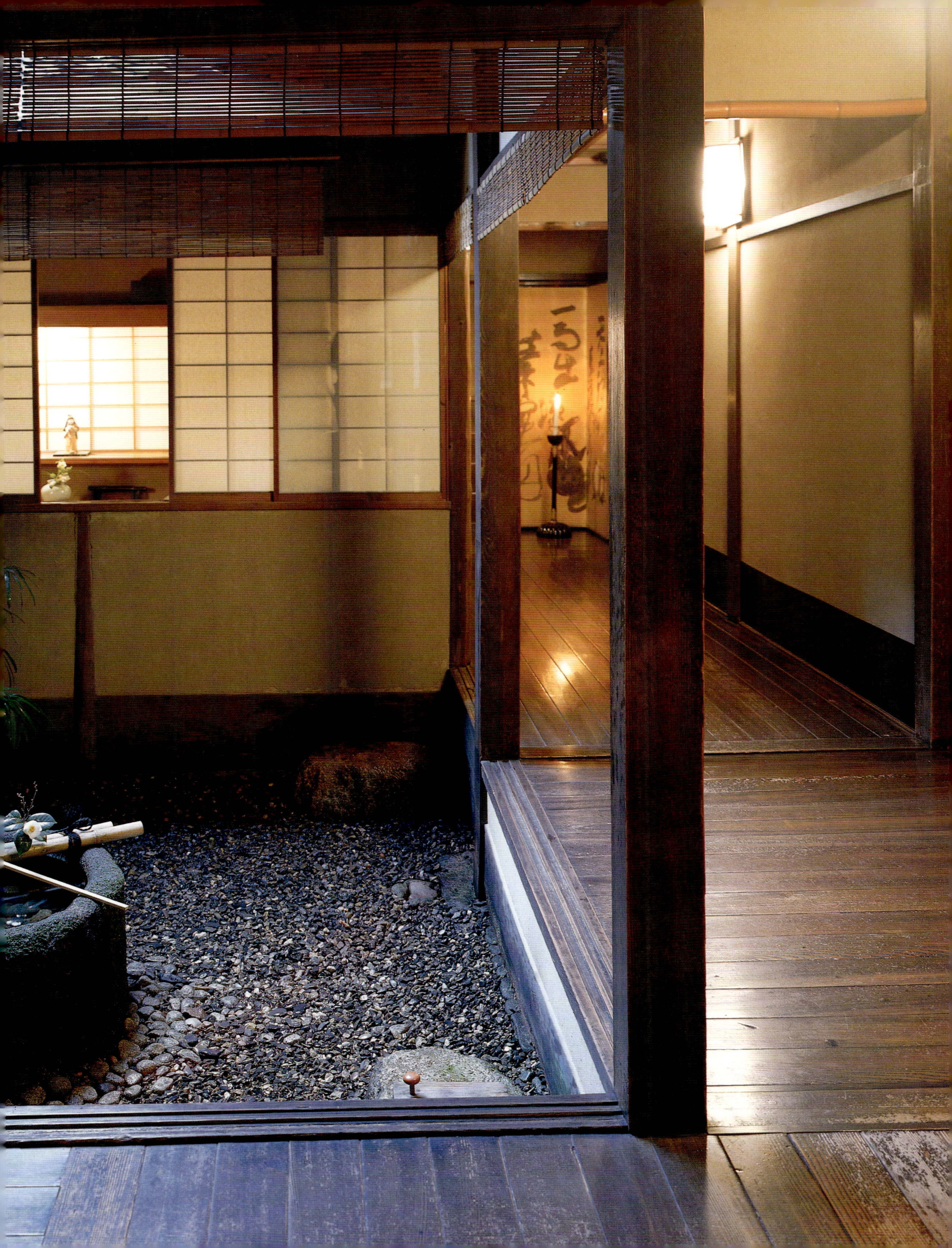

Three Centuries and Eleven Generations

300年、11代

The Tawaraya Inn has been handed down through the family for 11 generations since it was built nearly 300 years ago. Nevertheless, this long history has not been preserved willy-nilly in this inn. The ardent nature and spirit of the enterprise can be seen in comments made by the present owner about how she has tried to achieve a fusion between things modern and those that are old, instead of stubbornly holding on to old things per se.

The Tawaraya Inn is extremely popular with foreigners but this is not merely because they have a yearning for the Japan of old. The real reason lies not in its 300 year history but more in the fact that this inn started in Kyoto and is still offering accommodation today. Kyoto is, after all, where much of Japan's distinctive culture was born and has developed, and what is more, is still carefully preserved to this day.

There is an intense sense of the Japanese intellect here in this building, which is built in the traditional *sukiya* style. This is particularly evident in the sense of completeness which exists between the interior and exterior created by the *tsubo-niwa* or small court gardens viewable from many of the 18 individually designed rooms. But this does not only apply to the rooms on the first floor, as it is also true of those upstairs from which views of the gardens have been skillfully accommodated. The spaces here are truly multipurpose, serving as places to sleep, places to simply sit and talk, and at times as places in which to eat, thus continuing the true functional concepts of traditional Japanese architecture.

There is an intense feeling of Japanese aesthetics here, too, expressed by the impeccably kept gardens, the lattice work and *fusuma* or sliding screens, both of which create a consciousness of space, and is further exemplified by the *tsukubai* or round stone wash basin, and even by the bath tubs of sweetly smelling Japanese cedar. But it is the manner of the staff that brings all these things together. Guests can experience in person the stylistic beauty which is derived from day to day life here. All these thing have made people realize over the past 300 years that the Tamaraya Inn is a wonderful place in which to stay.

俵屋は、江戸宝永年間以来創業300年、11代に亘って営々と受け継がれている、京都の宿屋だ。とはいえこの宿は、ただ漫然とその歴史を守り続けてきた訳ではない。「古いものを頑なに守ることではなく、常にモダンなものとの融合を心掛けています。それもモダンが決して邪魔をしないように」という当主の言葉からも十分窺える、進取の精神と濃やかな気質。外国人に特に人気、といわれるそのゲストにしたところで、ただ古きゆかしき日本のノスタルジーを味わいにきているのではない。

それは300年という長さもさることながら、この宿が京都で始まり、京都で続いていることに深い意味がある。日本の文化のあらゆるものが京都に生まれ、京都で育まれてきたこと、そして未だ大切に生き続けているからだ。

ここには、日本の知恵が集約されている。数寄屋造りの一つひとつすべてに渡って違う18の部屋。外部と内部の一体感を生む、坪庭を眺めるための部屋の数々。勿論1階だけでなく、2階の部屋からも「庭」が堪能できる工夫が凝らされている。ベッドルームであり、リビング・ルームであり、時としてダイニングともなる居室。日本建築の持っている機能的な考えが伝わってくる。

ここには、日本の美が集約されている。手入れの行き届いた庭、空間を意識させる障子や襖、蹲、槙の木でできたシンプルで美しい風呂桶等々。そしてそれらを結び付ける空気の流れ、スタッフの起居振舞。ここでは日常の生活に根ざした様式美を、我が身を以て味わうことができる。

そういったすべての感覚が、300年もの間、俵屋を一流の宿として人々に認めさせ続けているのだろう。

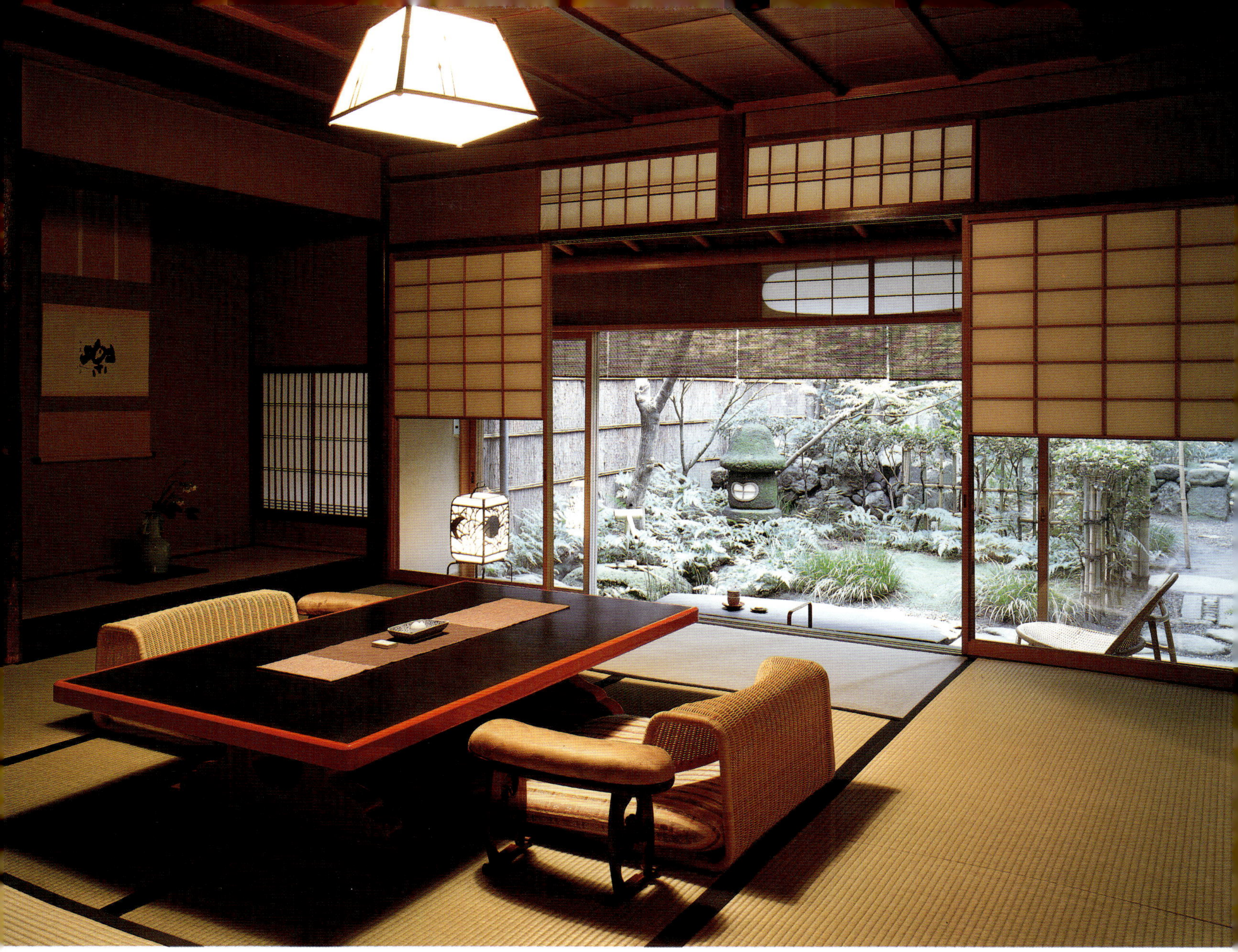

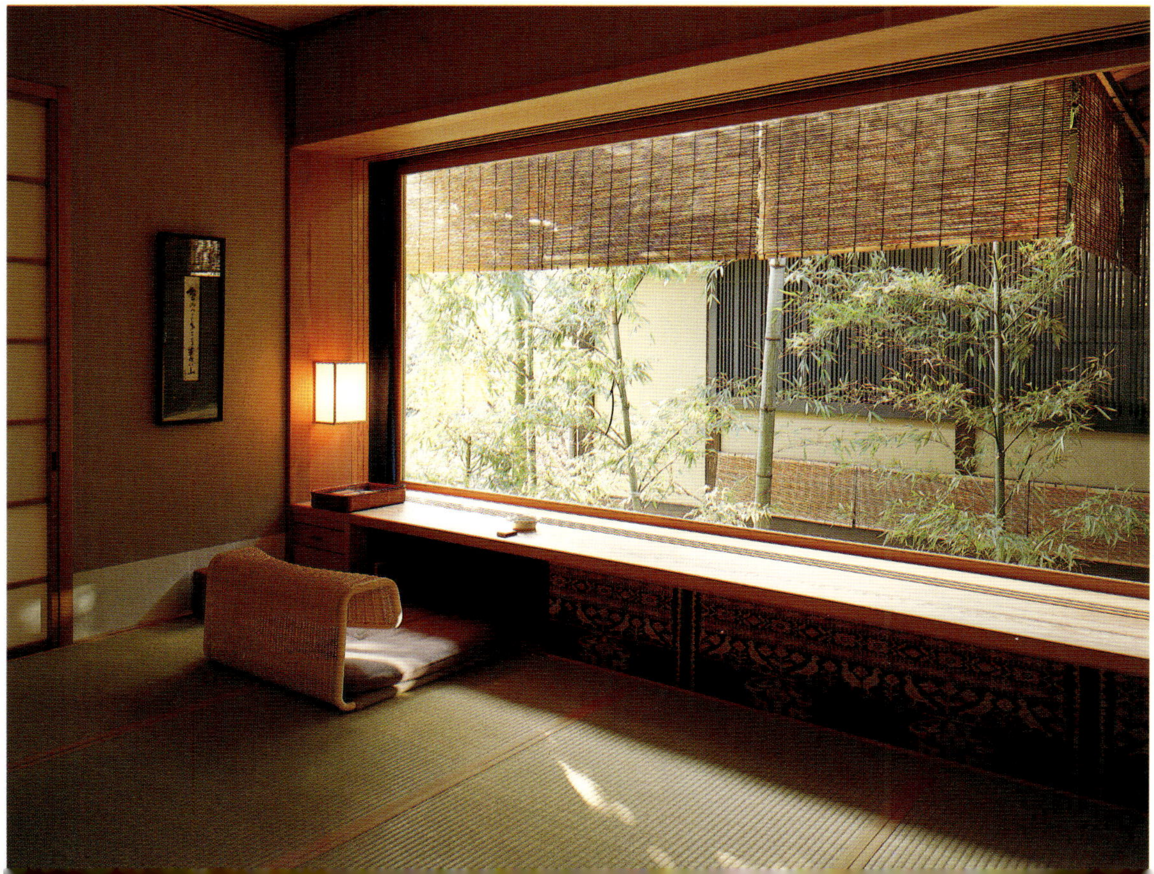

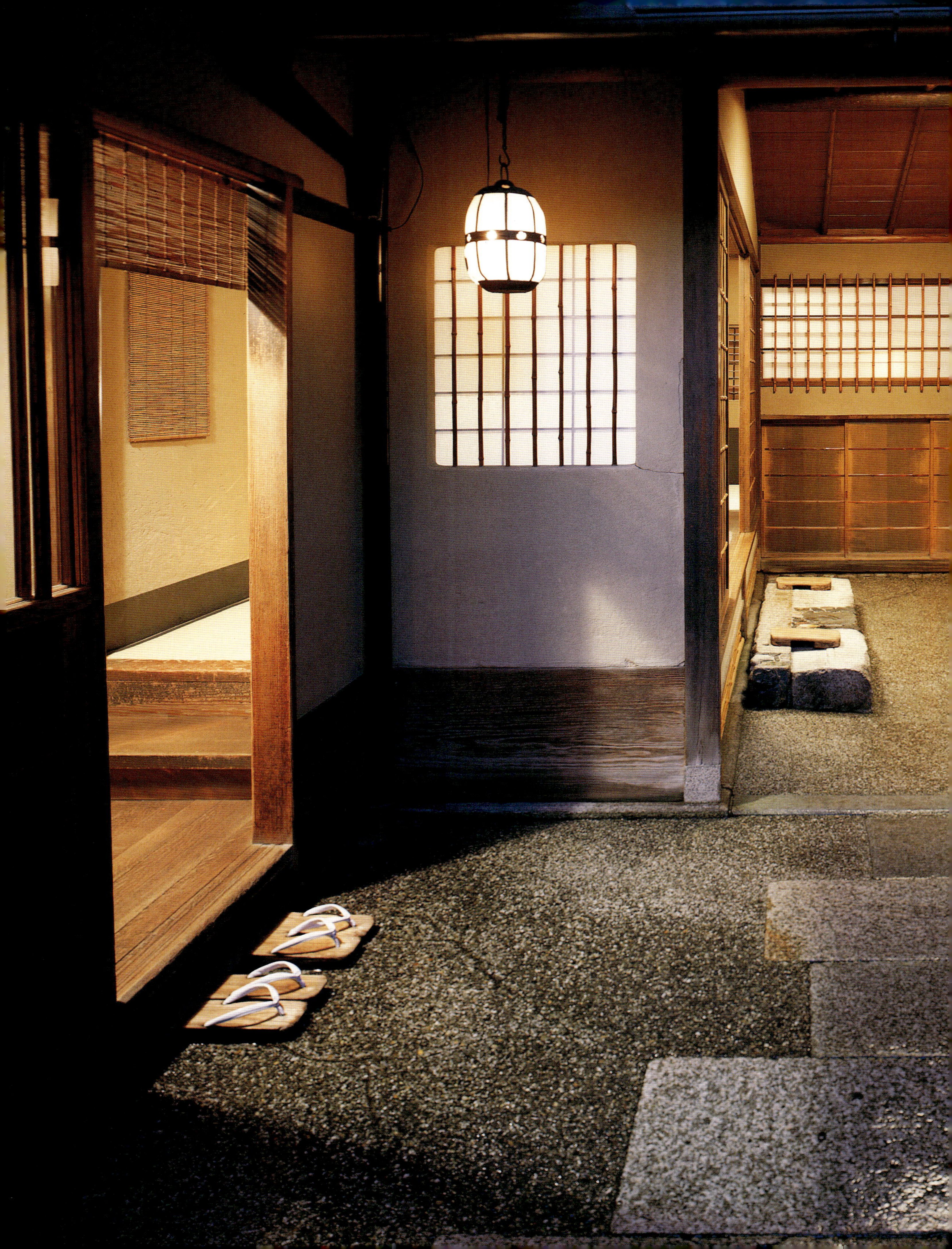

Page 87 <Top> Midori-no-ma guest room with view of garden, <Bottom> Kasumi-no-ma, a second floor guest room
Page 88 Entrance
Page 89 <Top> Lobby
Page 90 <Top> Bedding, <Bottom> Bathroom and Tsubo-niwa, a Japanese style courtyard
Page 91 Fuji-no-ma guest room

P. 87　上　客室「翠の間」から庭を見る、下　2階客室「霞の間」

P. 88　玄関
P. 89　上　ロビー
P. 90　上　夜具、下　浴室と坪庭

P. 91　客室「富士の間」

▲ 翠の間　Midori-no-ma

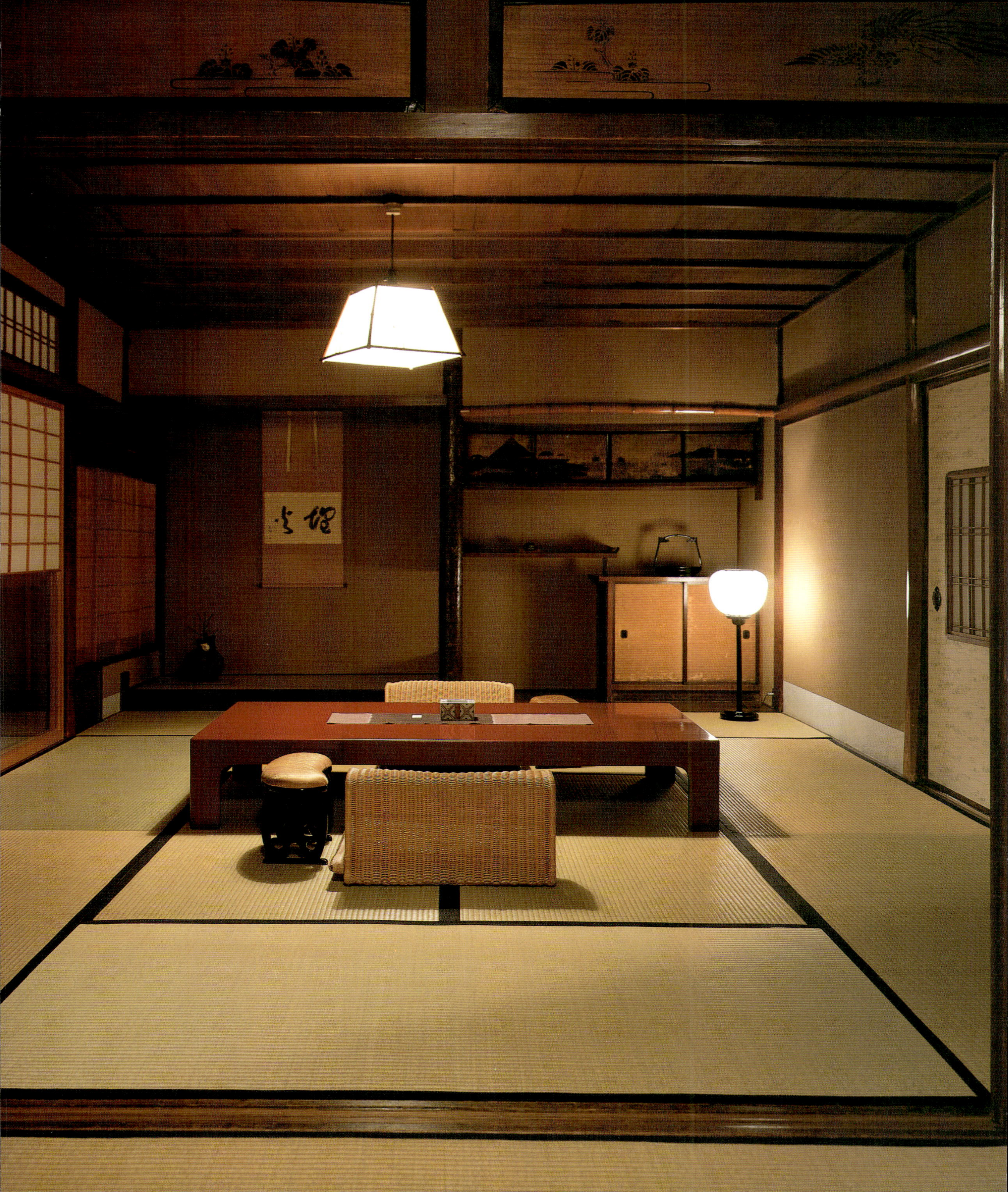

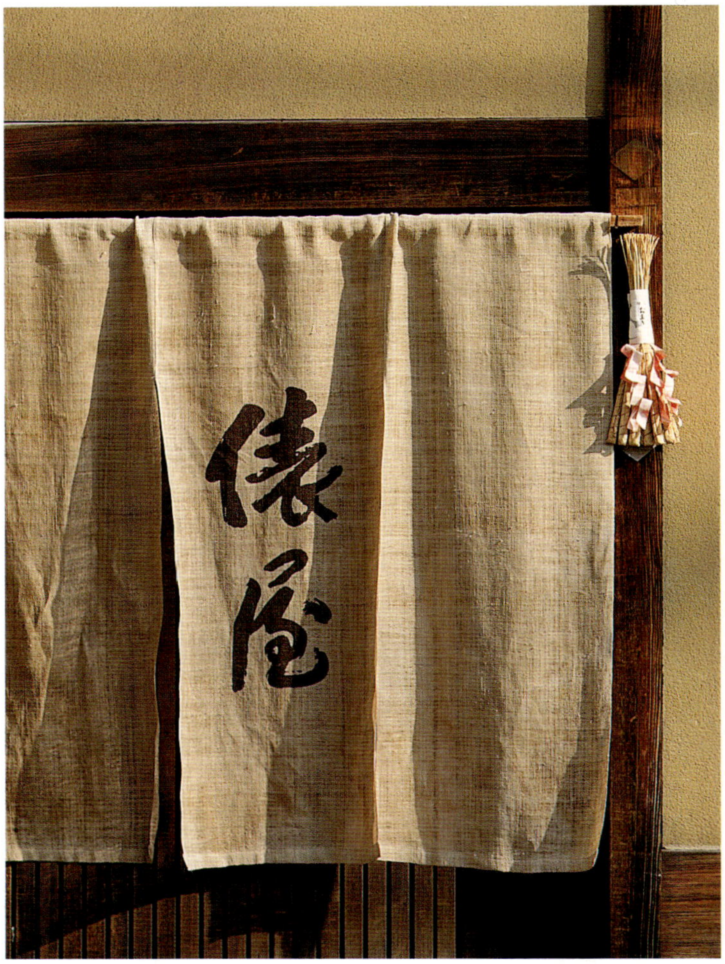
俵屋

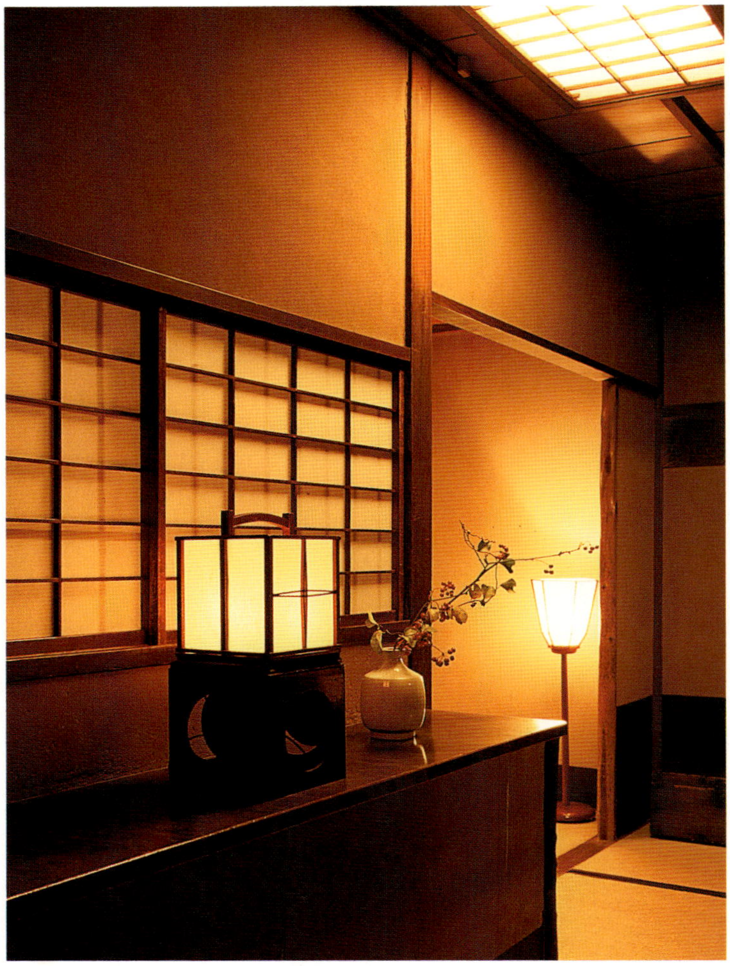

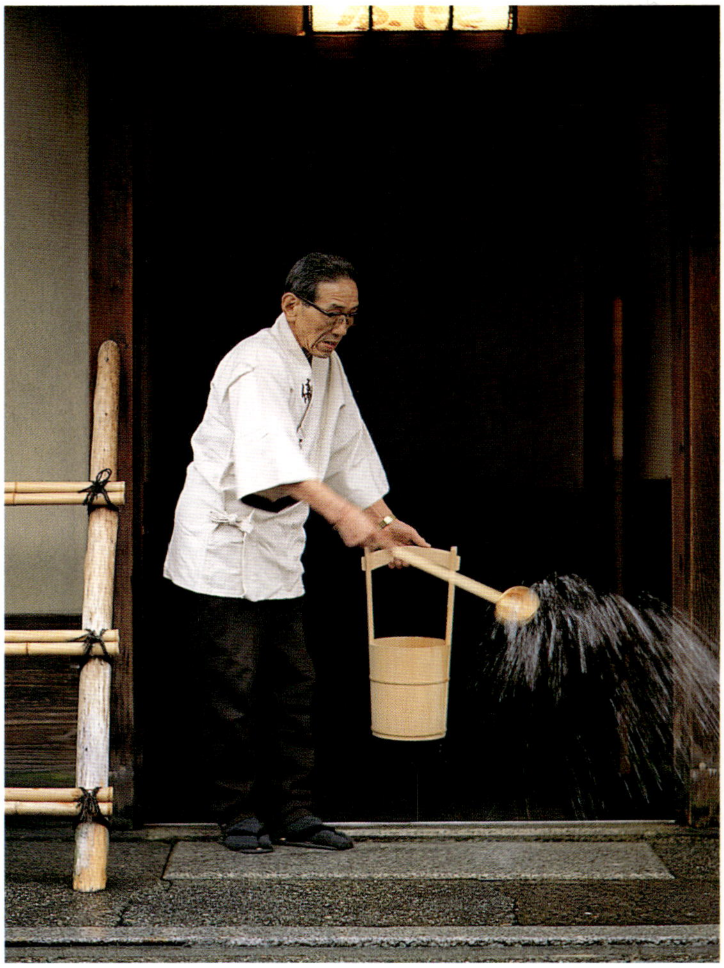

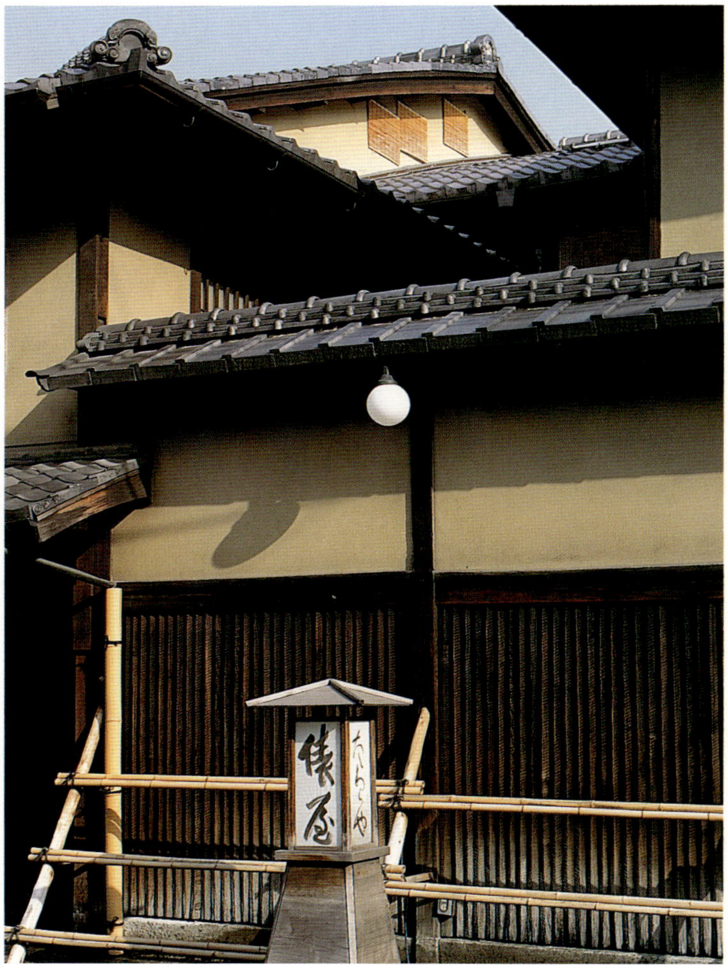
俵屋
たわらや

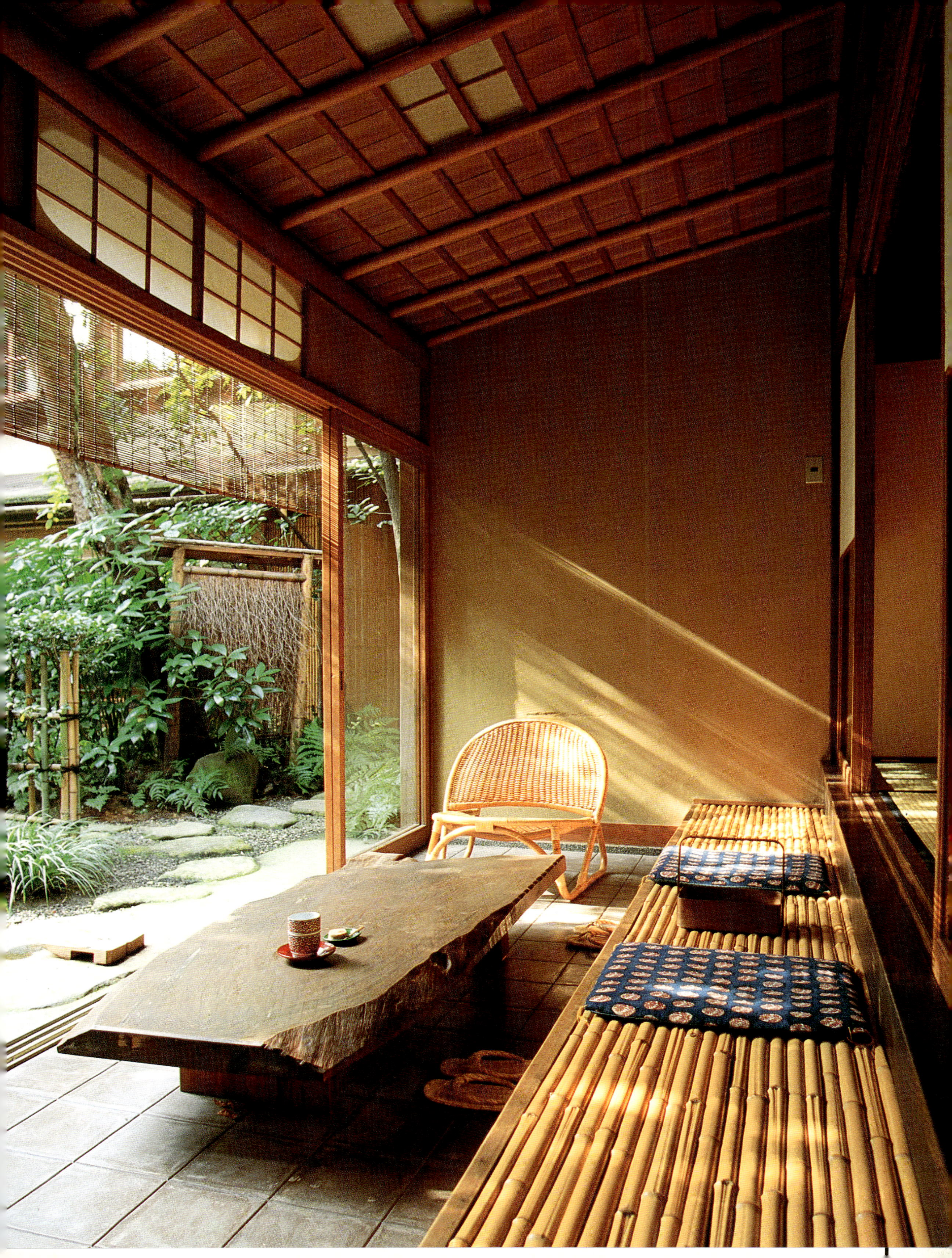

Interview

Tawaraya Inn
Proprietress: Mrs. Toshi Okazaki Sato
俵屋旅館
第11代当主　佐藤年

What is so special about this Japanese inn?
Basically, it is the 300 year history since it was established. However, it has not been simply a matter of keeping the traditional as it stands because we have tried to achieve a fusion of things ancient and modern, In doing this, we have been very careful not to let modern additions, such as new facilities, interfere with the overall atmosphere of the inn.

Secondly, from the professional point of view, we try to offer value for money by assuring comfort, excellent food and cleanliness. Furthermore, we make certain to give our guests individual attention in an effort to sustain these. We are also very careful to offer things which are good for the health and well being of our guests. For example, silk is used for night attire in the winter and linen in the summer, which insures a good night's repose.

What about your guests?
Two thirds of our guests are Japanese and the remainder are from abroad, but we are careful that the numbers of foreigners does not exceed that. On average Japanese spend two nights with us and those from overseas three. Generally speaking, they are usually over 40 years of age. What is remarkable is that foreign artists, whatever their genre, stay here because they like it. Also top executives from all over the world spend their vacation here, too.

What do you think are some of the blessings of having a business in Kyoto?
That is a very important point. Kyoto has a culture all of its own, an indigenous culture, unique it its location. For this reason it can be said that the style of the accommodation we offer is only possible in Kyoto.

What do you usually pay special attention to?
We do not have a "service manual" at Tawaraya. Each member of staff goes about their business with solicitude. For example, it is only a small point but the bath water is run three hours before a guest arrives and the temperature which falls about one degree an hour is kept at a constant 45° C in winter and 40° C in summer. We try to be thorough in everything we do.

What minor points do you consider to be important?
I normally take great pains to make exhaustive studies so that we may be able to offer new things in comfort. I myself love to concoct things and for this reason, my room has turned into something of a research studio. At present, I am looking into whether it would be feasible or not to have silk sheets because, if that were the case, then our guests would be even more comfortable during their stay with is. It might not be directly to do with the question but the thing which is most important as far as the nature of the staff is concerned is, they must be sensitive to things. Such people are suited to our type of service. There are 40 members of staff to serve 18 guest rooms. Most of them have been with us for a long time and are like part of the family.

What do you think will become necessary in the future?
An accumulation of inconspicuous and attentive basics will also, I think, be essential in the future.

What future plans, if any, do you have?
I want only to continue maintaining the present state of affairs, while preserving the size. However, I intend to carry out maintenance work in order to insure the comfort of our guests.

Finally, what would you do if you were to build a new hotel?
I have no idea where it would be but I think I would like to build a hotel that would promise simplicity and no service, the kind of hotel where you can wave the quests good-bye without having to strain one's nerves until they are out of sight!

——こちらの特徴を教えて下さい。
創業300年の歴史があります。しかし伝統を守ることだけではなく、「古さとモダンの融合」を常に心掛けています。そうしてそのモダン（注：新しい設備など）も、全体の雰囲気を邪魔しないよう細心の注意を払っています。

第2に、プロの気持ちとして、お金に見合うものを提供することを心掛けています。具体的には、「快適」であること、「おいしい」ものが食べられること、「清潔」であること。その上で、それらを支えるマン・ツー・マンのサービスがきちんと行なわれることです。

それからお客様の身になって、健康にいいものを提供することも大切にしています。例えば、寝具は冬は絹、夏には麻を使い、気持ちの良い睡眠が取れますように工夫しています。

——ゲストの特徴を教えて下さい。
国内からのお客様が3分の2、外国のお客様が3分の1、特に外国からのお客様がそれを越えないように注意しています。平均的な滞在日数は、国内の方で2泊、外国の方は3泊といったところです。全体的には、40代以上の方ということが共通しております。特徴が顕著なのは外国の方で、特に、ジャンルを問わず芸術家の方々には好んでお泊まりいただいています。次には、休暇でいらっしゃる各国のトップ・エグゼクティブの方々といったところでしょうか。

——京都でビジネスをすることで、どんなことが恵まれていると思いますか？
とても重要なことですが、ここには文化のオリジナリティがあるということです。その土地が持っていて、その土地に生まれる独自の文化が存在している。ですから、京都ならばこそできるスタイルだといえます。

——普段から気を付けていることは何がありますか？
俵屋には、サービスのマニュアルがありません。従業員の一人ひとりが、心を尽くすという行動をもって、サービスを行なっています。細かなことですが、お風呂のお湯は、お客様の到着する3時間前にはっておきます。冬は45度、夏は40度、1時間に1度ずつ下がることを前提に行なっています。すべてにこういったことを徹底しています。

——小さなところでは何が大切だと思いますか？
常に快適で、新しいものを提供できるようにと、徹底的に調べることに腐心しています。私自身は、何かをつくり上げていくことが好きです。実は建築家になりたかったのです。そのために自分の部屋は、研究室のようになってしまっています。今は、絹でシーツができないかと研究中です。それができればお客様により快適にお泊まり頂けると思っているからです。

直接関係ないかも知れませんが、従業員の資質として最も大切なことは、「ものに感動ができること」だと思います。そういった人が、私たちのようなサービス業に向いています。

——今後どのようなことが必要になってくると思いますか？
目立たない細かな基本の積み重ねが、今後ともとても重要だと思います。

——将来計画がありましたら？
この規模を守りながら、現状を維持していくことだけです。但し、常に快適に過ごしていただけるように、しっかりとメンテナンスは行なっていきます。

——もしあなたが新しいホテルを創るとしたら？
場所は決めていませんが、「シンプルで何にもしないこと」が約束された、そんなホテルを創りたいと思っています。送り手が細心の神経を使わないですむような（笑）。

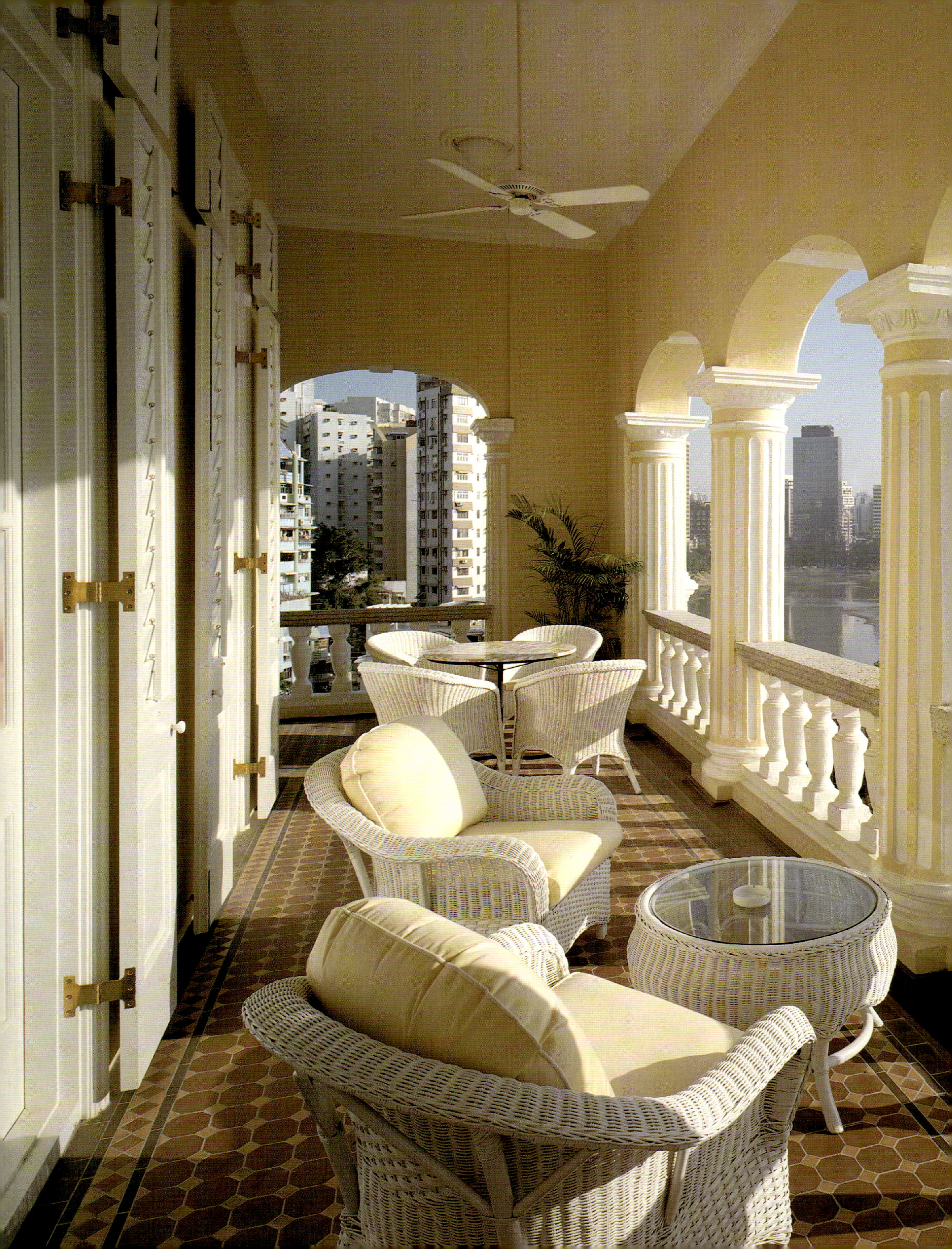

Hotel Bela Vista

Macau

ホテル・ベラ・ヴィスタ／マカオ

Page 98 View of Macau from the terrace of one of the Bela Vista Suites
Page 99 Another form of 'spiritual warmth' in the bar

P. 98　ベラ・ヴィスタ・スイートのテラスからマカオの街を見る
P. 99　上　バー・コーナー

An Amalgamation

中国＋ポルトガル＋香港＝

The Hotel Bela Vista was resurrected on 26th September 1992 in a joint venture by the government of Macau and the Mandarin Oriental Hotel Group of Hong Kong. It is a hotel with only eight rooms.

Macau is due to be returned to China in the near future, two years after Hong Kong in 1999. A confused mixture of China, Portugal and Hong Kong can be seen here in its social evolution. In a country, which has no large industries, casinos are a big source of income and this has added more fuel to the general confusion.

Bela Vista was originally built as a private residence 110 years ago but it is 40 years since it was first used as a hotel. The latest renovations have been completed in the style of a fashionable high class residence which has existed in Portugal for centuries. Its fascinating exterior is the height of perfection. Standing on top of Penna, a small hill, it seems proud of its pre-eminent notability as one of Macau's land marks.

Each room has been decorated in its own particular style and is known by its individual name. The scale and atmosphere are such that guests find it difficult to believe they are staying at a hotel.

All things taken into consideration, it must be the Verandah Restaurant from where people can enjoy a superb view that is the real selling point here. The fifty seated verandah is always bustling with local people who visit constantly all day long. It makes one realize how essential it must be to people living in the town as a place where they can relax. About five minutes away by car is a sister hotel called the Mandarin Oriental Hotel Macau, where guests staying at the Bela Vista may use facilities such as the pool or gym. This is just one of the amazing systems to be found here. When the change-over comes, they should be very grateful.

If it had not been for the link up between the management of the Mandarin Hotel with its established reputation and the government's consideration to somehow restore this hotel, then this project would probably have never been realized after all. Macau's future dreams are obviously entrusted to this hotel.

1992年9月26日、ベラ・ヴィスタ（＝良い眺め）は甦った。それは、マカオ政府と香港のマンダリン・オリエンタル・ホテル・グループとのジョイントによって、再び陽の目を見ることとなった。それも、たった8室のホテルとして。

香港に遅れること2年、1999年の中国返還を間近に控えたマカオ。ここでは中国とポルトガル、そして香港が出会い、混沌とした社会が形成されている。大きな産業を持たないこの国では、カジノが大きな収入源。それがより一層混沌に拍車を掛けている。

110年前に個人の邸宅として建てられたベラ・ヴィスタは、ホテルとして使われるようになってから、既に40年ほどの歴史を持つ。今回の改装では、ポルトガルに古くからある、上流階級の家のイメージで仕上げられている。その魅力的な外観は、ベラ・ヴィスタの真骨頂。ペンニャの小高い丘の上に建ち、マカオのランドマークとして抜群の知名度を誇る。一つひとつの部屋には、それぞれ独自のインテリアが施され、それぞれに違った名前が付けられている。大きさといい、雰囲気といい、どうしてもホテルに泊まっているような感じがしない。

ここでの売り物は何といっても、高台を利用した眺望が十二分に楽しめる「ベランダ・レストラン」。50席あるベランダは、日がな一日ひっきりなしに訪れる地元の人で、いつも盛況。ベラ・ヴィスタが、憩いの場として、この街になくてはならない存在だということに気が付く。車で5分程の距離にある姉妹ホテル、マンダリン・オリエンタル・ホテル・マカオのプールやジム等、さまざまな施設が利用できることも、ここでの魅力あるシステムのひとつ。色々な意味で切り替えが必要な時には、実にありがたい。

この古いホテルを何とか甦らせようという政府の思い入れと、マンダリン・ホテルの定評あるマネージメント力が結び付かなければ、到底このプロジェクトは実現しえなかっただろう。ここには、マカオの夢が託されている。

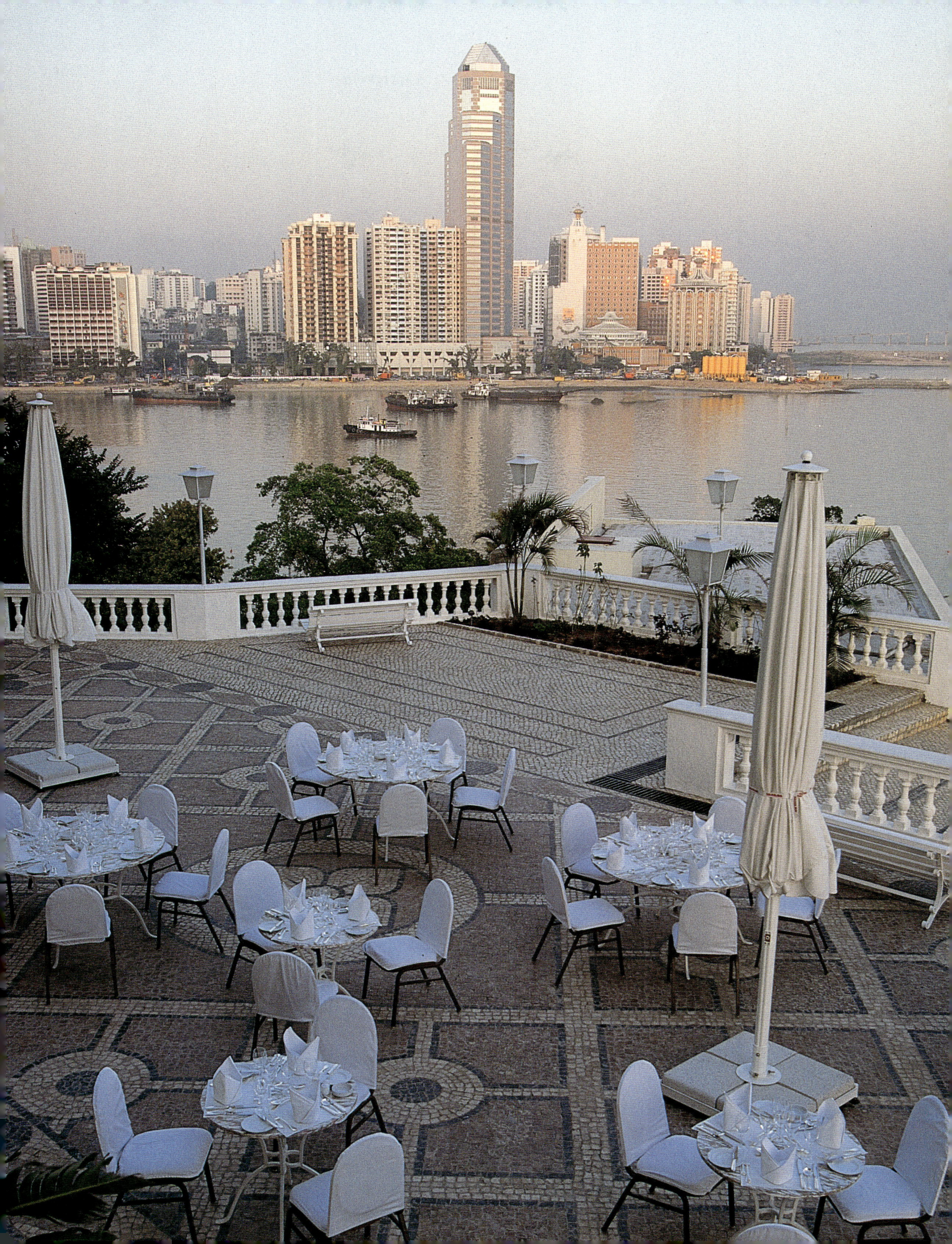

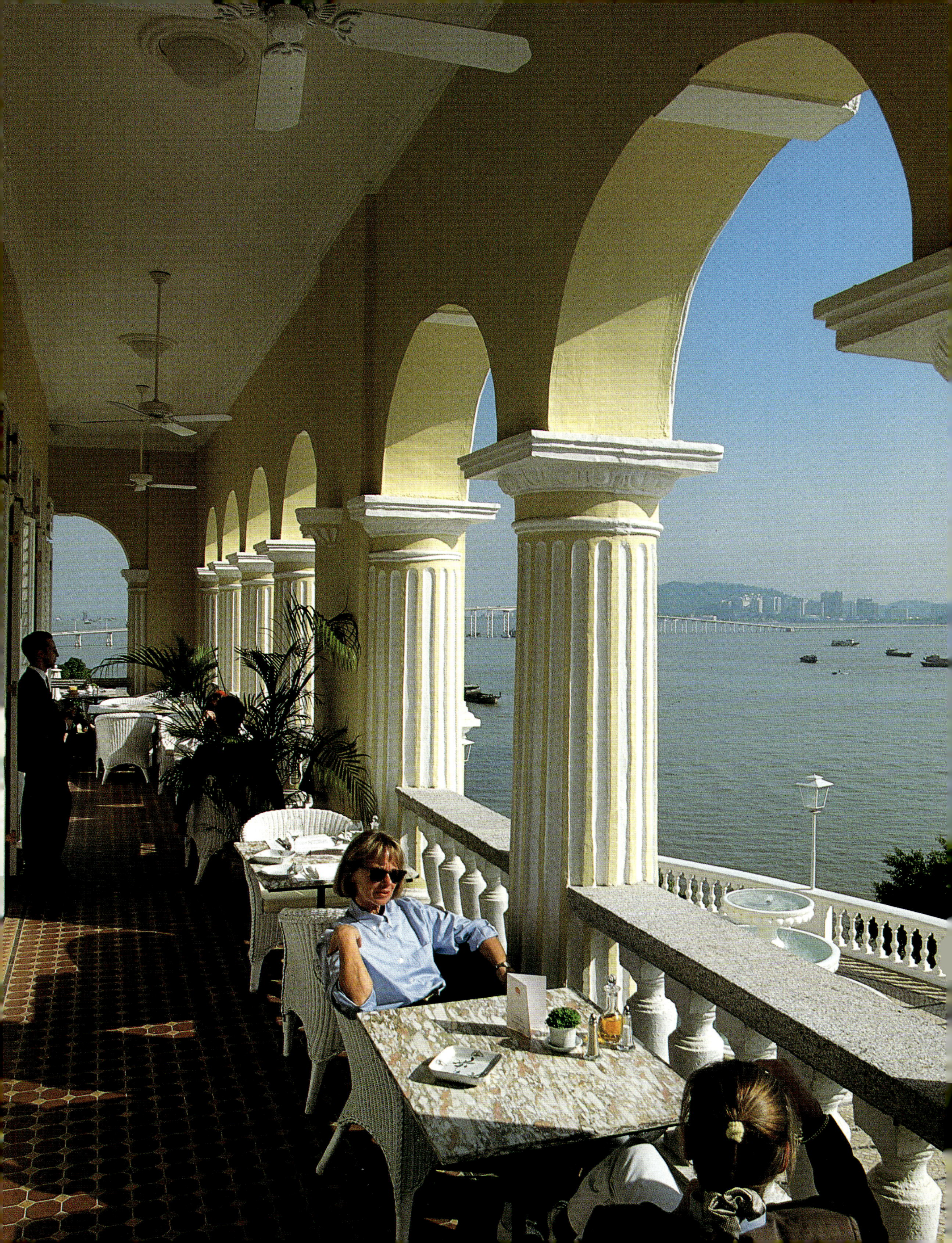

Page 101 Downtown Macau can be seen from terrace
Page 102 Terrace of Verandah Restaurant
Page 103 <Top> Interior of restaurant, <Center> Bar counter, <Bottom> A corner of terrace
Page 104 <Top> Bedroom, <Center left> Bathroom, <Bottom left> A corner of bathroom
Page 105 Reception

P.101 テラスから街を見る
P.102 「ベランダ・レストラン」のテラス
P.103 上　同レストラン内部、中　バー・カウンター、下　テラスの片隅
P.104 上　ベッドルーム、左中　バスルーム、左下　バスルームの片隅
P.105 レセプション

Bela Vista Suite

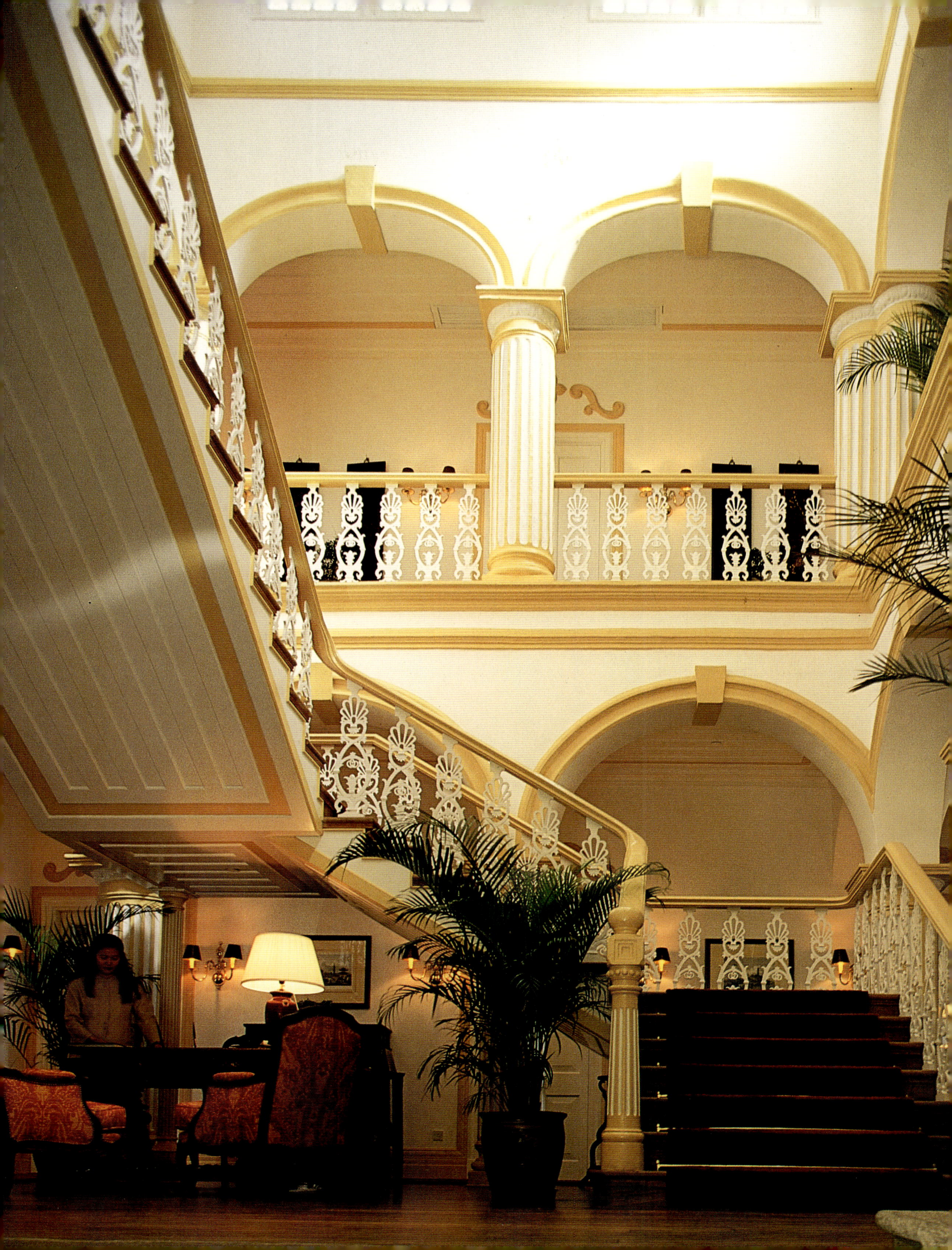

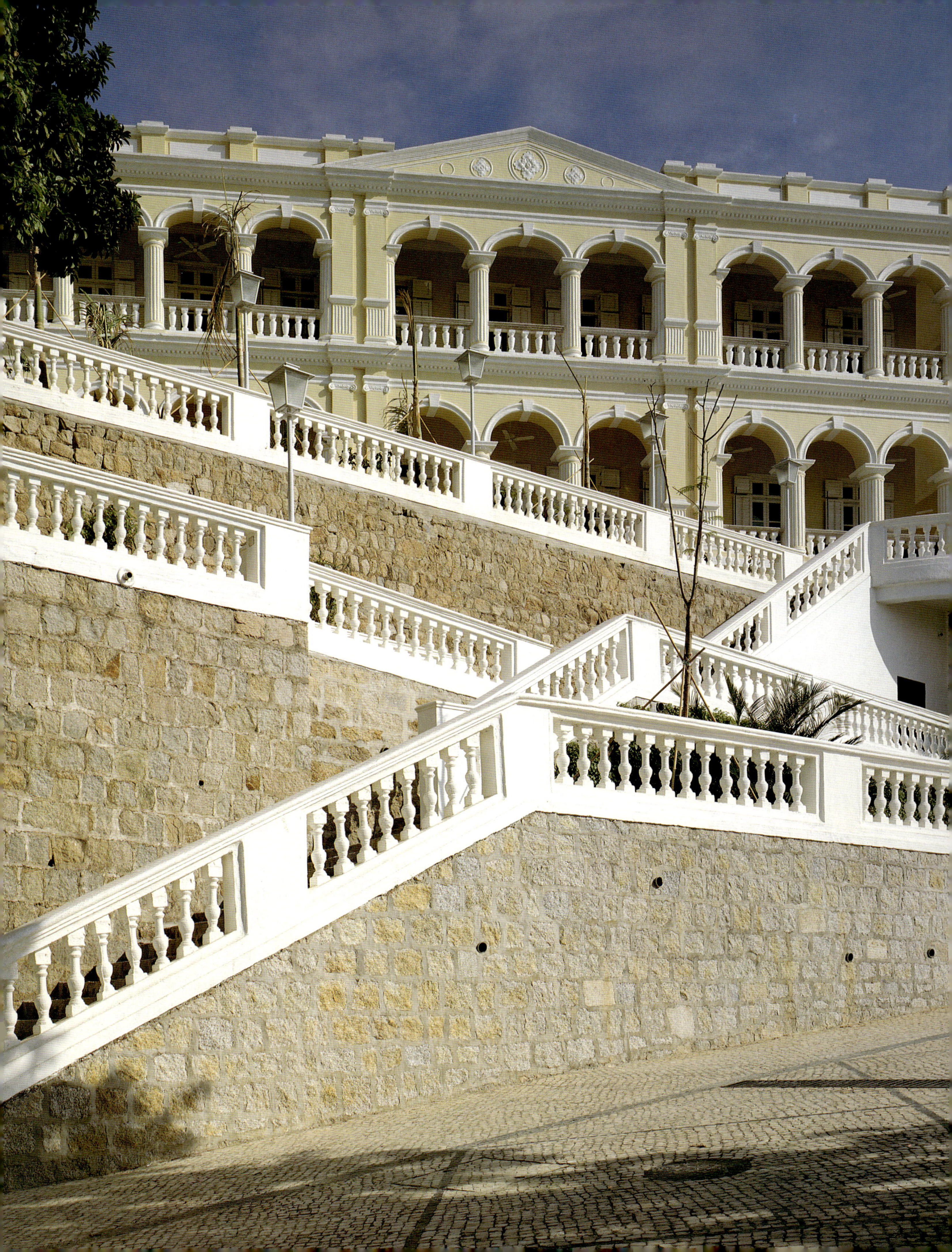

Page 106 Bela Vista, one of Macau´s land-marks, sits on top of Penha Hill
Page 107 Exterior of the hotel at night
Page 108 <Top left> Embroidered laundry bag, <Top right> Soap rack over the bath, <Center left> Sign in front of the hotel, <Center right> Bath towel, <Bottom left> Pumice stone inscribed with the hotel's logo <Bottom right> Facade
Page 109 <Top> Exterior, <Bottom left> Bela Vista of old

P.106　丘の上に建つベラ・ヴィスタ
P.107　ホテル外観の夜景
P.108　上左　刺繍のほどこされたランドリー・バック、上右　バスタブ・ネット、中左　入口サイン、中右　オリジナル・タオル、下左　ロゴマークの入った敷石、下右　ファサード
P.109　上　ホテル外観、下左　昔の姿を記す写真

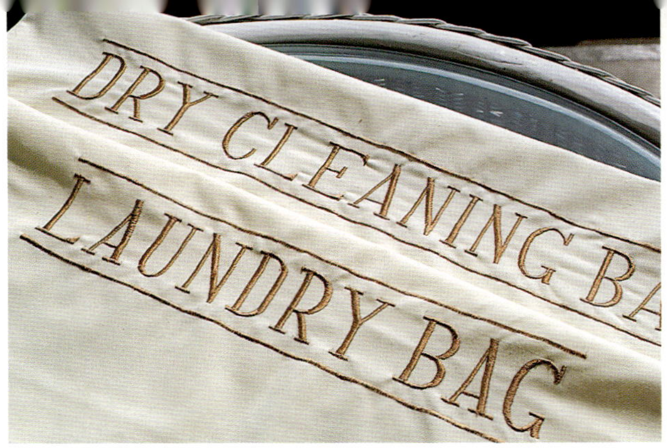
DRY CLEANING
LAUNDRY BAG

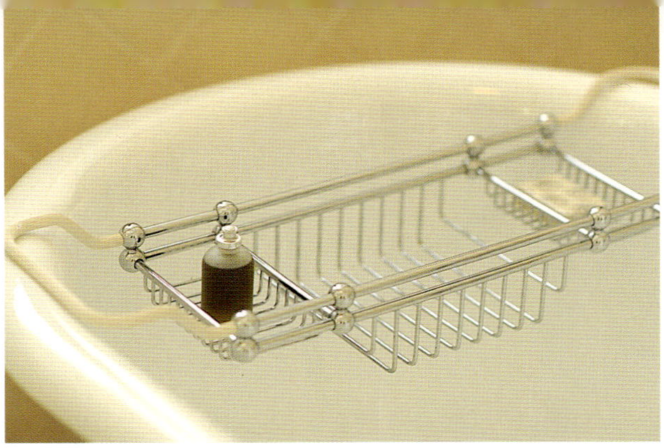

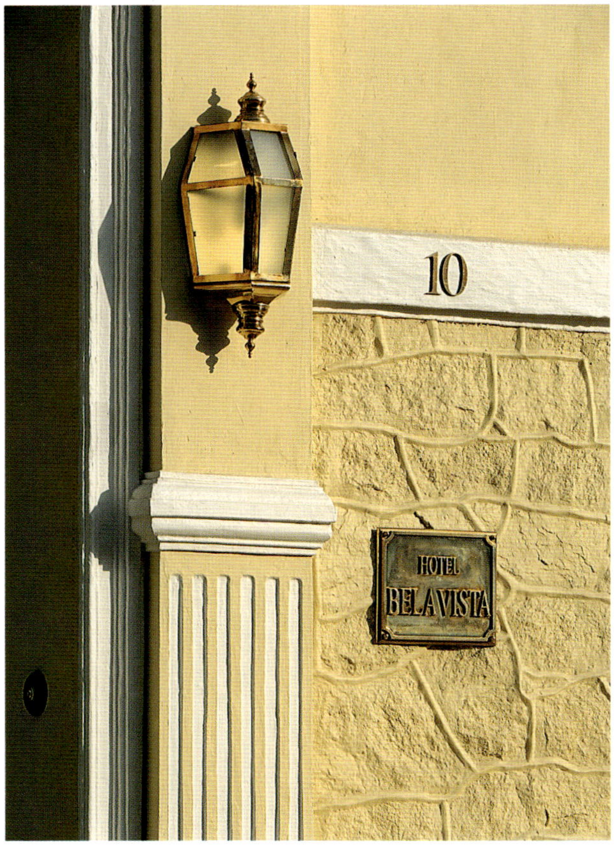
10
HOTEL
BELAVISTA

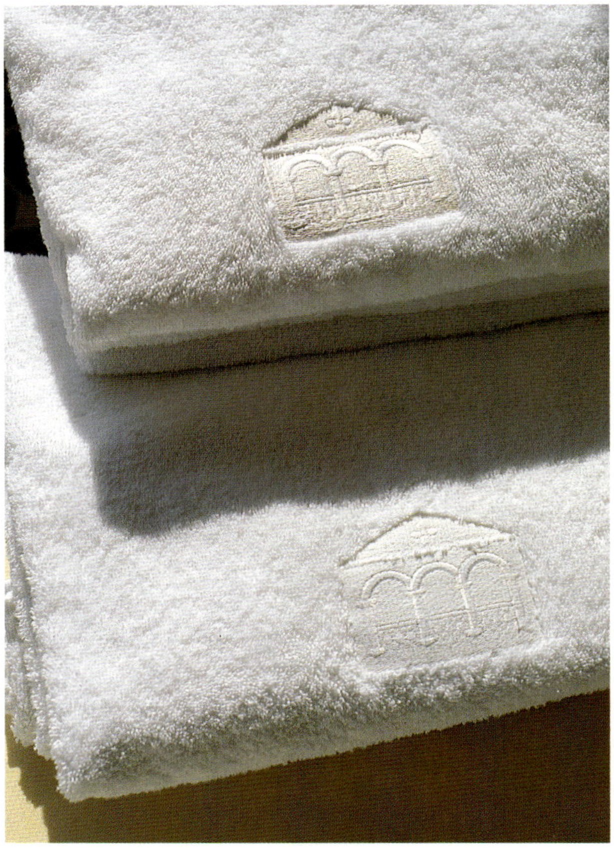

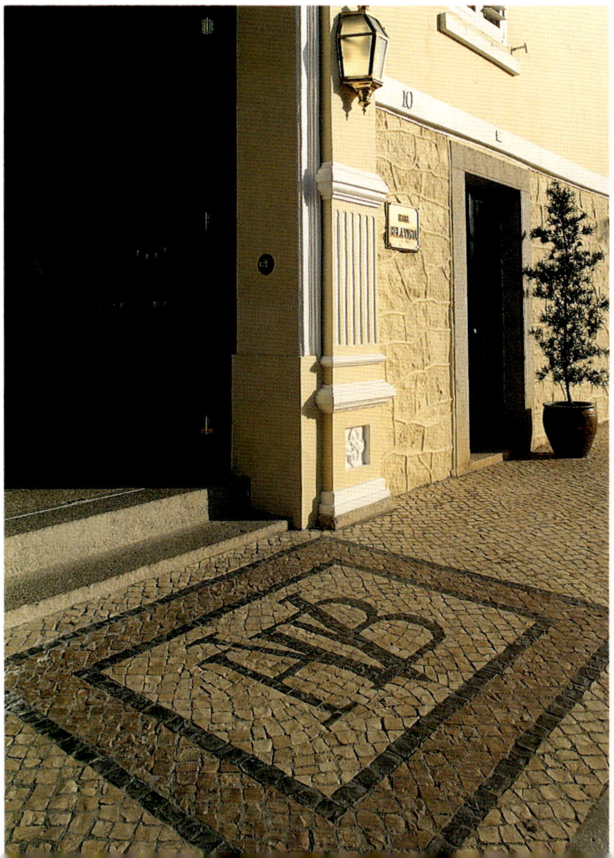

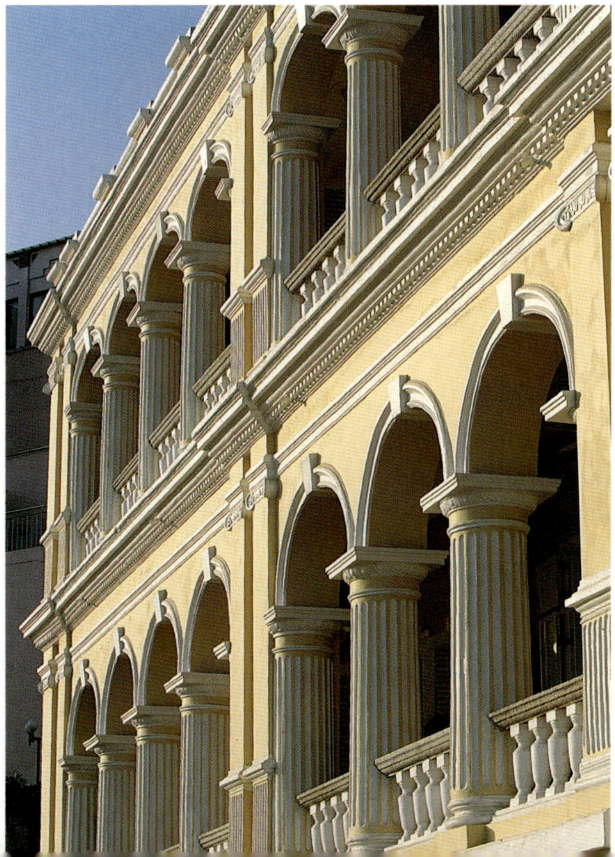

General Manager Mr. Brian E. Williams

総支配人　ブライアン・ウイリアムス

Hotel Bela Vista

The Duxton
Singapore

ザ・ダクストン／シンガポール

Page 110 Exterior of the hotel

P.110　ホテル外観

Redevelopment Sired Small Urban Hotel
再開発で生まれた、小さな都市型ホテル

The Duxton is a new hotel, which made its debut in October 1991 as part of a redevelopment project of the Tanjong Pagar district in a corner of Singapore's China Town. Although it is basically a Chinese design, it has a subtle air of the European about it without distracting from the neighborhood atmosphere. All hotels in Singapore have until now been huge concerns, catering for tourists and business people alike. Most of these hotels are grouped in overcrowded conditions around Orchard Street, the busiest shopping street in town but the Duxton is one of the few hotels, which have been established next to the financial district with an eye to the business sector. It naturally follows, therefore, that most of the guests staying at the hotel are foreigners on business in the district. As all the guests are young, well travelled business people, who are not fond of large scale hotels, they seek a stylish service from reception. Even though the hotel is not widely advertised, many of the reservations are made by people who have heard about The Duxton by word of mouth. Guests must be satisfied with the service offered as they invariably come back to stay again and again.

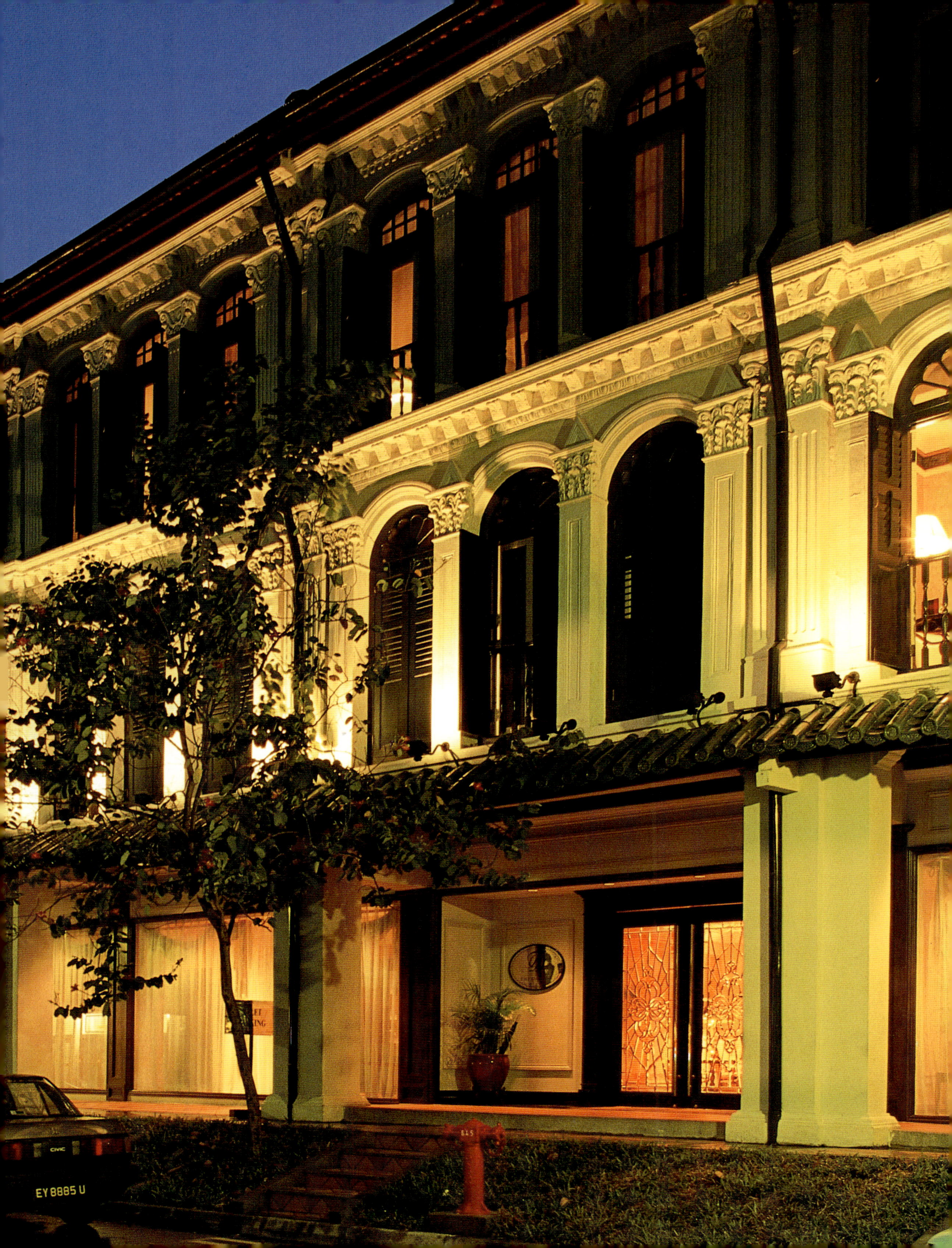
EY 8885 U

The number of rooms is very small but the variation is fairly complete. It is very difficult to demand spacious accommodation in view of the type of urban hotel it is, but this is covered by the maisonette type deluxe suite and is supplemented by the patio outside the windows of the garden suite.

The L'Aigle d'Or French restaurant adjoining the lobby rapidly gained a reputation among Singaporians after it opened as a place to enjoy a really authentic French meal and it is now acknowledged as being one of the most popular restaurants in Singapore.

The Duxton has many potentials. It is a very small urban hotel with only 49 rooms, situated in a superb location in the redeveloped area of China Town, and it is now attracting a good deal of attention as Singapore's latest experiment in hotel accommodation.

シンガポールのチャイナタウンの一角、タンジョン・パガー地区の再開発によって、1991年10月に誕生した新しいホテル。それが、ザ・ダクストンだ。周囲に雰囲気を損なうことなく、「中国」をベースにしながらもヨーロッパの香りをうまく伝えている。今までのシンガポールのホテルといえば、ビジネス、観光共に大きなタイプと決まっていた。そして、その多くのホテルが街一番の繁華街、オーチャード・ロードの回りに集中している過密状態の中、このホテルはビジネスの中心、金融街に隣接する数少ないホテルのひとつ。当然の帰結として、ビジネスでこの街を訪れる外国人が宿泊の中心となる。それも大きな規模を好まない、旅慣れた若いビジネスマンばかりなので、受け入れ側にもスマートなサービスが求められる。あまり大々的な広告をしていないにも関わらず、噂を聞いての予約が入り、リピーターとして定着しているというので、そのサービスが認められているのだろう。

部屋の数こそ少ないが、バリエーションはかなり揃っている。都市型ゆえに広さを求めることは難しいが、それでもメゾネット・タイプでは容積でカバーし、ガーデン・スイートでは、窓の外のパティオがそれを補っている。ロビーに続く、フレンチ・レストラン"L'Aigle d'Or"「ラーグル・ドール（金の鷲）」は、本格的なフランス料理を食べさせるということで、シンガポーリアンの中でも瞬く間に評判となり、今や押しも押されもしない、人気レストランのひとつに成長している。

49室と都市型ホテルとしては極めて少ない部屋数、チャイナタウンというロケーション、そして地域の再開発によって新しく生まれたこと等々…。色々な可能性を秘めているザ・ダクストンは、シンガポールの新たな試みとして注目されている。

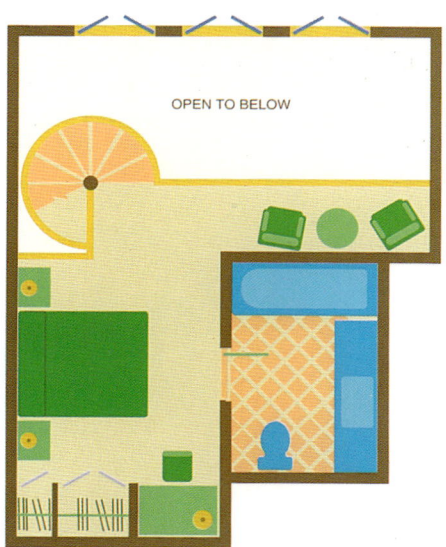

Deluxe Suite

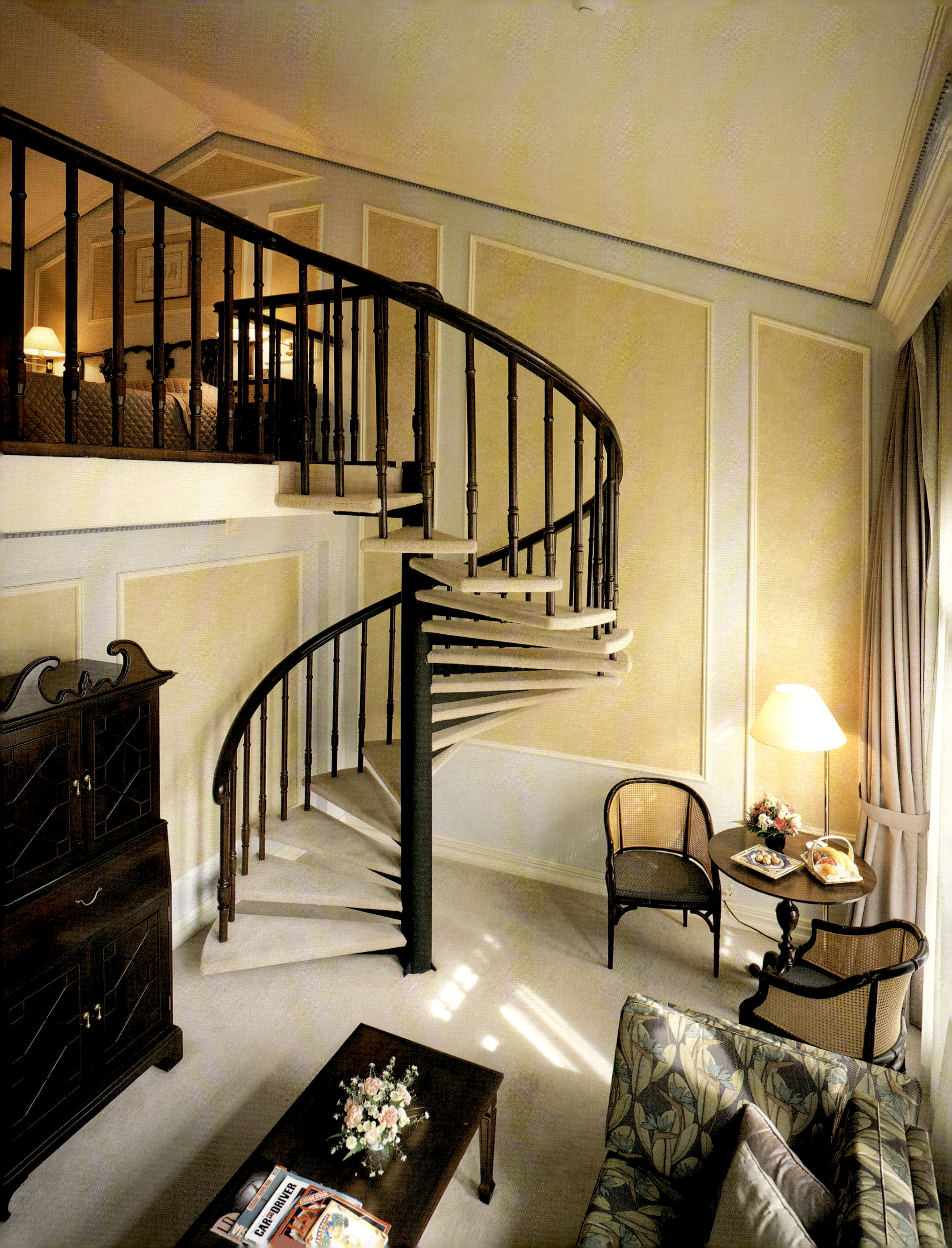

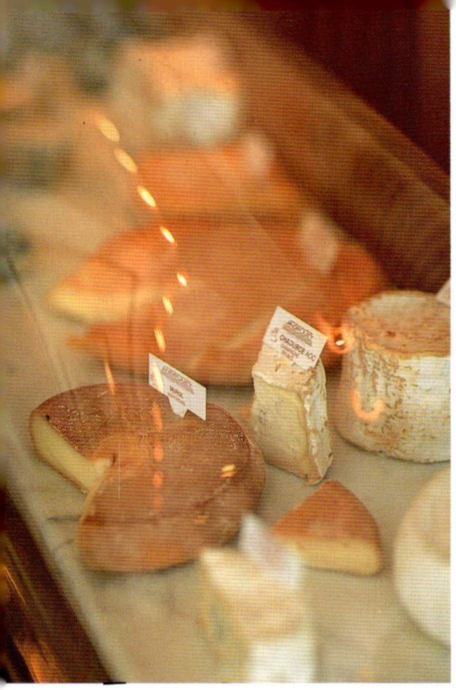

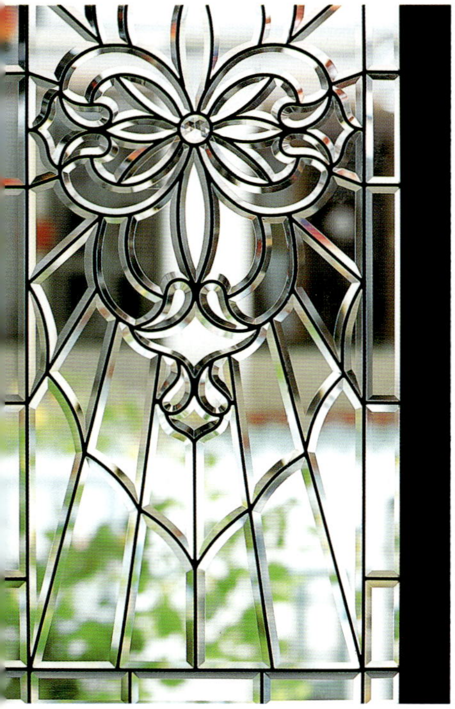

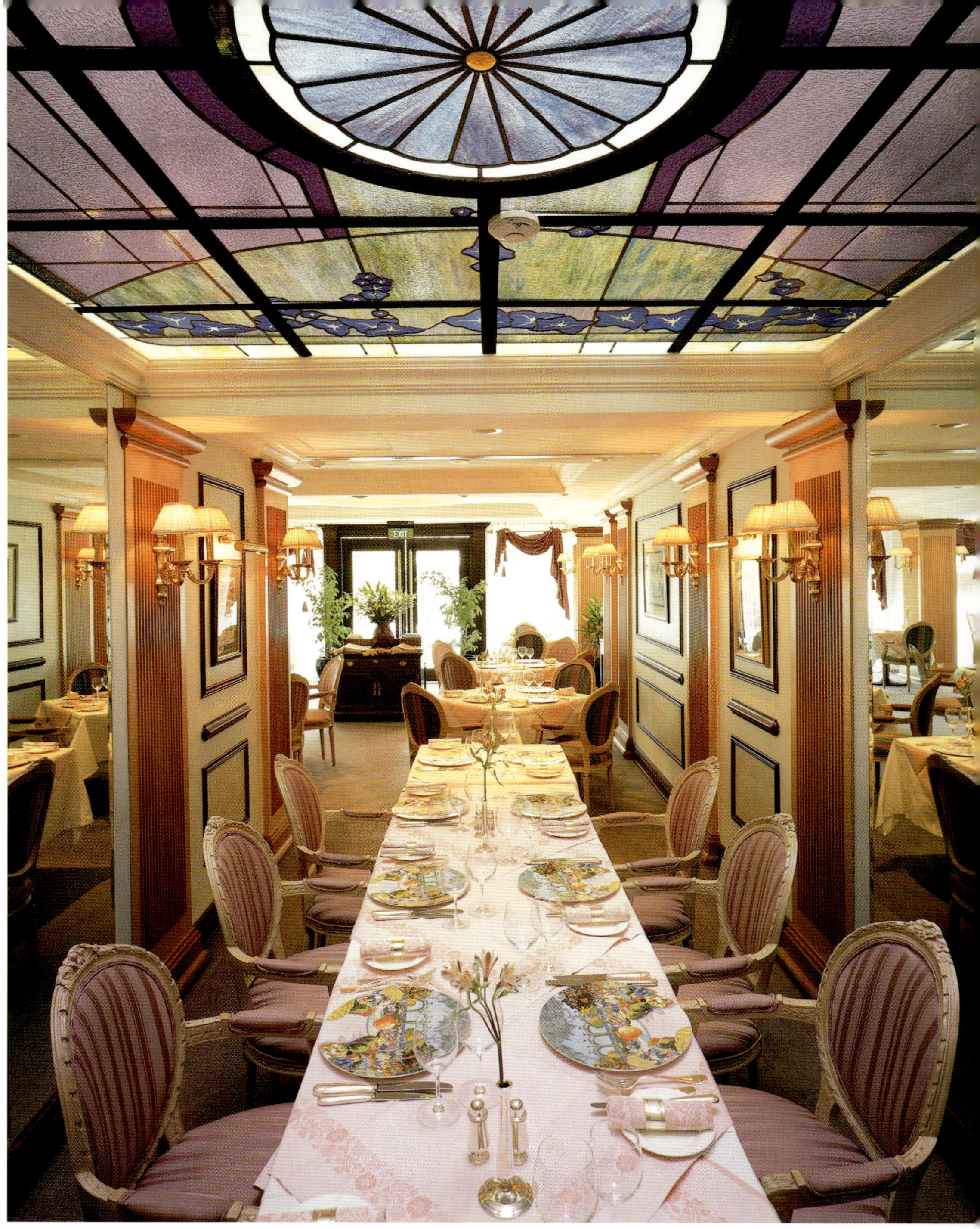

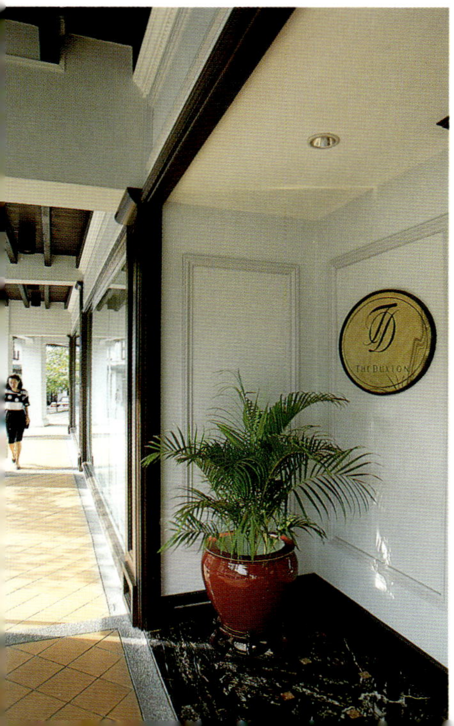

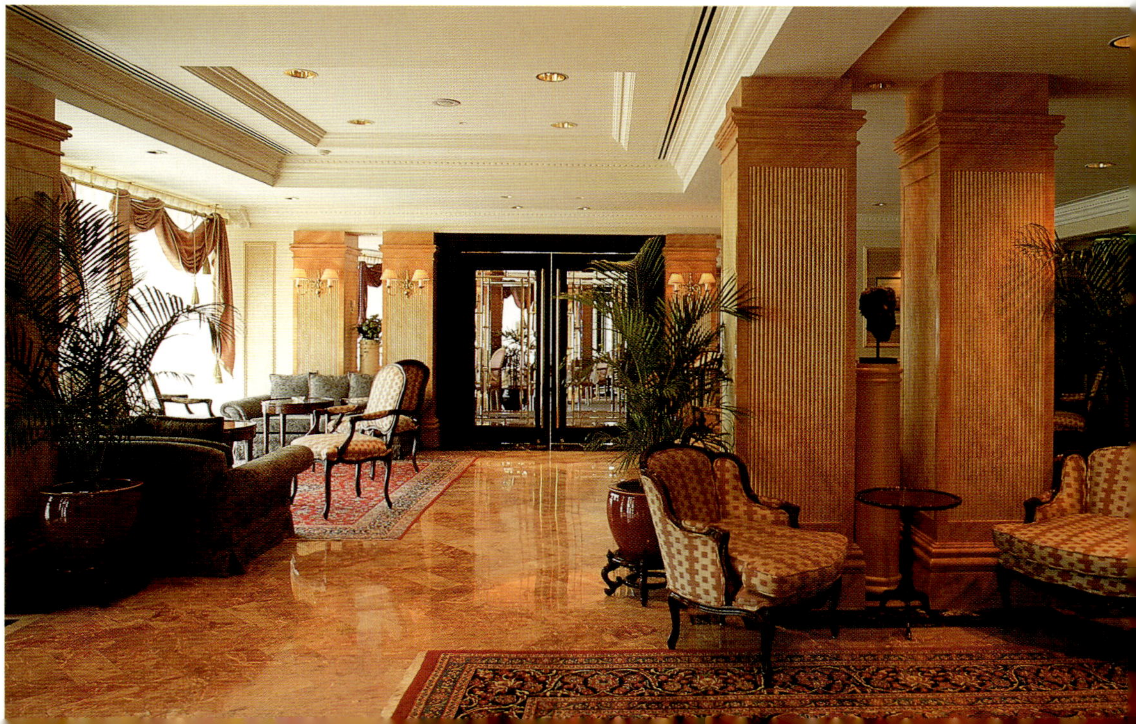

Page 112 <Top> View of the living room from the second floor of the Deluxe Suite, <Center> Interior of Garden Suite
Page 113 Interior of Deluxe Suite
Page 114 <Top right> Interior of the restaurant, <Bottom left> Interesting arrangement in a corner of the entrance, <Bottom right> Entrance of the restaurant seen from lobby
Page 115 <Top> Look-ing toward the financial district from the hotel, <Bottom> China town

P.112 上 「デラックス・スイート」の吹抜からリビング・ルームを見る、中 「ガーデン・スイート」の内部
P.113 「デラックス・スイート」の内部
P.114 上右 レストランの内部、下左 エントランス・コーナー、下右 ロビーからレストラン入口を見る
P.115 上 ホテルのあるタンジョン・パガー地区から見る金融街、下 チャイナタウン

Director Ms. Margaret Wong

取締役　マーガレット・ウォン

The Duxton

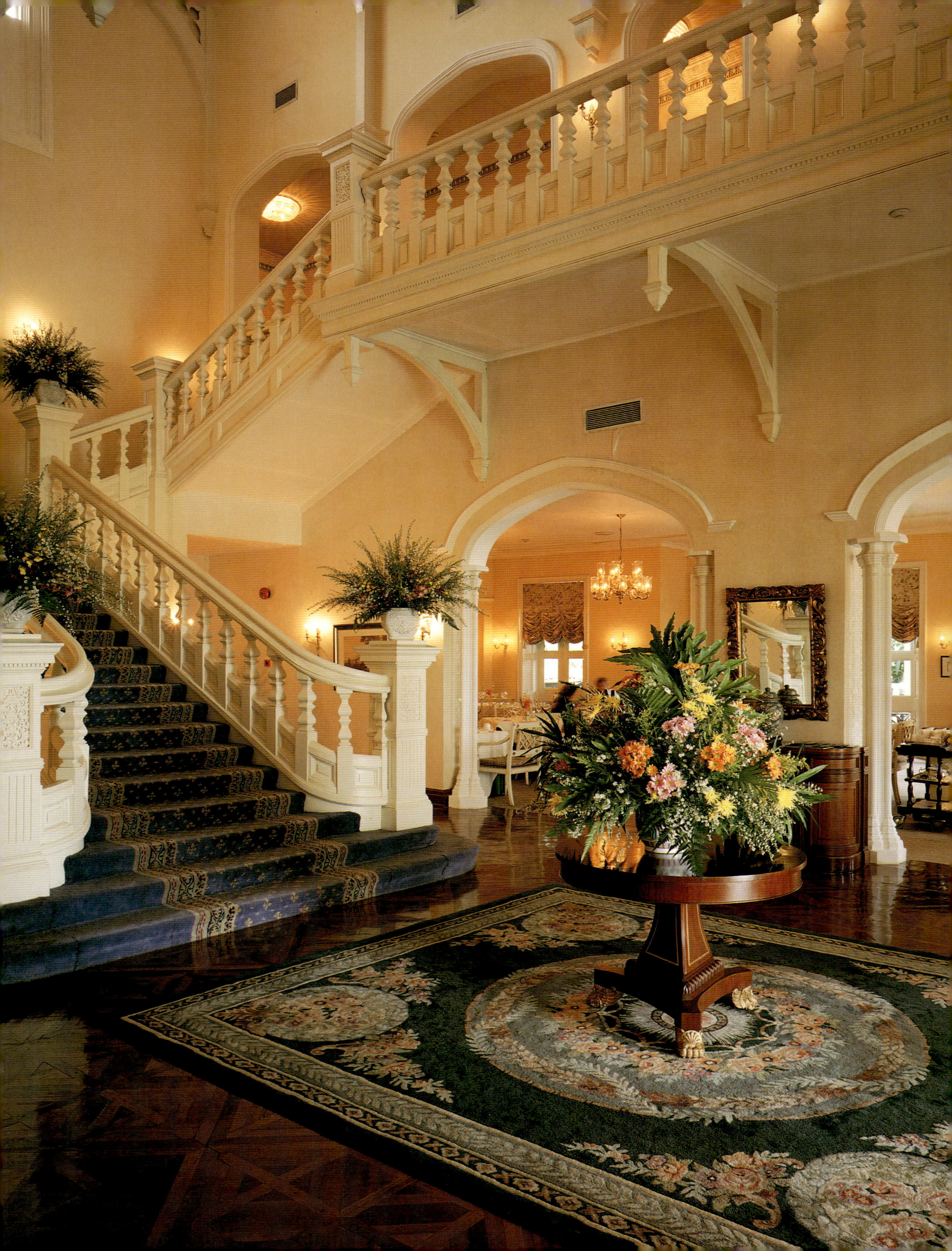

Carcosa Seri Negara
Kuala Lumpur

カルコーサ・セリ・ネガラ／クアラルンプール

Malaysia's Reception House
マレーシアの迎賓館

Set in the middle of a luxuriant forest with commanding views of Kuala Lumpur stands a 13 room hotel, called the Carcosa Seri Negara. Even though it is within the city limits, it is unbelievably peaceful there.

The history of the building reflects the modern history of Malaysia itself, being built as the residence of Sir Frank Swettenham, the first English Governor to Malaya in 1896. When Sir Frank first visited the outskirts of Kuala Lumpur some 8 years previously, he was highly delighted with the jungle there and had considered it as an ideal spot for sometime before proposing it. A small river was dammed to form a lake and the surrounding jungle was transformed into a park called the Lake Gardens which are frequented by the residents of Kuala Lumpur. The Governor's residence was built on the top of a hill overlooking these gardens.

The house, which is called Carcosa or Beloved Place when loosely translated, was completed in 1901 and King's House, a guest house, which was already under construction on the same hill, was eventually finished four years later. Since then, it has experienced countless numbers of changes and it was eventually given to England as a 'thank you' present to mark Malaysia's independence in 1957. Thirty years later in 1987, it was once again returned to the Malaysian government and was formerly opened as a government hotel in the presence of her Majesty Queen Elizabeth II in the autumn of 1989, after restoration work had been carried out.

The hotel is government owned but managed by Amanresorts, which has its headquarters is Hong Kong. The general managers are a young British couple, whose sincere manner has helped along with the very personalized service - a butler is assigned to each guest - to establish this small hotel as a true gem among Asian hotels.

The manager and his wife say that they change the type of service to suit the needs of the guests, depending on whether they are visitors of state, a family or a honeymoon couple. This is one of the most outstanding examples of the way in which this husband and wife team consider their guests. Not only that, they seek a flexible and expedient answer to everything. Take for example, breakfast; guests may have this important start to the day in any place of their choice, be it on the terrace, the verandah, by the pool or of course in their suite or in the dining room. They would probably even be willing to set out breakfast on the lawn, if it were requested. This must be the only hotel where such luxury can be enjoyed.

Facilities are scattered over the 40 acre site. The Carcosa consists of seven guest rooms, the main dining room, bar lounge, three function rooms and a business center. The Seri Negara has six guest rooms, a tea room and a function room.

Even now that it is a hotel, it still fulfils an important role as a reception facility and when state guests are received, the hotel is obviously closed to the public. However, anyone may stay there at all other times. By allowing people to stay here and experience the same degree of service and hospitality as visiting dignitaries, the government benefits amicably from the arrangement. The Malaysian government, which up until now has devoted its attention solely to business policies, is beginning to put some of its energies into the tourist industry. The significance which this hotel has in this respect is considerable. A man of foresight, Sir Frank Swettenham certainly bequeathed a great asset to Malaysia.

クアラルンプールを一望する、うっそうとした森の中に、たった13室のホテルがある。市内に隣接しながらも、ここには信じられない静寂が確保されている。カルコーサ・セリ・ネガラ、この小さなホテルの歴史は、すなわち近代マレーシアの歴史だといわれている。

1896年、英国人としては初のマレー駐在の提督、フランク卿の家の建設が始まった。遡ること8年、クアラルンプールの町外れを初めて訪れたフランク卿は、そこにあったジャングルが大変気に入って、この場所をかねがね考えていた、パブリック・エリアの最適地として進言した。小川は塞き止められ、湖となり、ジャングルは、現在"レイク・ガーデン"と呼ばれ、市民に親

119

しまれている公園へと変貌していった。そのレイク・ガーデンを見下ろす丘の上に、提督の家は造られることになった。カルコーサ（直訳できる言葉はなく、「親愛なる場所」というのが適訳といわれている）と呼ばれるその家は、1901年に完成し、同じ丘の上に前後して進められていたゲスト・ハウス（今日のセリ・ネガラ）も1904年に完成した。その後何回かの大きな変遷を経た後、1957年のマレーシア独立に際して、この場所は英国にそのお礼として贈られたものの、30年後の1987年には、再びマレーシア政府に返還された。修復を加えた後の1989年秋、こけら落としとしてエリザベス女王をお迎えして、このマレーシア政府所有のホテルは、正式にオープンした。

ホテルの所有は政府だが、マネージメントは、香港に本拠を置くアマンリゾーツが行なっている。総支配人の若い英国人夫妻のマネージメントに対する真摯な態度と、個々のゲストに専属となるバトラーを始めとする、スタッフたちの濃やかな対応がひとつとなってこの小さなホテルを、アジアの中でも特出したものとして位置付けている。

「国賓の方から、家族連れ、新婚旅行までお客様の要求に合わせて、サービスの内容を変えます」という総支配人夫妻。ここの最も優れた点のひとつだ。それだけに、柔軟性のある、臨機応変な対応がすべてに求められる。その端的な例は、朝食に表われる。1日の始まりの大切なひとときを、このホテルでは、ゲストの望むあらゆる場所で可能にする。ダイニングルームやスイートはいうに及ばず、ベランダでもテラスでもプールサイドでも、望むところすべてで。芝生の上にさえも快く、セット・アップしてくれるだろう。ここでしか味わうことのできない贅沢といえる。

約5万坪の敷地内に施設は点在する。カルコーサ棟に7つの客室、メイン・ダイニング、バー＆ラウンジそして、3つのファンクション・ルームとビジネスセンター。そしてセリ・ネガラ（＝「美しい国」）には、6つの客室、ティールームそしてファンクション・ルーム。

ホテルとなった現在も、迎賓館という役割を担っている。国賓を迎える際には、当然のことながらホテルとしてはクローズされる。それでも、それ以外の時は誰でも泊まることができる。迎賓館に泊まり、同等のサービスが受けられるとは、政府も仲々粋な計らいをしてくれる。マレーシア政府は、今迄のビジネス一辺倒の施策から、観光事業にも力を入れ始めているという。そういった中で、このホテルを持つ意味は大きい。フランク卿の先見の明が、マレーシアに大きな財産を残した。

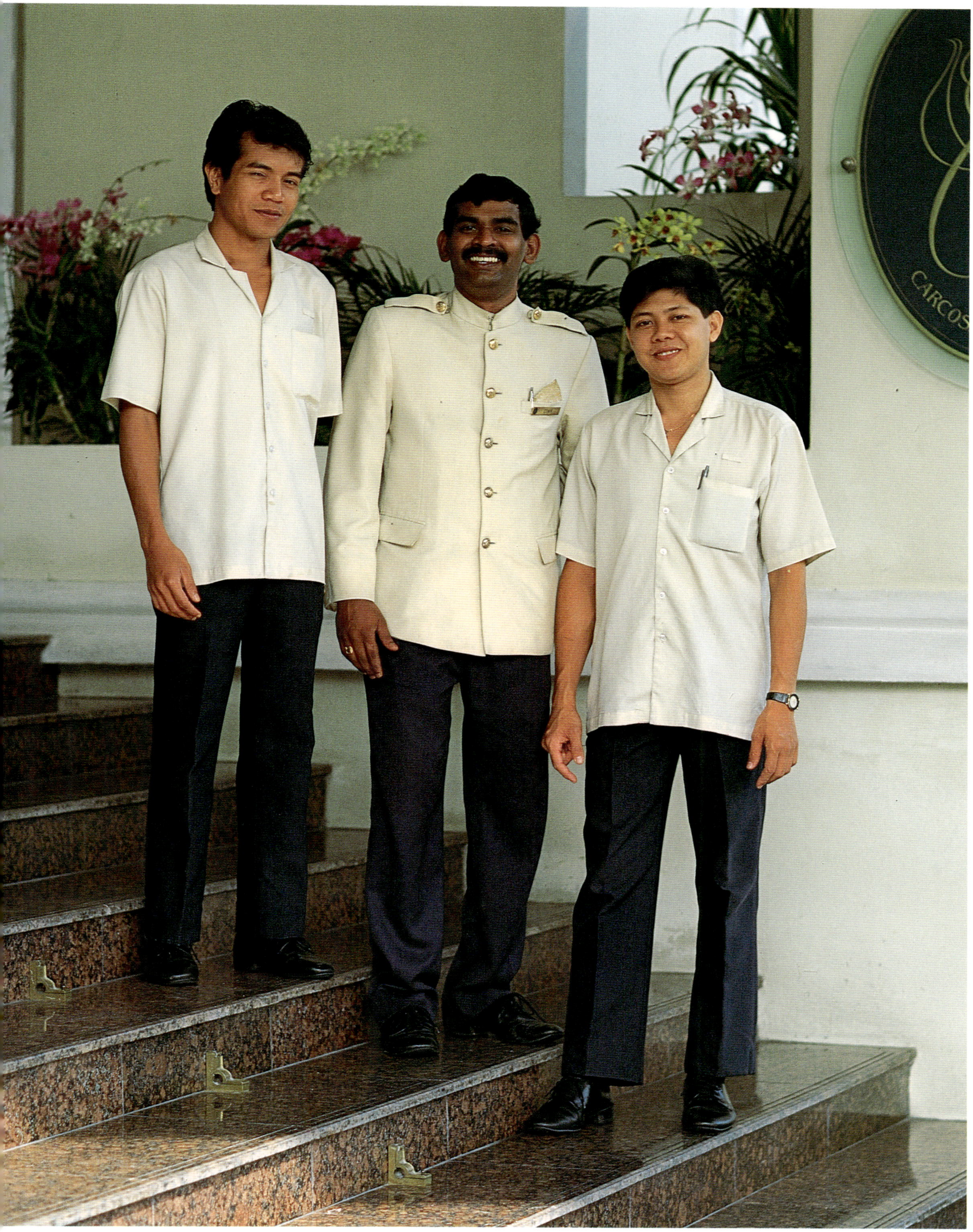
CARCOS

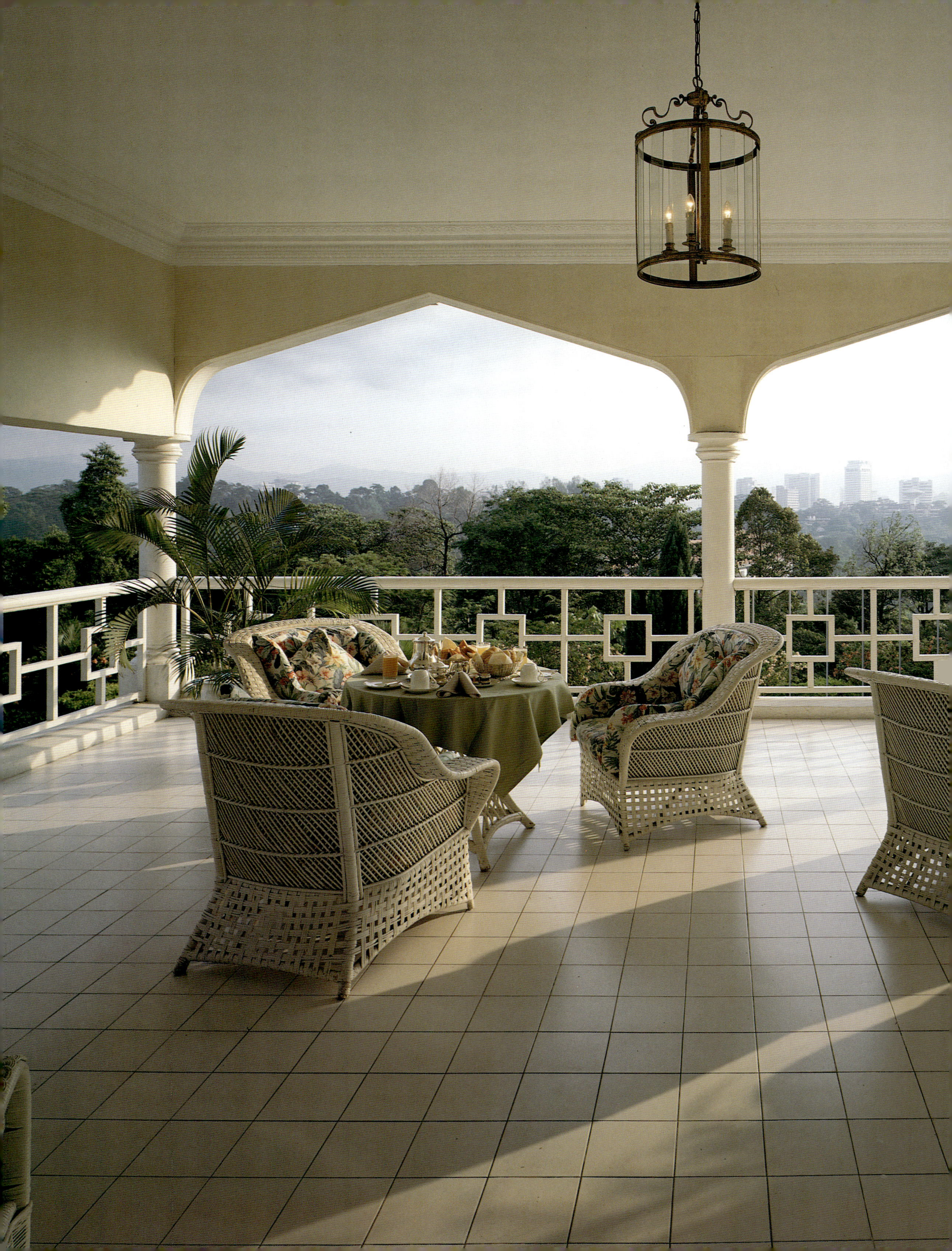

Page 116 Main lobby of the Carcosa
Page 118 Sunday Curry Tiffin
Page 119 Exterior of the Carcosa

Page 120 Mahsuri, the main dining room
Page 121 Butlers
Page 122 Breakfast at the Verandah
Page 124 <Top> Exterior of the Seri Negara, <Bottom> Afternoon tea in The Drawing Room of the Seri Negara
Page 125 <Top> Bathroom of Seri Makmur, guest room, <Bottom> Bedroom

P.116　メイン・ロビー（カルコーサ棟）
P.118　毎週日曜日に開かれるカレー・ブランチ
P.119　カルコーサ棟の外観
P.120　メインダイニング「マースリ」
P.121　臨機応変のバトラーたち
P.122　「ベランダ」での朝食
P.124　上　セリ・ネガラ棟の外観、下　アフタヌーンティーが楽しめる「ザ・ドローイングルーム」（セリ・ネガラ棟）
P.125　上　客室「セリ・マクムー」のバスルーム、下　同ベッドルーム（セリ・ネガラ棟）

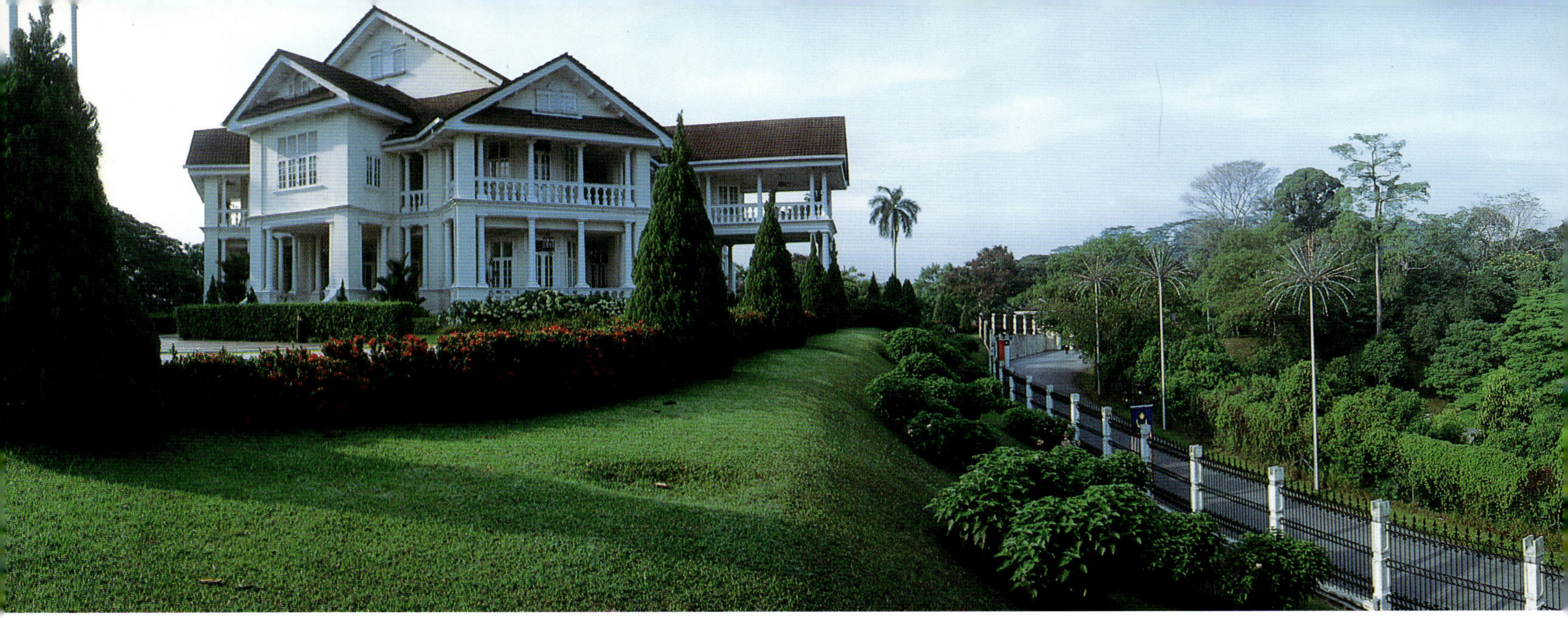

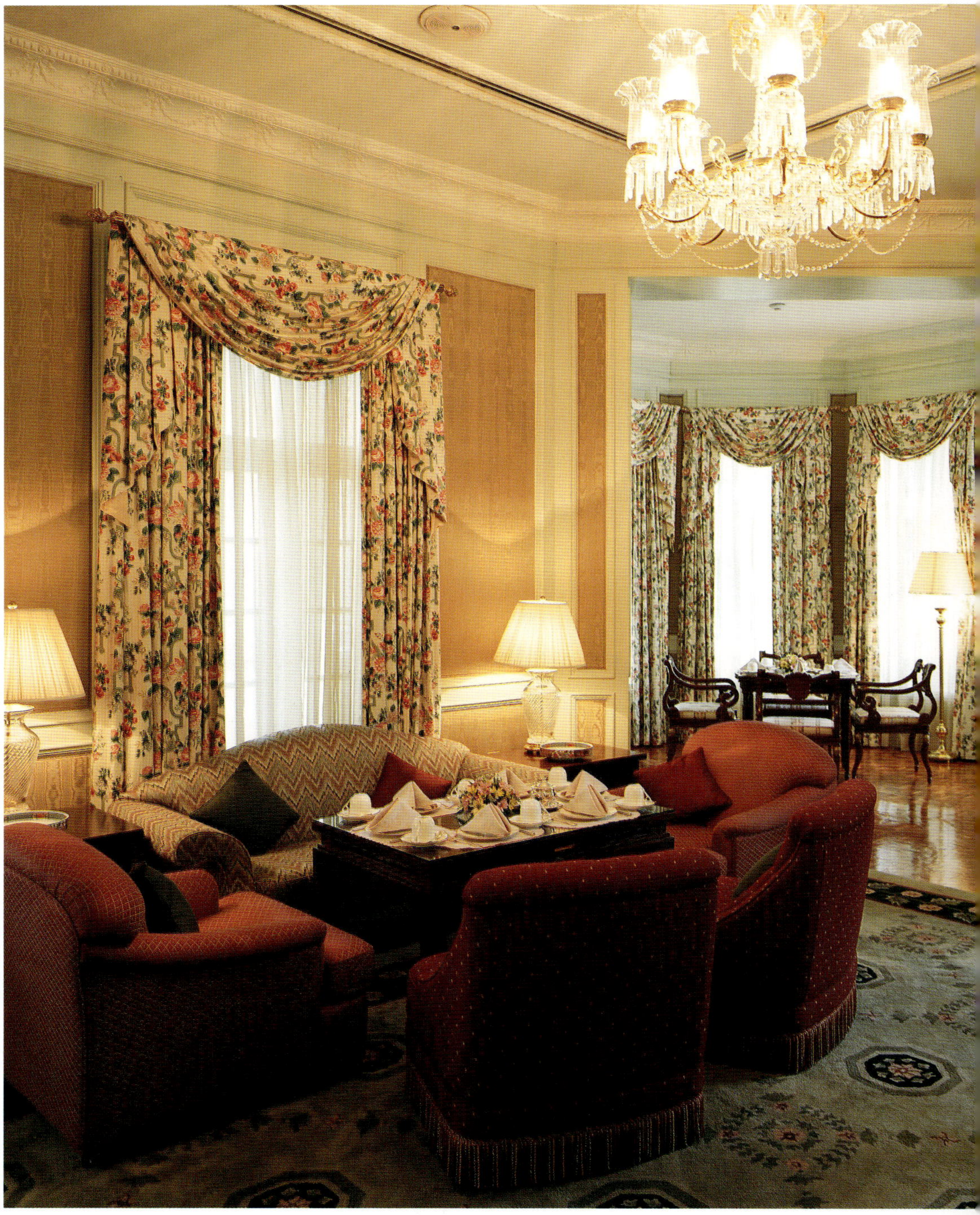

Seri Tandjung

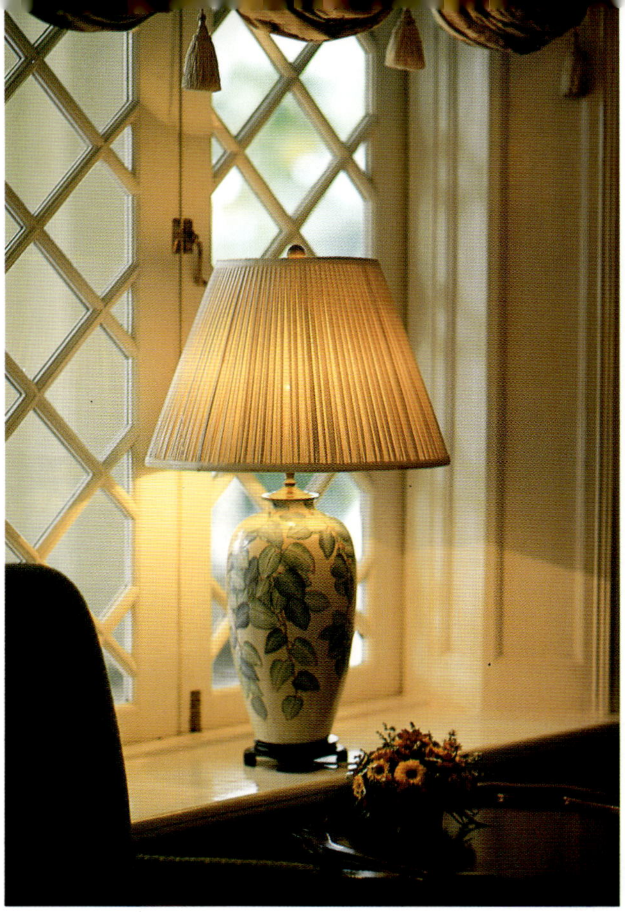

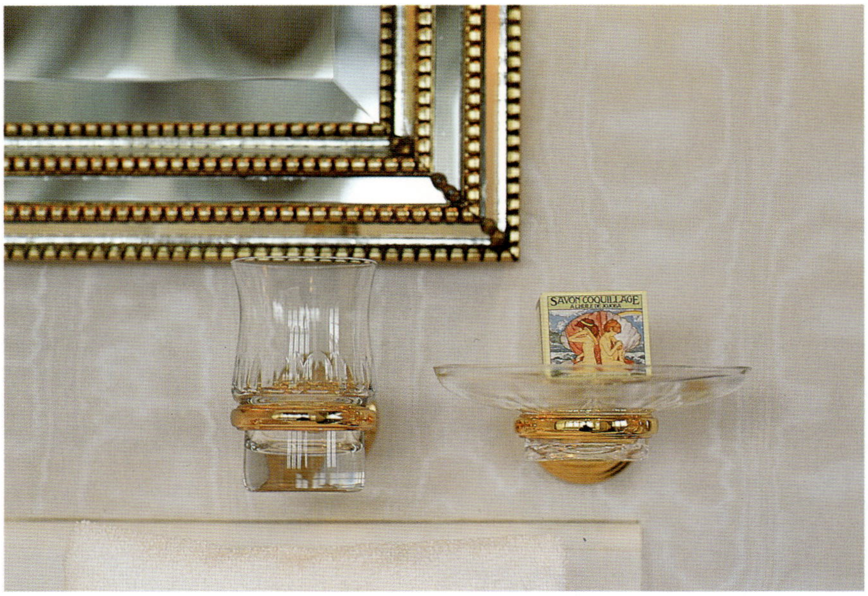
SAVON COQUILLAGE

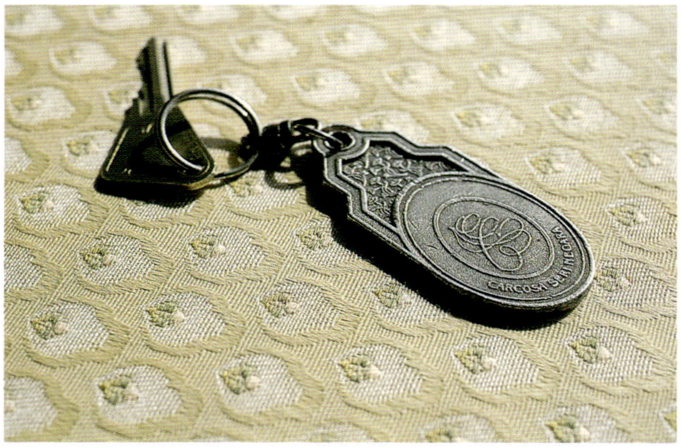

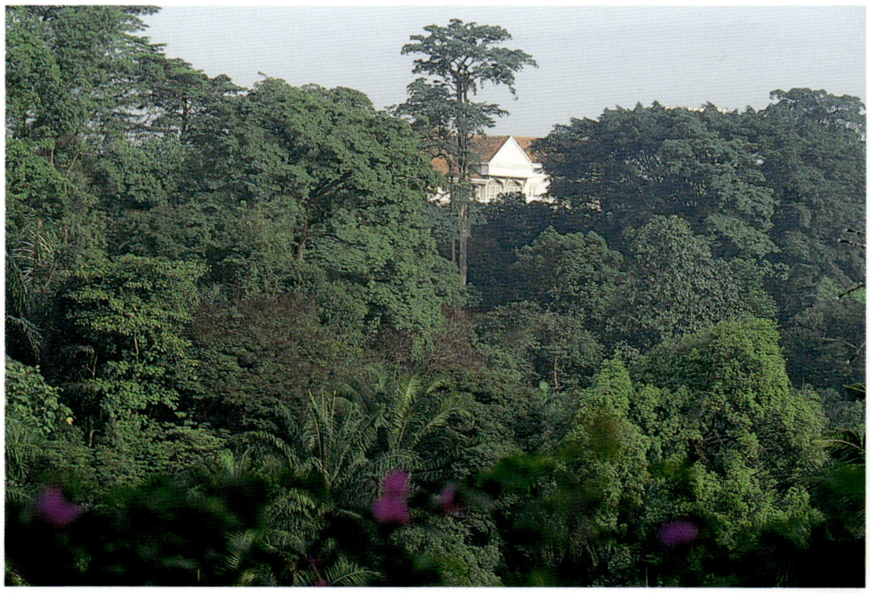

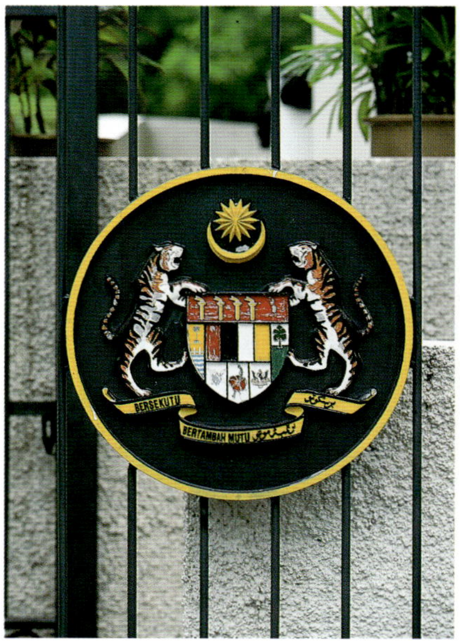
BERSEKUTU
BERTAMBAH MUTU

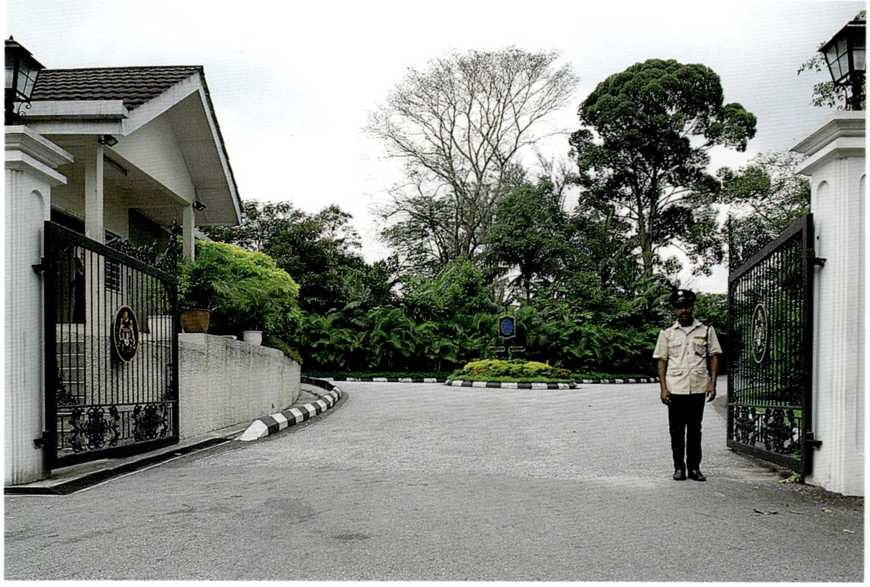

Page 126 <Top left> Window of The Drawing Room, <Top right> Bathroom, <Center left> Tin key ring, <Center right> View of the Carcosa from the Seri Negara, <Bottom left> Plate decorated with the hotel's crest, <Bottom right> Main gate
Page 127 <Center> Hall of conference room, <Bottom> Pictures of V. I. P.'s in the bar

P. 126 上左 「ザ・ドローイングルーム」の窓辺、中左 錫製のキーホルダー、下左 迎賓館としての紋章、上右 バスルーム、中右 セリ・ネガラよりカルコーサ棟を見る、下右 ホテルの正門
P. 127 中 会議室のホール、下 バーに飾られたVIPの写真の数々

General Managers Mr. & Mrs. Shaun & Beverly Matthews

総支配人　マシューズ夫妻

Carcosa Seri Negara

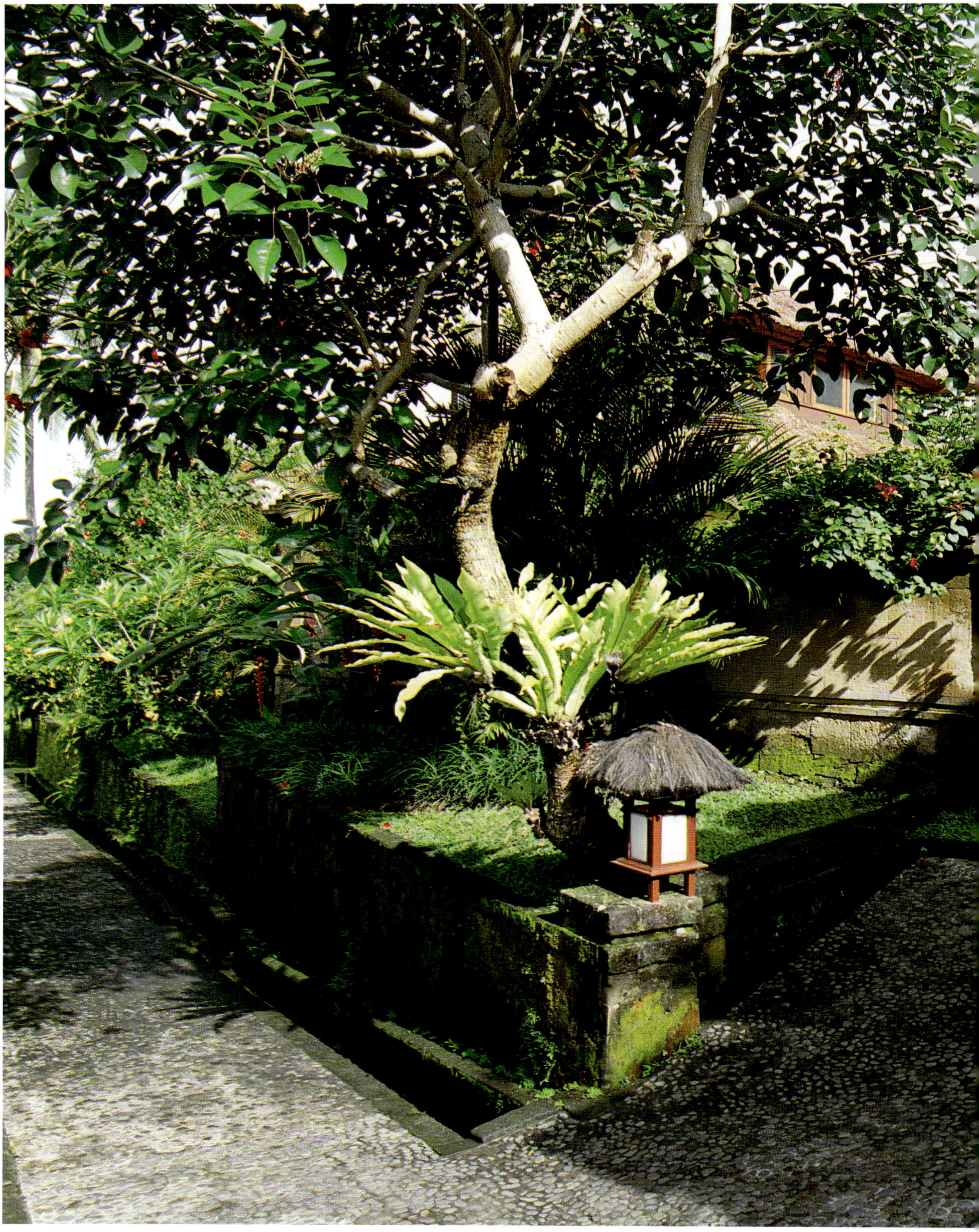

Bali

Amandari

Ubud, Bali

アマンダリ／バリ島ウブドゥ

Page 130 Dynamic stage reflected in pool at night　P.130　左　夜のプールに浮かぶ幻想的なステージ
Page 131 Each cottage is linked by beautiful paths　P.131　下　各コテージを結ぶ美しい路

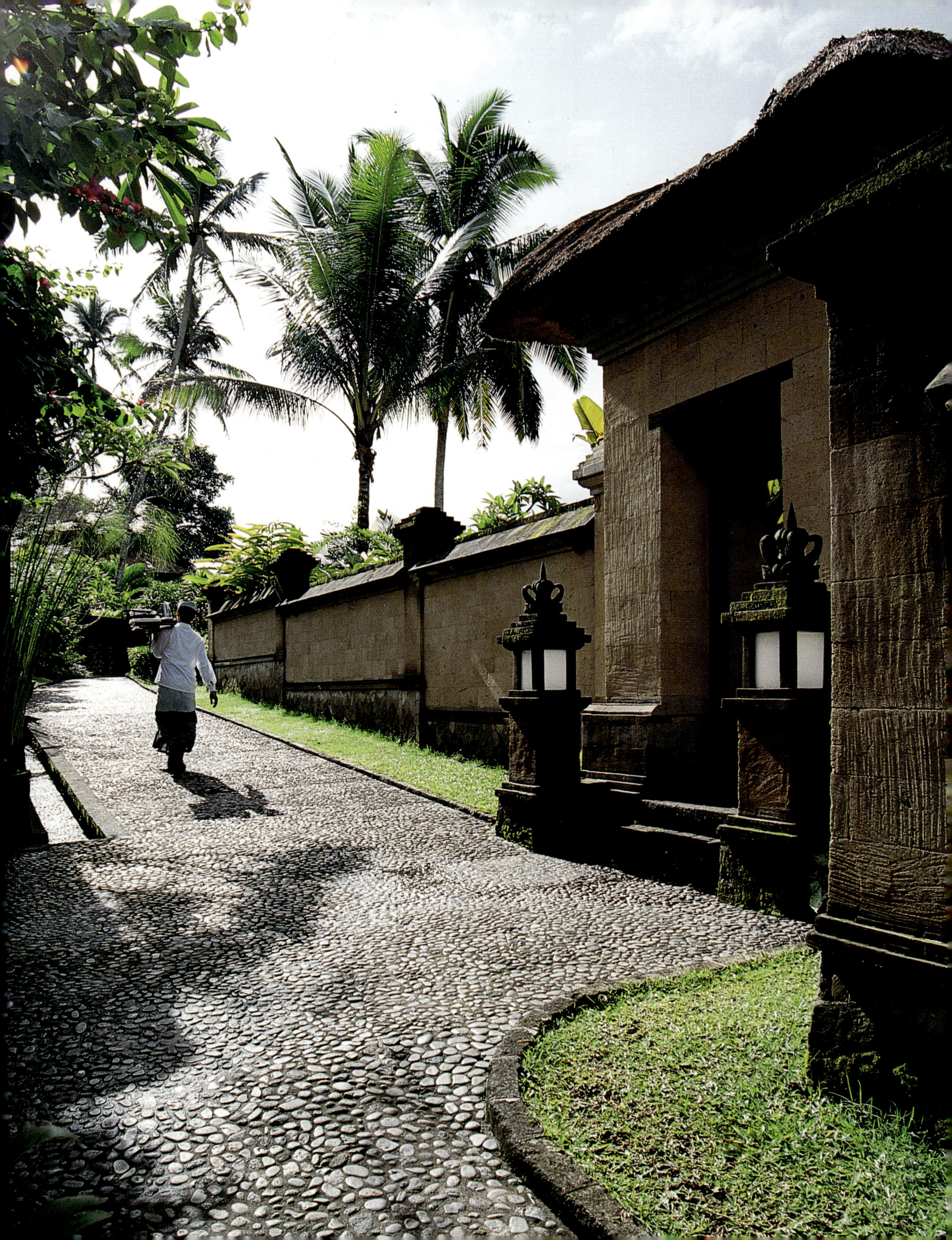

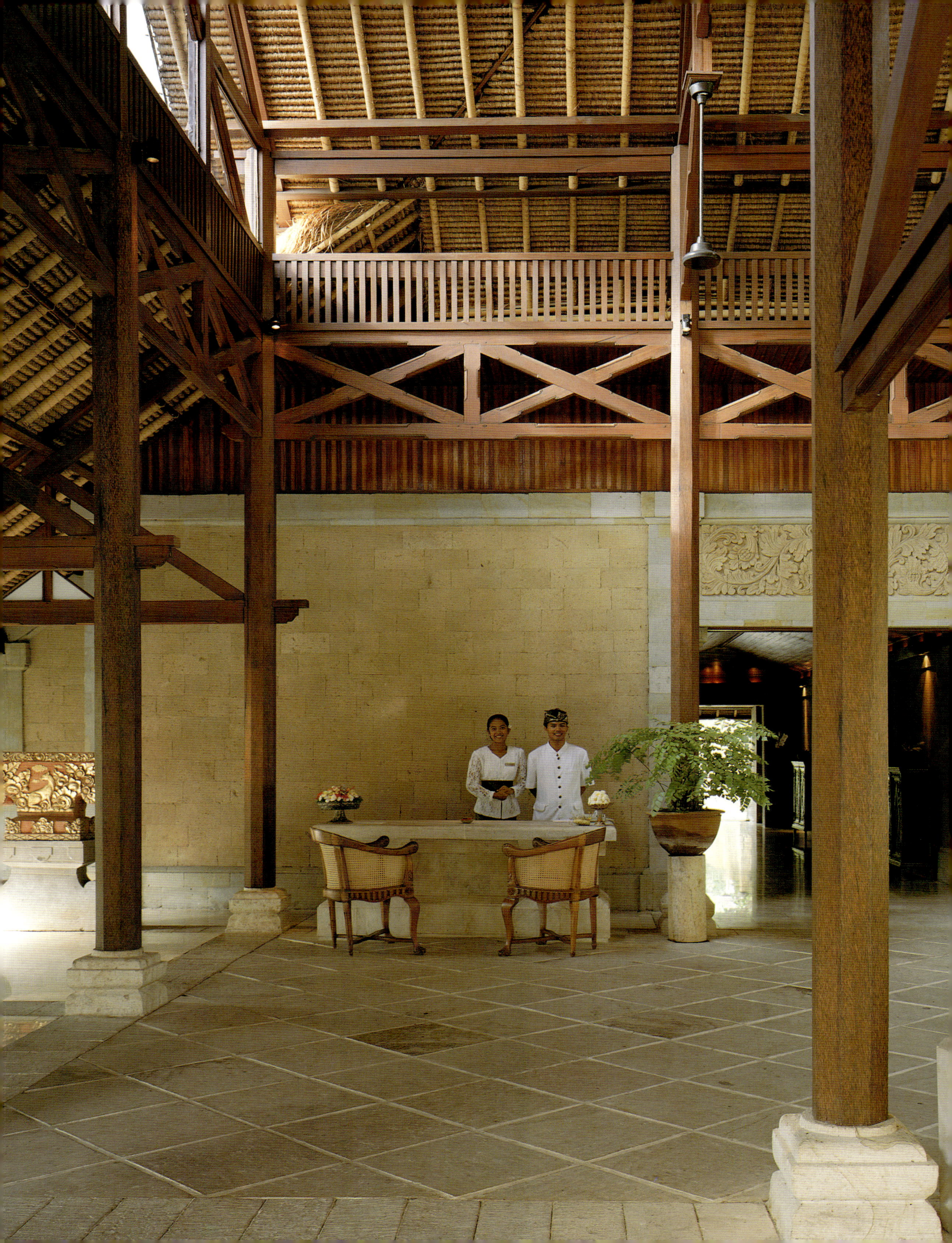

Page 132 <Left> Open Lobby
Page 133 Lobby Cottage seen from outside
Page 134 <Top> Second floor of restaurant, <Bottom right> Looking toward pool from restaurant

P.132　左　開放的なロビー空間
P.133　ロビー棟の外観
P.134　上　レストラン（2階）内部、下右　レストランからプールを望む

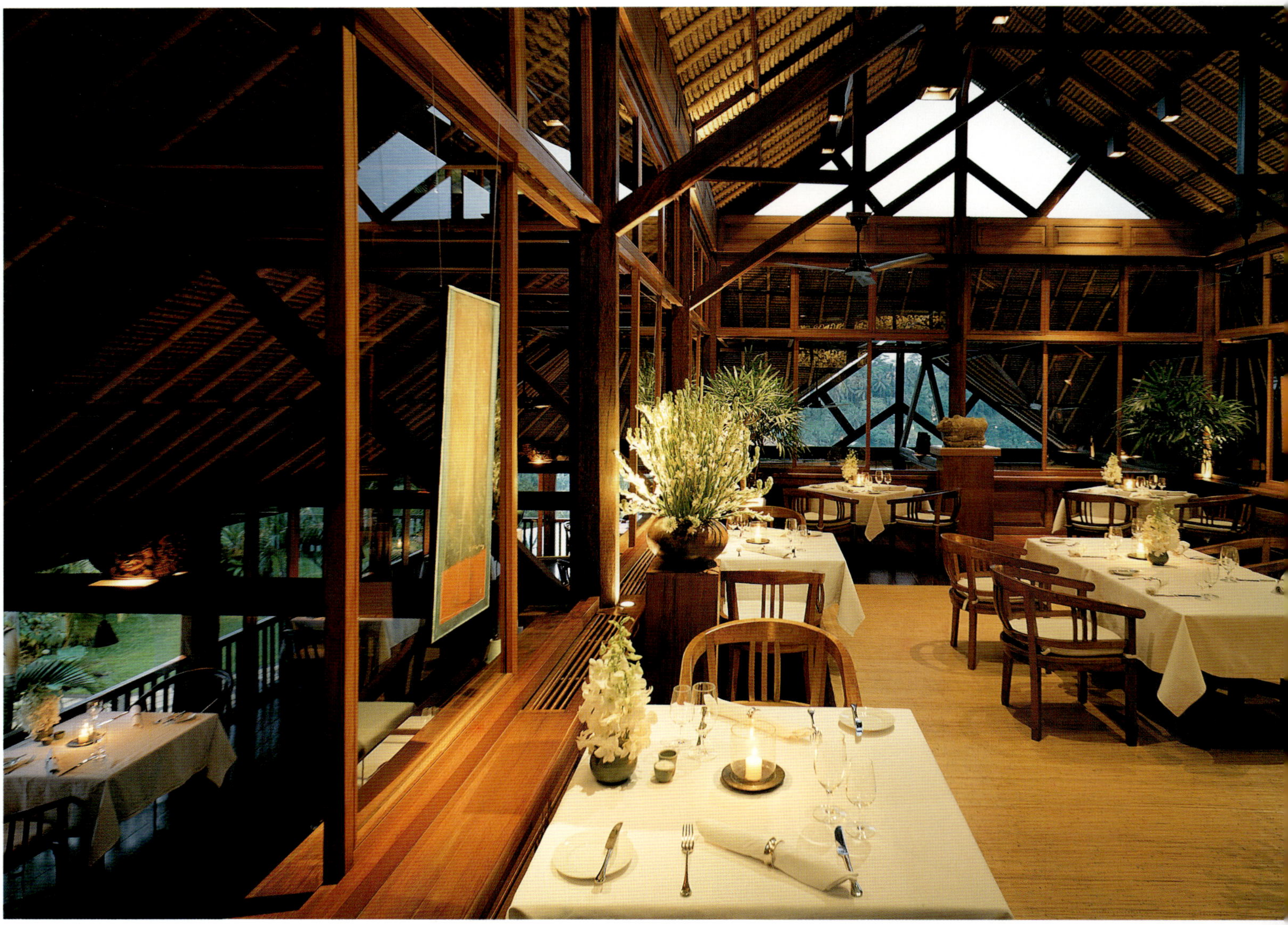

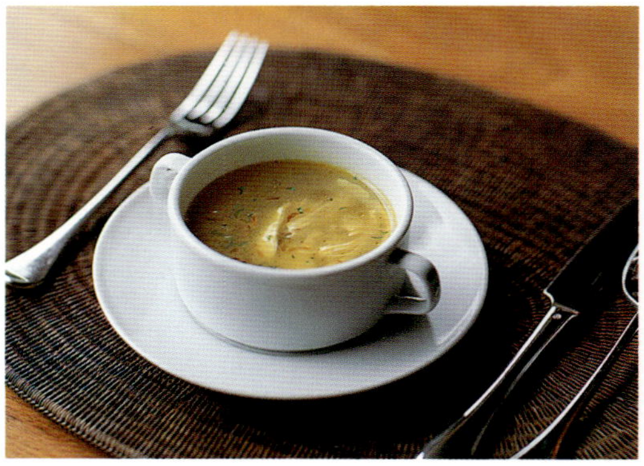

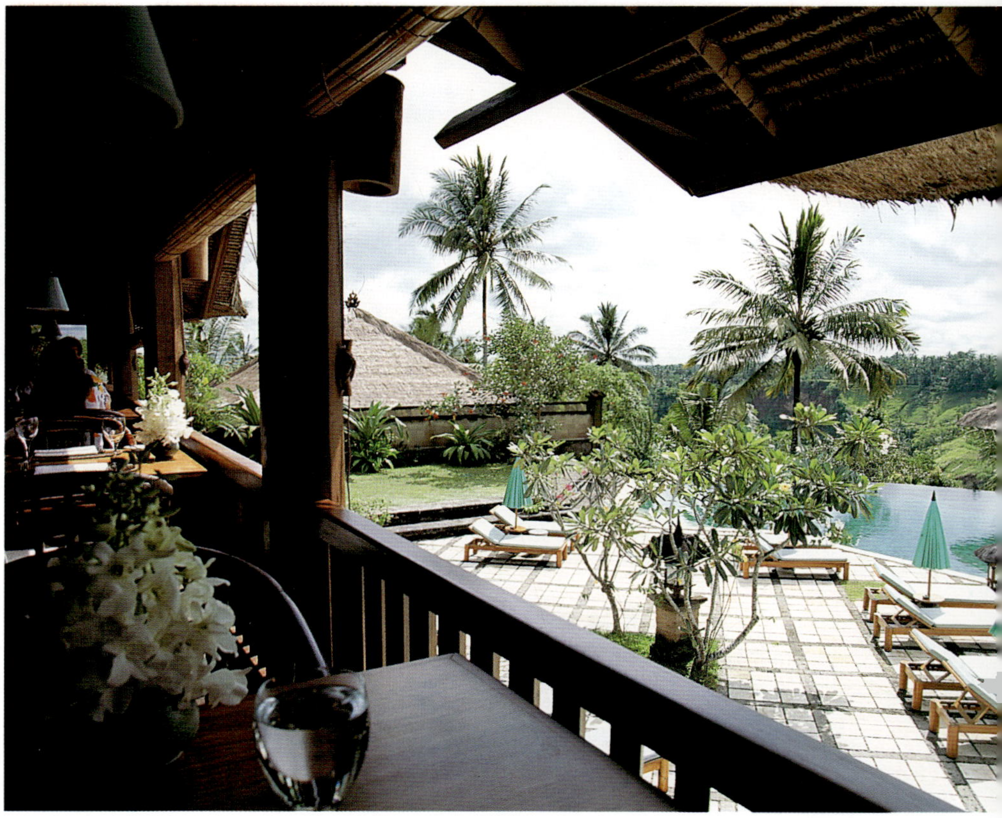

The Height of Perfection
「完成度」を楽しむ

In Bali, it is said that the gods dwell in the mountains. Ubud, which is in the heart of those mountains, has been widely known as an artists' village since time immemorial. Situated as if in hiding in a corner of Kedawatan, a settlement on the outskirts of this village, stands the Amandari, a super resort which opened in October 1989. The approach to this hotel contrasts conspicuously with the sudden open space with which one is confronted and it must be a very impressive sight to all who visit. The reputation of the Amandari spread very rapidly after it was built and is well known throughout the world. All the suites have been built as detached cottages indigenous to Bali. The modern interiors are a perfect match for the traditional exteriors and express correctly the resort's theme of 'simplicity and elegance'. The combined efforts of Peter Muller, the architect, and Neville Marsh, the interior designer, who have both been working in Australia, have brought a new style to Bali.

There are basically two types of cottages. One is a single stories suite with a terrace and the other is a duplex suite with a bedroom upstairs. In the duplex suite, there is a strong feeling of grandeur in the marble floors of the symmetrical space in the living room, whereas the bedroom on the second floor with its multi use of wood, on the other hand, has a softening effect so that the overall composition is an extremely balanced one. In the case of the terrace type, however, even though fundamentally there is a common symmetrical space, it is doubtful whether or not it is possible to enjoy both the open feeling during the day and privacy at night in the single room, where no spatial divisions can be made as in the duplex type. Some of both the single storied and terraced cottages have their own private pools.

Not unlike Japanese paper covered *fusuma* screens, the shutters are located inside the windows. They are arranged in such a way that light from outside is completely shut out, when they are closed, or floods in, when they are open. Happily guests can choose the type of suite to suit their taste.

Perhaps the finest thing about the Amandari is firstly that as a hotel, it is almost perfect and that both the space and nature around it provide a vital accent to the whole complex rather than relying on the more usual kind of perfectly appointed scenery and effective 'bunching' of elements to be found in many famous resorts.

Corridor like paths connect the cottages, which fit so aptly into the landscape and views of the terraced rice paddies and forest can be enjoyed from the pool side. These, together with the wonderful restaurant and feeling of openness in the lobby, are all without exception of the highest quality. Obviously it is impossible to forget the overwhelmingly hospitable service and the effort needed to maintain such conditions. Because neither of these relies on anything in particular, it has been possible to realize an ideal situation where the staff is attentive in every way.

They seem to have achieved the impossible, even in the ratio of foreigners, who come from all parts of the world, with a third of the guests coming from North America, a third from Europe and the rest from Asia and Oceania. As far as age is concerned, the greater proportion of guests are between 20 and 45 years old but it seems that people of any age enjoy the life here.

Amanresorts started development of three different types of hotel on the island with the Amandari. This was followed in the spring of 1992 with Amankila, a beach resort in Candi Dasa in the east. Amanusa, which is situated next to a golf course in Nusa Dua, in the south, was opened in the autumn of the same year. The same hotel group, therefore, has created three totally different types of hotel on one island. It is indeed a very interesting experiment which deserves attention.

バリでは、神は山に棲むという。その山の懐に抱かれたウブドゥは、古くからアーティストの村として広く知られている。その村外れの集落、ケダワタンの一角に、身を隠すかのように位置する、スーパーリゾート、アマンダリ。躙り口のようなアプローチは、突然拡がる空間との対比を際立たせ、訪れたものに確かな感動を与える。オープンは、1989年10月だが、瞬く間にその名は、世界に広まることとなった。部屋はすべてが独立したバリスタイルのコテージ。モダンなインテリアと、バリスタイルの外観がうまくマッチして、ここのテーマとする「シンプル＆エレガント」を正に表現している。建築はピーター・ミューラー、インテリアはネヴィル・マーシュ、共にオーストラリアで活躍する2人のコンビネーションが、バリに新しいスタイルをつくり上げた。

コテージには、2つのタイプが用意されている。寝室が2階にあるデュプレックス・スイートと、平家建てのテラス・スイート(どちらにもプール付きのタイプがある)だ。デュプレックスのタイプでは、1階のリビング・ルームに、大理石の床に代表されるような、緊張感の高いシンメトリーな空間があり、一方ベッドルームの2階は、木を多用した柔らかな効果をうまく演出、バランスの取れた構成となっている。テラスタイプの場合は、基本的にはシンメトリーな空間は共通だが、デュプレックスのような空間の性格分けができない分、昼間の開放感と夜のプライベートな空間、両方がひとつの部屋で楽しめるように工夫が凝らされている。日本の襖のような扉が窓の内側に納まっていて、開ければオープン、閉めれば光を完全にシャット・アウトできる仕組みになっている。どちらにせよ、好みによって部屋のタイプが選べるのが嬉しい。

　ここアマンダリの最も優れた点は、絶対的な景観や集客効果の高い観光名所などがないことで、自然と空間の緊張感や、ホテル自体の完成度が高められたことにあると思う。景観にジャスト・フィットしたコテージ、それらを結び付ける回廊のような通路、森や棚田を眺めるプール、おいしいレストラン、そしてオープン感覚のロビー。どれを取ってもクォリティーがすべて高いところで揃えられている。勿論、その状態を常に保ち続けるメンテナンス力と、ホスピタリティ溢れるサービス体制も忘れることができない。何れにしても、何かに頼ることをしなかったために、すべてに行き届いた理想的なものができ上がった。気になるゲスト像だが、北米、欧州、太平洋圏(アジア・オセアニア)が共に3分の1ずつと、ここでも理想的な配分。年齢層は、20代後半から40代後半までが大半で、どの年代においても、生活を楽しむ人たちに変わりはないという。

　アマンリゾーツでは、このアマンダリを皮切りに、既にバリ島の中に3つの違ったタイプのホテルの展開を始めた。1992年春には、東部チャンディダサにビーチリゾート、アマンキラ。同年秋には、南部ヌサドアにゴルフコースに隣接する、アマンヌサをオープンさせている。ひとつのホテル・グループがひとつの島の中に、3つの違ったタイプのホテルを共存させるという、注目に値する面白い試みだ。

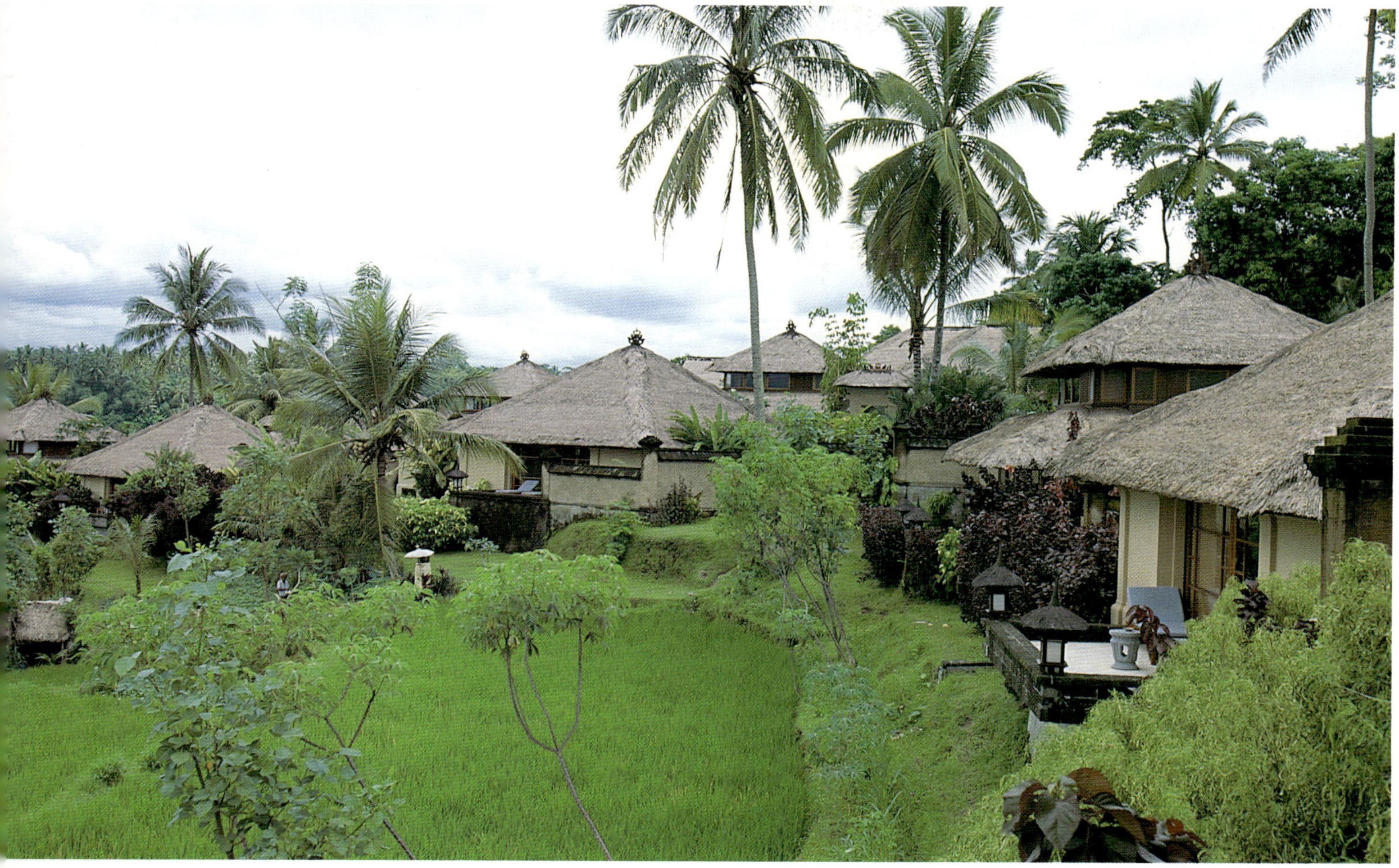

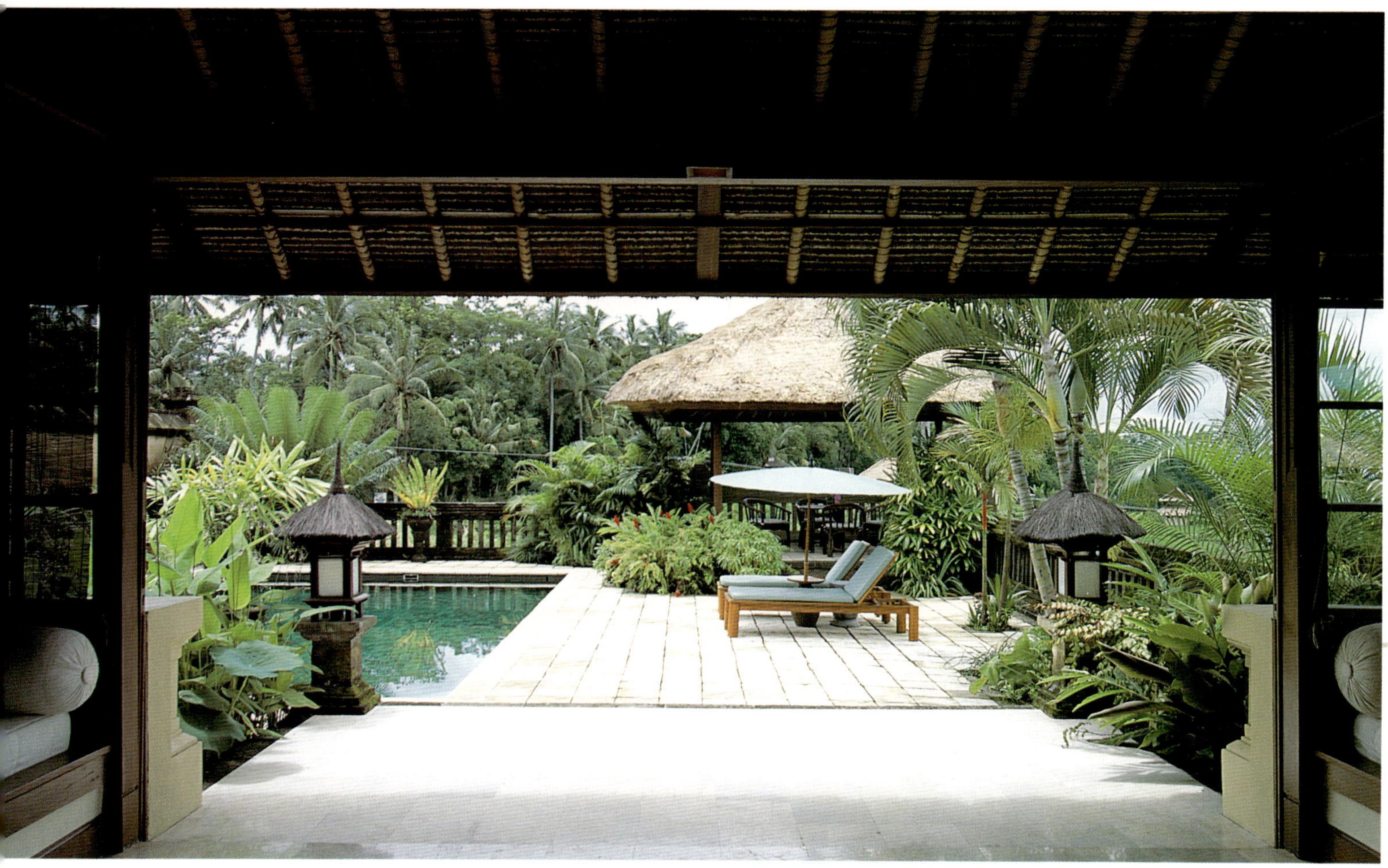

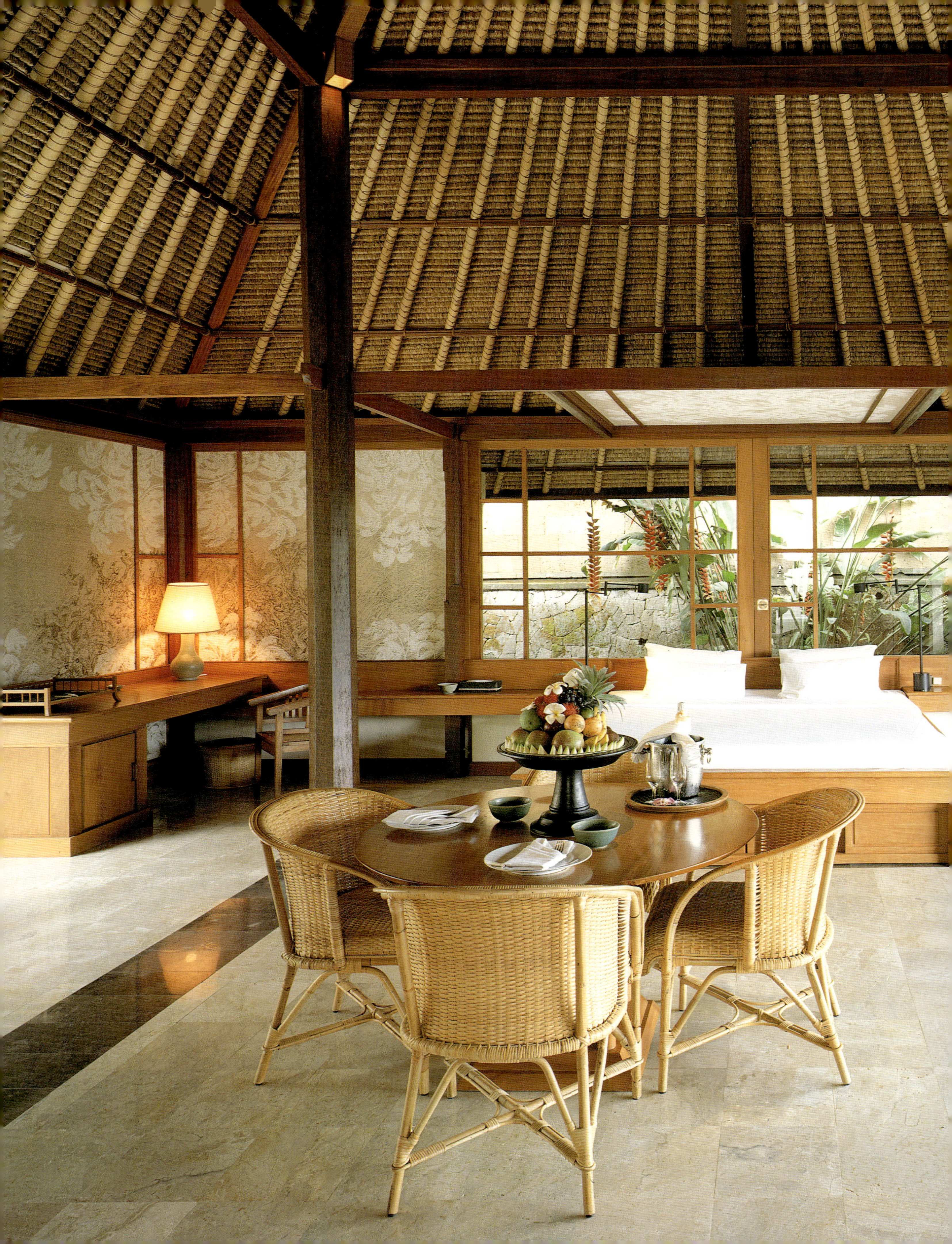

Terrace Suite

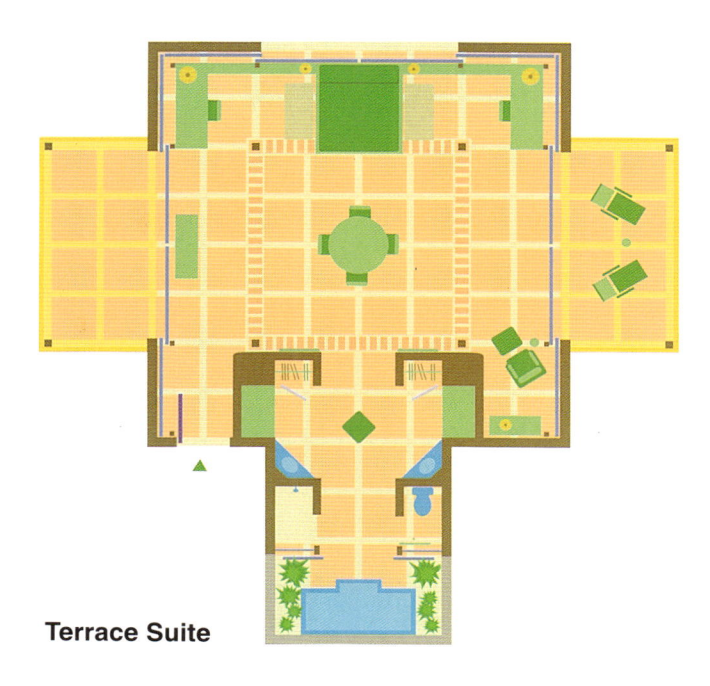

Page 136 <Top> View of terraced rice paddies from the terrace, <Center> Entrance to cottage, <Bottom> First floor study of Duplex Suite
Page 137 <Top> View of cottages, <Bottom> Amandari Suite with pool
Page 139 Functional Terrace Suite

P.136 上 棚田を眺めるためのテラス、中 コテージ・エントランス、下 「デュプレックス・スイート」2階の書斎コーナー
P.137 上 コテージが連なる景観、下 プール付きの「アマンダリ・スイート」
P.139 機能的にまとめられた「テラス・スイート」

140

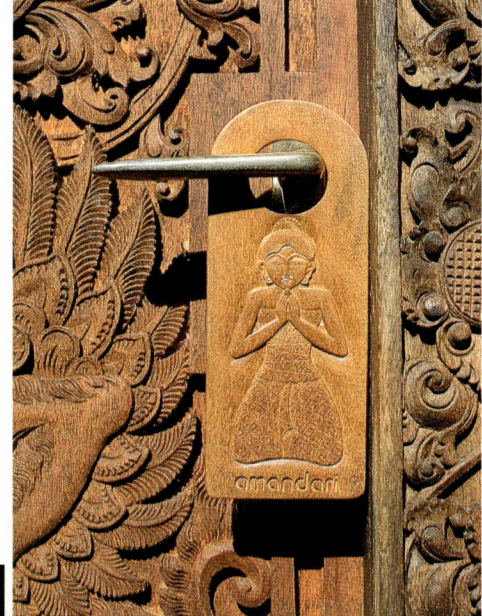

General Managers Mr. & Mrs. Henry & Char Gray

総支配人　グレイ夫妻

1	2	
3	4	
5	6	
7	8	9

Page 140
1. Entrance to cottage
2. Pool and stage
3. Corridor like path
4. Cafe next to the lobby
5. Corridor leading from lobby to restaurant
6. Shop dealing in industrial art objects
7. Wooden "Do not disturb" sign
8. Each room has a selection of fruit
9. Upstairs bedroom in Duplex Suite

Page 141 <From top>
Some of the stone figures which adorn the site, Dance practice, Library

P.140　1．コテージ入口　2．プールとステージ　3．回廊のような通路　4．ロビーに続くカフェ　5．ロビーとレストランを結ぶ廊下　6．バリの工芸品を扱うショップ　7．"Do not disturb"の木製プレート　8．各部屋に備え付けのフルーツ・コンポート　9．「デュプレックス・スイート」2階のベッドルーム

P.141　左上から　敷地のあちこちに置かれた石像、ホテルで行なわれるダンスの練習風景、ライブラリー

Amandari

Tandjung Sari

Sanur, Bali

タンジュン・サリ／バリ島サヌール

Page 142 View of dawn breaking over the sea as seen from the bar   P. 142　バーから見た夜明けのビーチ

Bali Experience
「バリの普通」を楽しむ

Out of all the many hotels, which have tried diligently to create a homely atmosphere for their guests, Tandjung Sari, or Cape of Flowers, literally started life out as a house. When it opened in 1962, it consisted of one Bali style unit of four rooms. This number has grown over the years to the present 29 rooms but it seems that the present owner does not intend to increase this number in the future.

Quite surprisingly, 90% of the hundred or so members of staff have been working at the hotel for over 20 years, so it may quite correctly be considered to be a family run concern.

Various reasons spring to mind as to why Tandjung Sari is one of the most popular hotels in Bali. Firstly, it is situated in Sanur, which was developed as a beach resort comparatively early on but has preserved its relaxed atmosphere. One of the big factors is that the spatial and cultural styles indigenous to Bali have been left in their natural form. But more than anything else perhaps, the owner's philosophy is colorfully reflected in this hotel. "I have", he states, "Been able to solve the problem of how best to satisfy guests' needs. The only thing is, I like to complete everything on the spot so some things inevitably are not really enough but I don't think that matters here. What is more important, on the other hand, is the fact that I personally concern myself with even the smallest details. A defiant will exists here to play the game in a business like way. He knows full well that this is the greatest thing that he can do himself and it something with which a big hotel could not hope to compete. Having been involved in some way since an early age, this knowledge was probably absorbed from his parents without his really knowing it.

Each suite is a detached cottage like a private house or a Bali style unit so that there is a personal homely atmosphere about them. All thirteen cottages are designed differently. In units where four buildings have been arranged in a cross, the partitionless bathroom plays a part in the structure of the remarkably open rooms. Nevertheless, privacy is sufficiently preserved, while it is possible to fully appreciate the benefits of the individuality of the accommodation provided by each building. It really is an incredibly well thought out unit.

Countless numbers of old things from Bali nonchalantly furnish the buildings so that it is like a veritable museum itself. The desire of the second generation owner, who is also an anthropologist, to create a museum like hotel, which would be absolutely impossible to imitate anywhere else, is reflected here too.

タンジュン・サリは、家から始まった。ホテルの多くが、ゲストに「家」をイメージさせることに腐心する中で、ここは正しく家からスタートしている。1962年にオープンした時、部屋数はバリスタイルのユニットひとつの4室。拡張を続けた現在でも29室、もうこれ以上増やすつもりはないという。驚くことに、100人以上いる従業員の(これだけでも驚くが)実に9割は、20年以上ここで働いているという。正に家族経営のホテルといっていい。

バリの中にあって、ヨーロピアンを中心に最も人気のあるホテルのひとつ。理由は色々思い浮かぶ。まずはサヌールという立地。比較的早くから開発されたビーチリゾートでありながら、落ち着いた雰囲気が保たれている。一般的なバリスタイルの空間や文化が、自然な形で残されていることも大きな要因だ。そして何よりこのホテルには、オーナーの哲学が色濃く反映されている。「どうしたらお客様が満足してくれるかを追及しています。ただ現地ですべて完結したいので、足りないものもあるけれど、ここはそれで良いと思う。そのかわり、私が直接ディテールまで拘わります」ビジネスライクに経営することとは対局にある、確かな意志がここには存在する。そしてそれが自分にできる最大のことであり、大きなところが絶対に太刀打ちできないことであることを良く知っている。小さい頃からここに携わり、知らず知らずの内に親から受け継がれた知恵なのであろう。

個々の部屋は、独立した民家風のコテージ、もしくはバリス

Page 144 <Top> "Do not disturb" sign, <Center> Children working at the hotel
Page 145 <Top> Interior of magnificent restaurant

P.144 上 "Do not disturb" のプレート、中 ホテルで働く子供たち
P.145 上 荘厳な感じのするレストラン内部

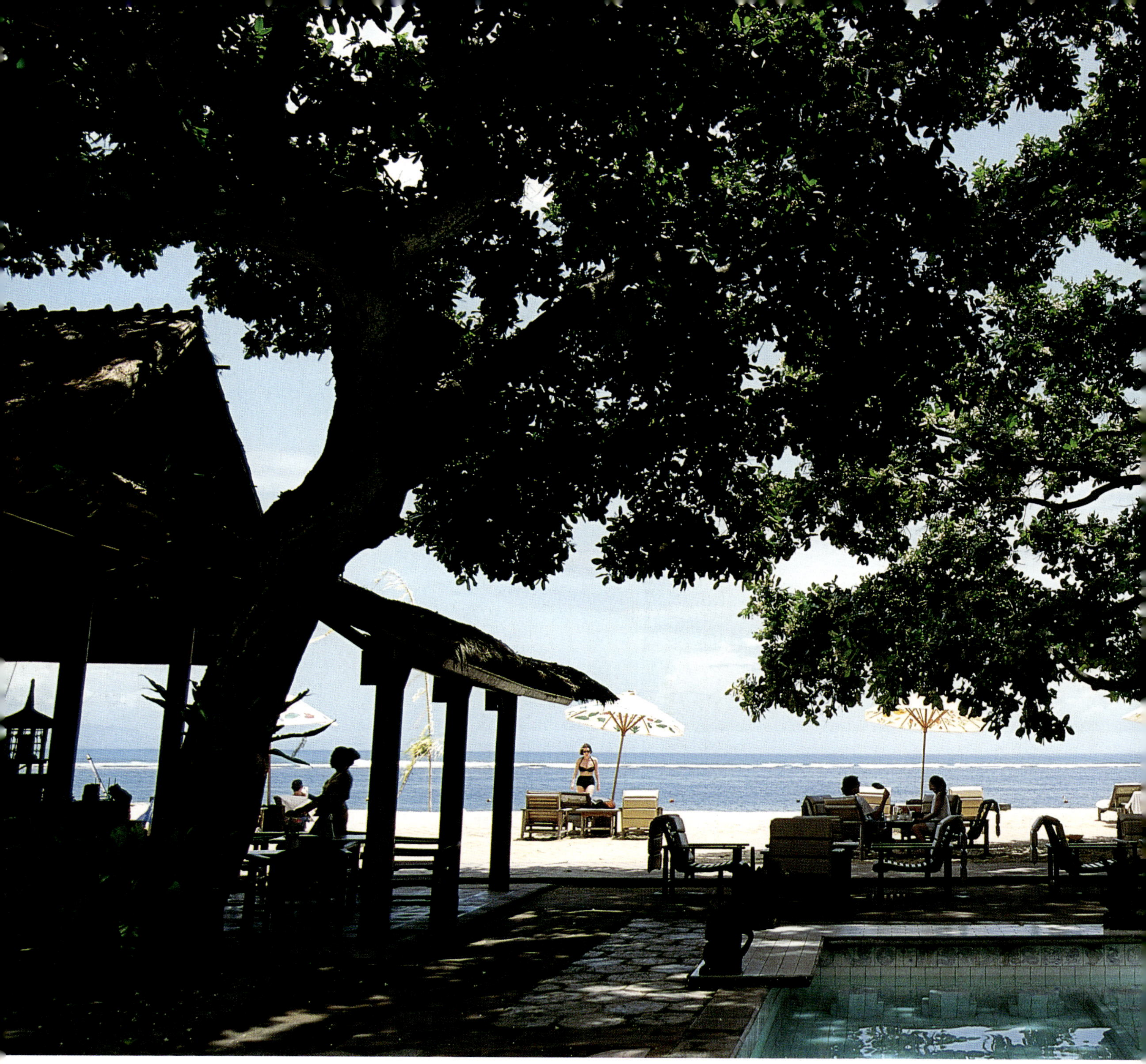

Managing Director Mr. Agusetiwan Wawo-runtu

取締役社長　アグスティアナ・ワオルントゥ

Page 146 <Top> Living room of unit type cottage, <Bottom> Bathroom of the cottage

Page 147 <Top left> Two-storied detached type cottage, <Bottom> Bedroom of detached type cottage

Page 148 Pool and bar overlooking the beach

Page 149 <Top> Semi-open reception

P. 146　上　ユニット型コテージのリビング　下　同バスルーム

P. 147　上　2階建の独立型コテージ、下　ユニット型コテージのベッド

P. 148　ビーチに面したプールとバー

P. 149　上　セミ・オープンのレセプション

Tandjung Sari

The library, restaurant, bar and lounge look out over three pools which have been set back from the sea below. They are all the result of the flawless work of Ed Tuttle, an American who lives in France. In fact, the very first hotel to be opened by Amanresorts the Amanpuri on phuket Island in Thailand was also designed by him. His clever ability to bring everything together is certainly one of his strong points. The atmosphere inside the limestone faced restaurant overlooking the sea is somehow 'stateless' but one step outside and there is no mistaking that this is sophisticated Bali. The modern contrasting theme colors of blue and yellow also contribute towards the quality of the hotel. At any rate, it has all the makings of an idyllic spot from which to enjoy the superb view. All that remains now is for us to pack our bags and leave for Bali.

アマンキラは、ただこの眺めを見るためにつくられた、といっていい。そのためだけに滞在するに、充分に値する眺めだ。とはいえ、バリの空港ングラ・ライからはかなり離れている。でも心配することはない。車による送迎は無料だし、もっと急ぐ向きにはヘリコプターによるアレンジも可能だ。という具合で、わざわざ来てみるだけのものは、既に用意されている。

海からセットバックしてレイアウトされた3つのプール、それらを見下ろすレストランとバー＆ラウンジ、そして落ち着いたライブラリー。この完璧な仕掛けは、フランス在住の米国人エド・タトルによるもの。実は、アマンリゾーツ最初のホテル、プーケット島(タイ)のアマンプリも彼の手による。その場所が持っている魅力を最大限に生かし、全体を手際良くまとめるのは、彼の最も得意とするところだ。ライムストーンで覆われた、海に面したレストランの中にいると「無国籍」の雰囲気だが、一歩外に出れば、そこにはソフィスケートされたバリが紛れもなく存在している、という具合に。テーマカラーのイエローとブルーのモダンな対比も、ホテルの高質化に貢献している。

とにかく「絶景を楽しむ」お膳立ては、すべて揃っている。あとは、出掛けるだけだ。

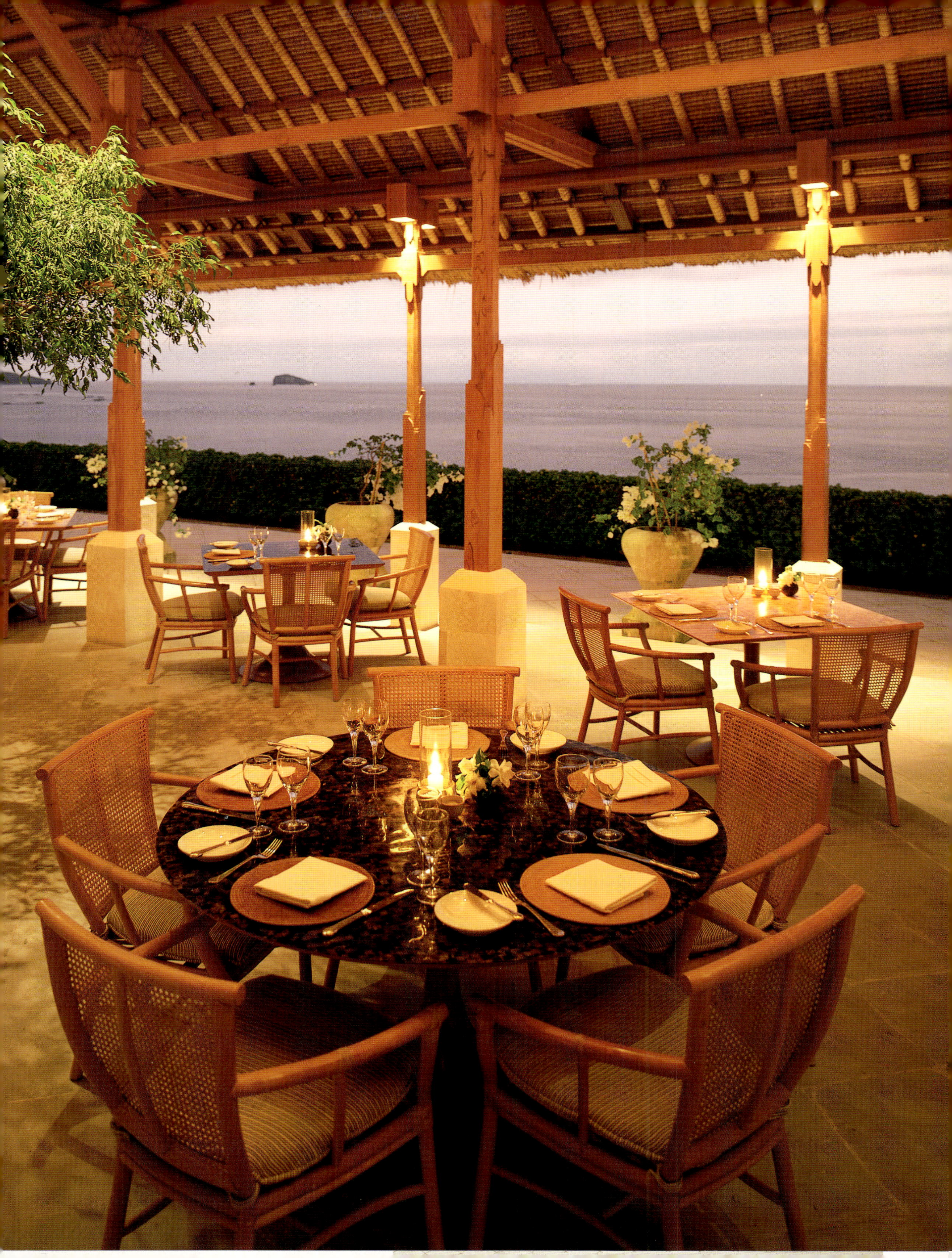

Page 156 Frangipani Cafe, Open air cafe facing the sea
P. 156　海に面したオープン・カフェ「フランジパニ・カフェ」

The Oberoi Bali

Legian Beach Bali

ジ・オベロイ／バリ島レギャンビーチ

Best of Bali

「オールマイティ」を楽しむ

About 15 minutes from the airport, through the noisy bustling Kuta streets, lined with shops and restaurants, lies a tranquil beach resort on the northern outskirts of the Legian area. It is the Oberoi Bali, the product of Oberoi Hotels, a unique hotel chain which has developed about twenty luxury hotels in Asia and the Middle East and has its headquarters in India. This hotel is the one and only one under the Oberoi management in Indonesia.

It started out life as a 63 room private club on a 6.1 ha (15 acre) site in 1974, but was taken over by the Oberoi Hotel chain in 1978. Twelve rooms were added in 1980 and with further additions, the number of rooms has risen to the present 75. The basic design consists of 4 rooms set out in the traditional lanai style. There are 15 of these plus 15 detached cottages, all of which are surrounded by independent outer walls. Six of the cottages have their own pools. A really elegant space has been secured even in the small lanai type with their 60sq.m. (646sq.ft) of marble floors. The renovations, which started in 1988, were aimed at perfecting the bathrooms. Various things including a shower booth were installed in an effort to upgrade the hotel and increase the comfort of the guests. The Australian architect, Peter Muller, who is a pioneer in giving the Bali style an international flavor, participated in both the renovations and the original design.

What makes this resort so special is the perfection of the facilities even though there are so few rooms. With its beach, pool, restaurant, open air cafe, bar and shops, it is a resort that has a feeling of versatility, capable of coping with any situation. However, having said that there is such a wealth of amenities does not mean that it is impossible to relax there. It may have something to do with the surrounding walls but even in the cottages with their enormous rooms, the atmosphere is such that guests feel as though they are staying in a holiday house. It does not matter whether they are there alone or with a group of friends, young or old, or even a couple, guests can enjoy the accommodation in their own way. This kind of resort is usually completely remote from its natural surroundings and there is a limit as to how it can be used, but this does not seem to be the case with Oberoi Bali. The common factor among the guests is that they are all people who have

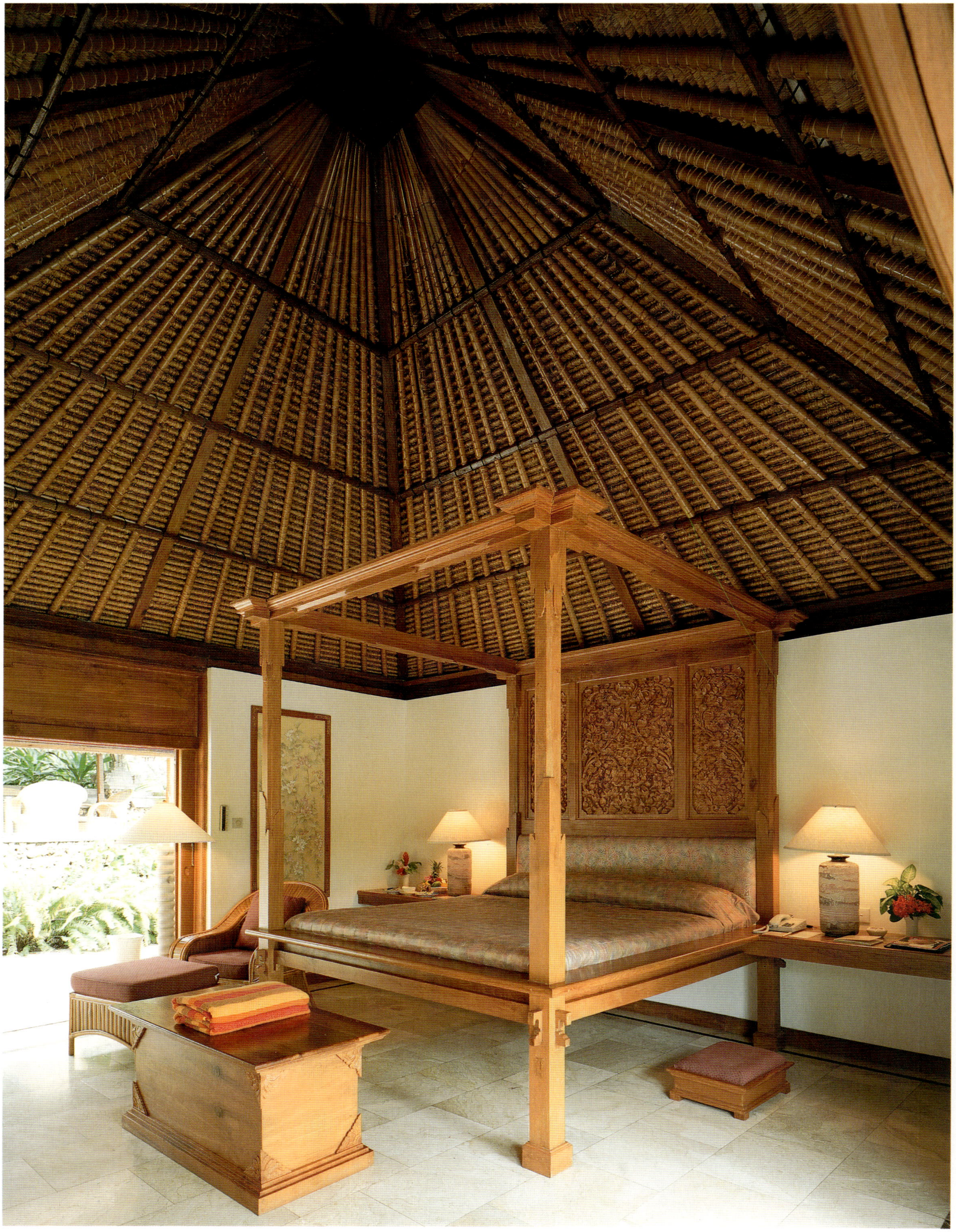

Luxury Lanai

161

Page 158 <Top> Cottages punctuate the skyline beyond lush vegetation, <Bottom> Pool overlooking the beach
Page 160 Bedroom of Presidential Villa
Page 161 <Top> Pool of Presential Villa, <Center> Bathroom of Deluxe Lanai, <Bottom left> Sign over entrance to Presidential Villa
Page 162 <Top> Various bar and restaurant signs
Page 163 <Top> Interior of the The Kura Kura restaurant, <Bottom left and center> Frangipani Cafe, <Bottom right> Interior of Kayu Bar
Page 164 Interior' of the lobby

Page 165 <Top> Steps leading to lobby cottage, <Center> Guests dancing in plaza by pool at night

P.158　上　緑の上に点在するコテージ、下　ビーチに面したプール
P.160　「プレジデンシャル・ビラ」のベッドルーム
P.161　上　同ビラのプール、中　「デラックス・ラナイ」のバスルーム、下左　「プレジデンシャル・ビラ」の入口サイン
P.162　上　各料飲施設のサイン
P.163　上　レストラン「ザ・クラクラ」内部、下左、中　「フランジパニ・カフェ」、下右　「カユ・バー」内部
P.164　ホテルロビー内部（左下がレセプション）
P.165　上　ロビー棟に続く階段、中　夜にはダンスの舞台となるプール脇の広場

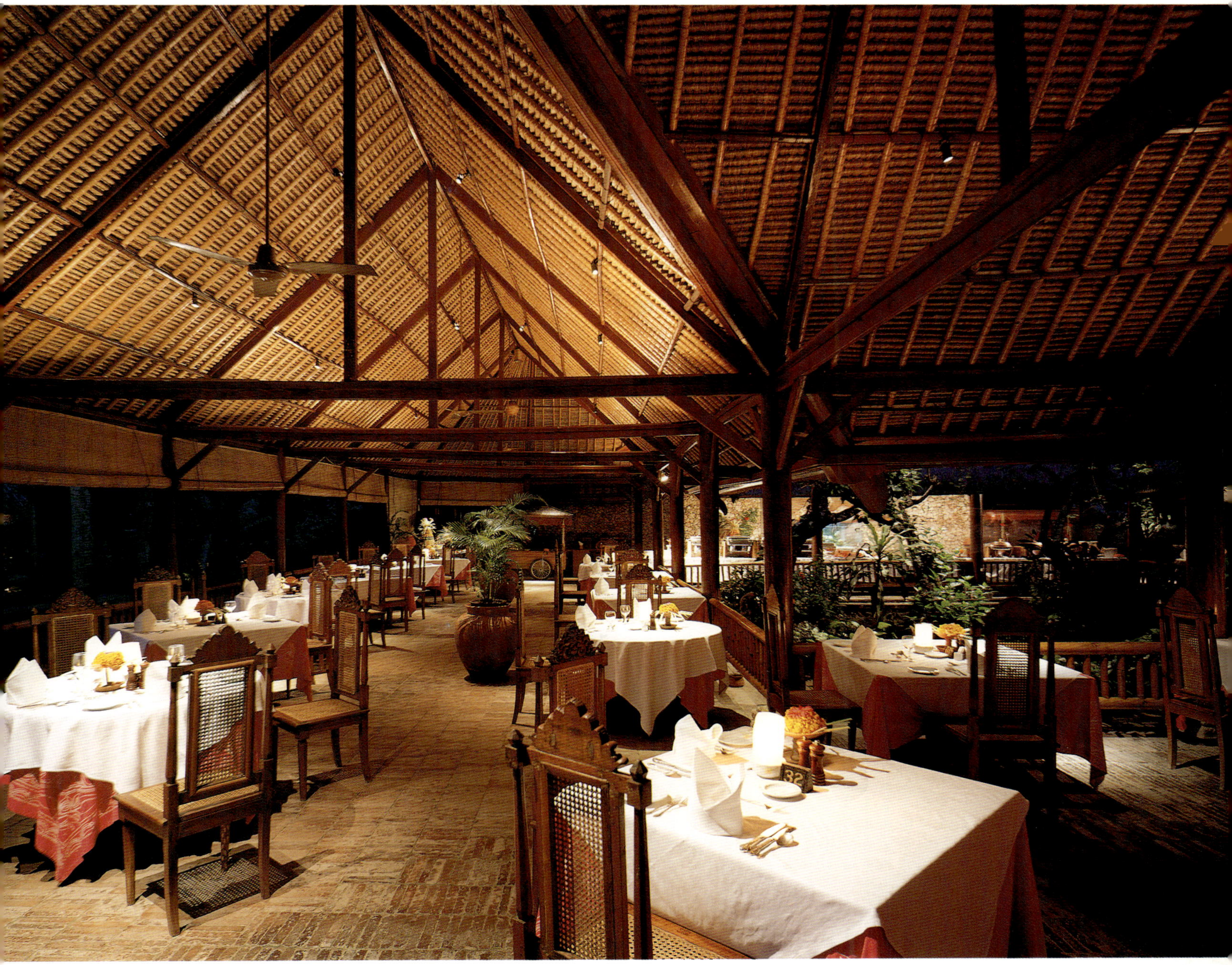
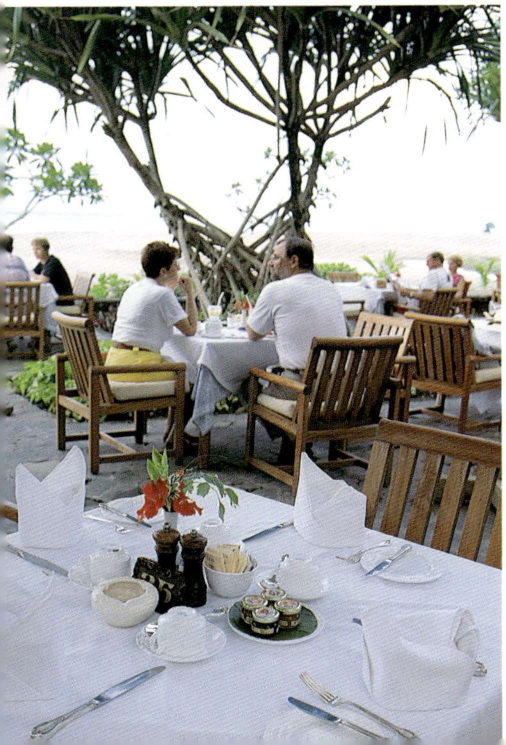
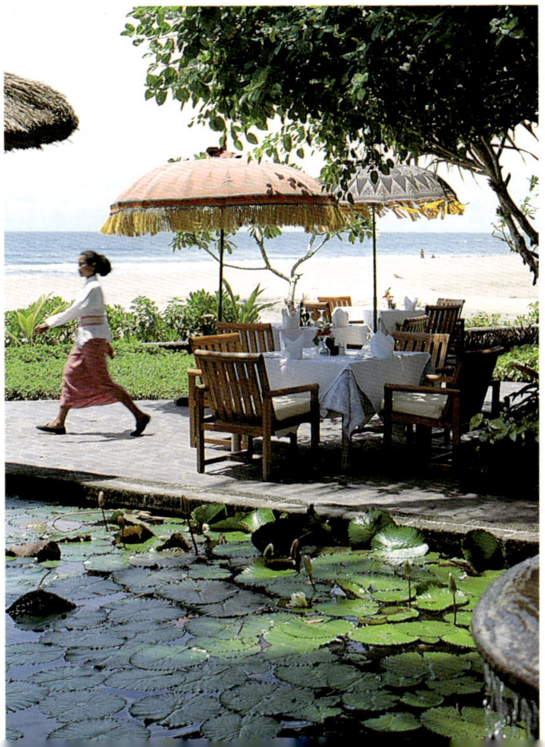
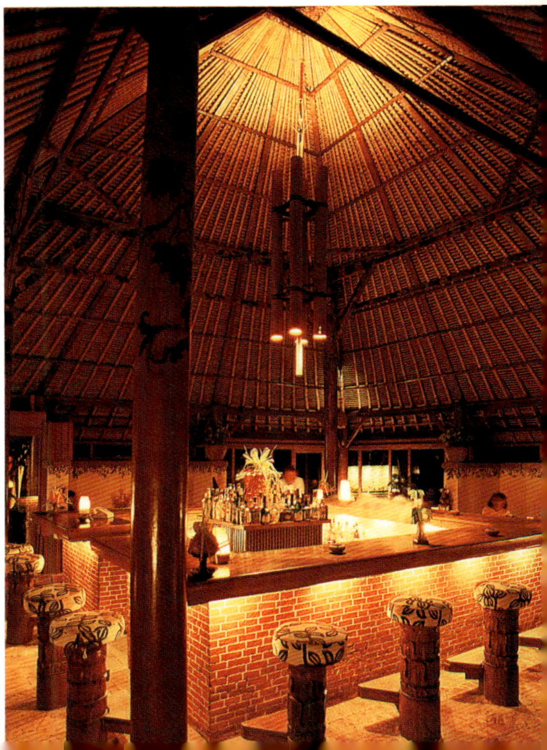

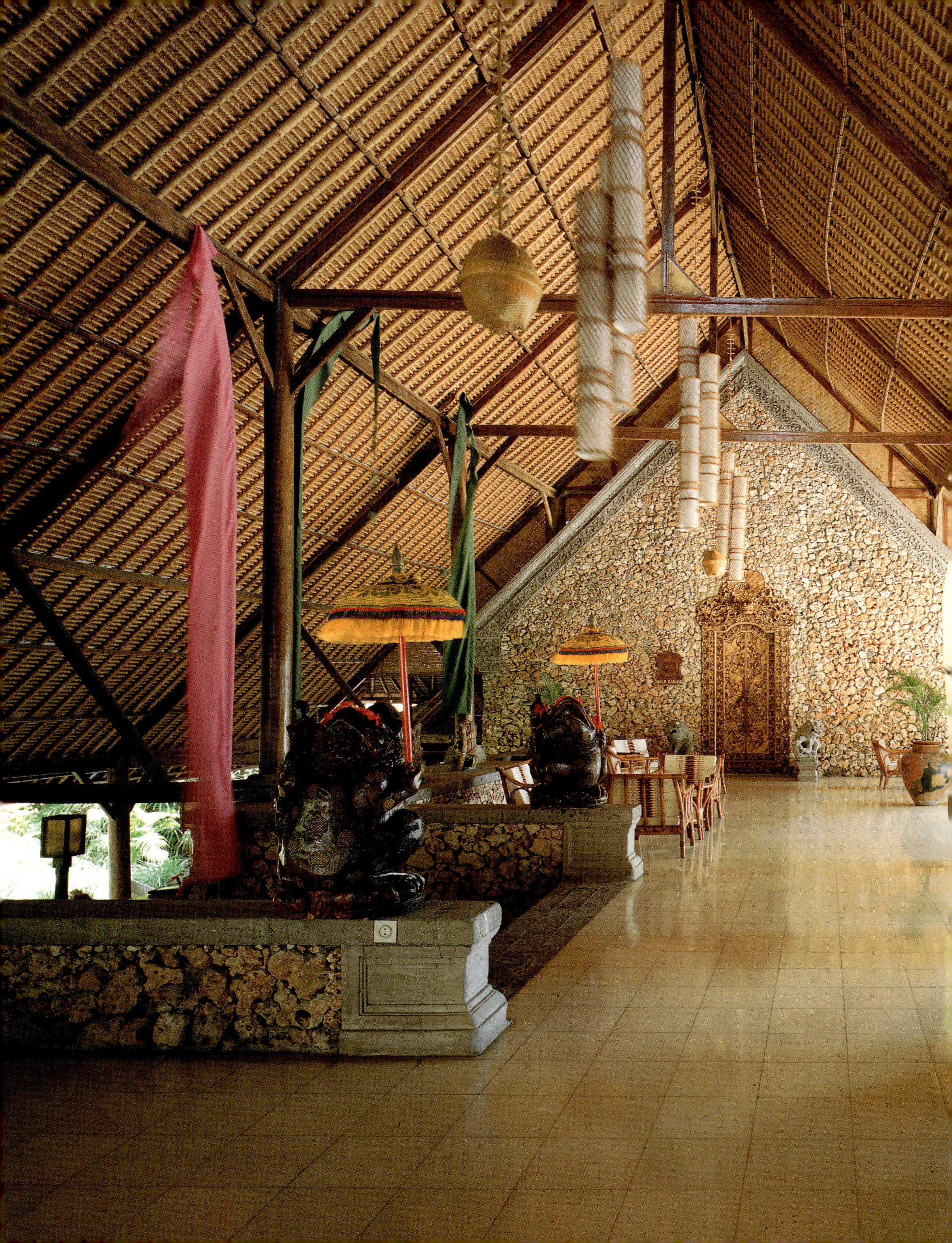

Room Division Manager Mr. Alexander Nayoan
客室担当支配人　アレキサンダー・ナヨアン

The Oberoi Bali

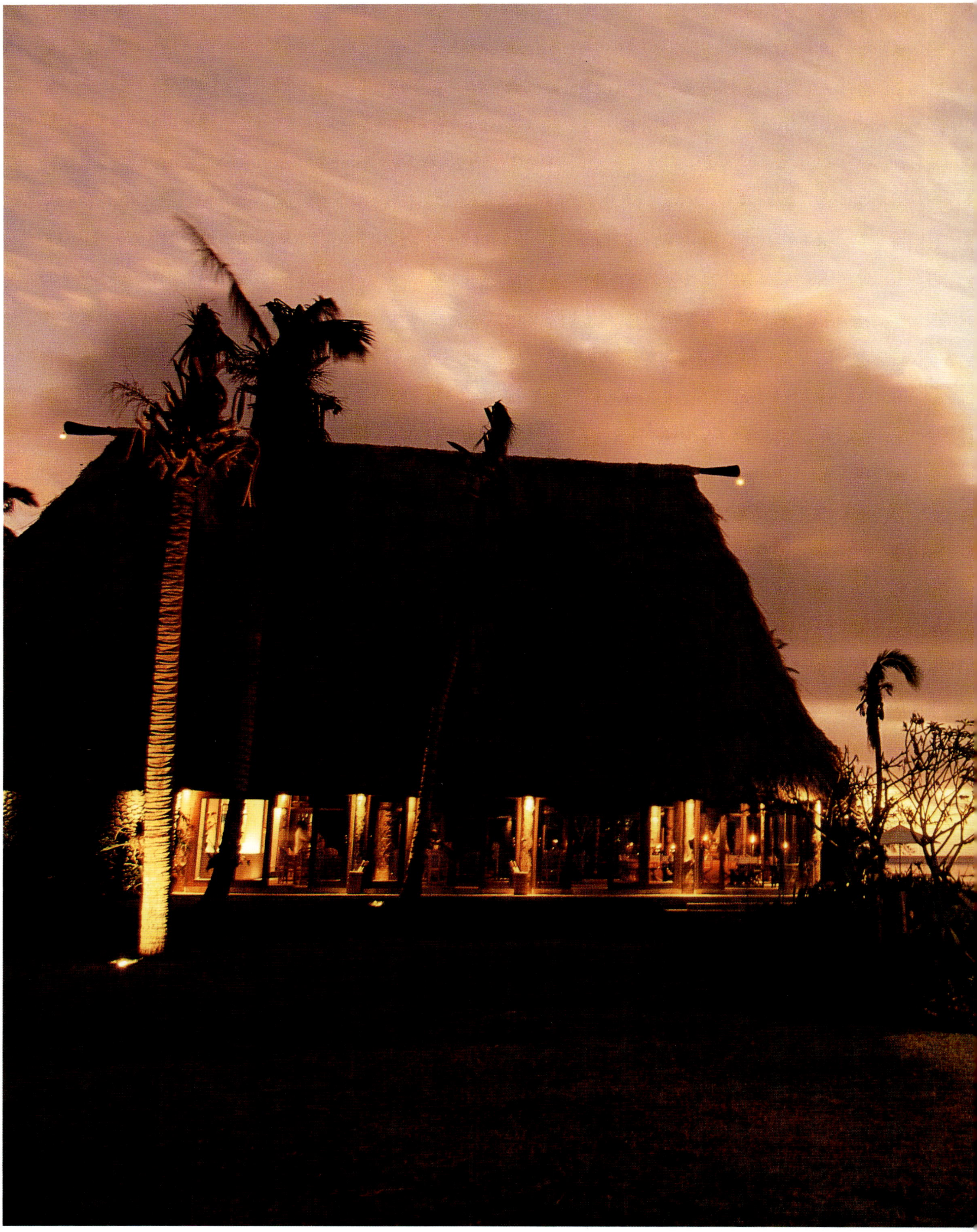

Oceania

Page 168 View of Original House from pool of courtyard
P. 168　中庭のプールから「オリジナル・ハウス」を見る

Mount Lofty House

Adelaide, Australia

マウント・ロフティ・ハウス／アデレード

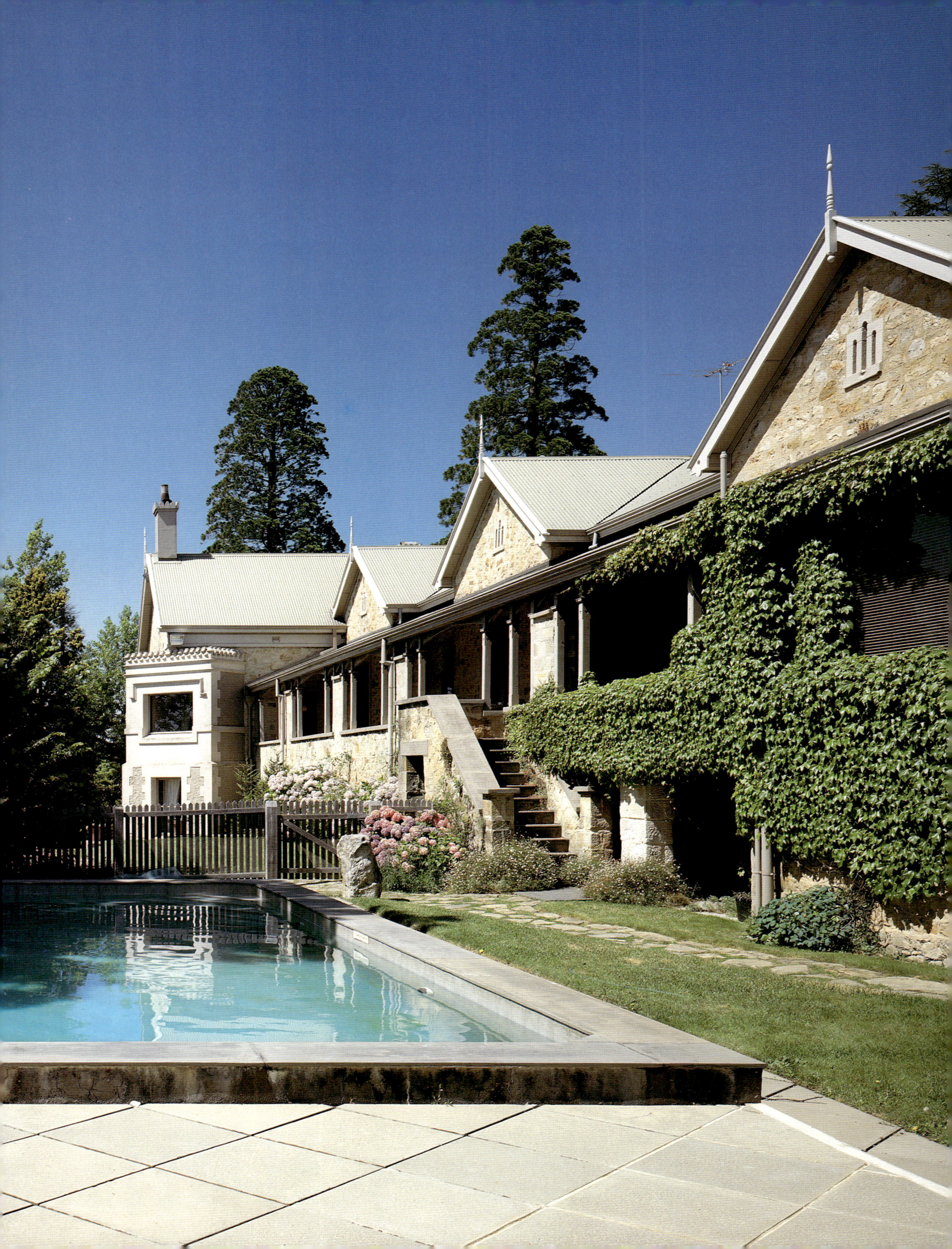

Ash Wednesday

「アッシュ・ウエンズデー」

Adelaide, with a population of 1 million is the 4th largest city in Australia and is also the state capital of South Australia. The city was well planned by William Light, an Englishman who first arrived in the area in the 1800s. Despite being an Australian city, Adelaide is one of the few cities which still retains a European flavor today. Mount Lofty House stands on the top of a hill about 20 minutes by car from the city streets of Adelaide. In that short time, however, the scenery changes dramatically and the view of Piccadilly Valley, which closely resembles an English Garden village with its immaculately kept gardens, is just like a hill resort. The change in countryside within such easy reach of the city must be invaluable to the people who live there. People undoubtedly frequent the place for lunch and dinner but it seems that many guests go to stay for conferences or a quiet weekend. It most likely serves as a guest house for the residents of Adelaide.

It is difficult to tell from the exterior of the building that it has been less than 10 years since Mount Lofty House opened as a hotel. It was in fact a natural disaster which marked the turning point for this building. Everything in the area, including this building which had stood there for over a hundred years was gutted in a bush fire known as Ash Wednesday on February 16th 1983. All that was left were the outer stone walls and the chimney. Ross Sands, who heard about the sad situation, bought it himself with a view to bringing the historical building back to life in a new form as a hotel. Being both owner and architect, he was able to put his heart and soul into devotedly rebuilding the image of an English country house.

Mount Lofty House appeared as a small 8 roomed hotel exactly 3 years after the fire on Ash Wednesday February 15th 1986. Obviously the existence of this hotel became a talking point because the support which it received was such that the Summit Wing was added in October 1988. Thus it expanded to its present form with 29 guest rooms, two restaurants and a conference room. Nevertheless, the original image of a country house and atmosphere have been faithfully preserved and the hotel offers a restful place, not readily available anywhere else, for its guests. The views and facilities may not be grand but it is the kind of hotel where tired souls from the city may relax and recharge their batteries before going home to face the new week on Monday.

I cannot help feeling that the reason why this hotel is able to exist is because of its accessibility to the city of Adelaide itself and the affluence of the people who live there.

オーストラリア第4の都市アデレードは、人口約100万人。南オーストラリア州の州都でもある。1800年代に初めてこの地に赴いた、英国人ウイリアム・ライト大佐によって、きちんとした都市計画がなされ、オーストラリアにあって、今でもヨーロッパの香りを残す数少ない都市である。マウント・ロフティ・ハウスは、そのアデレードの市街地から車で20分ほどの丘の上に建つ。

　ところが、僅か20分でその景観は見事に一変する。手入れの行き届いた庭園と、どこか英国の田園風景を想いおこさせるピカデリーの谷の眺めは、さながら高原の避暑地のイメージ。僅か20分の一変は、アデレード市民にとっても価値のあることに違いない。確かに、ランチやディナーで使われ、週末や会議で滞在するパターンが多いという。正に、アデレード市民のゲスト・ハウスとして存在する。

　マウント・ロフティ・ハウスは、その外観から窺い知ることは難しいが、ホテルとして営業を始めて、実はまだ10年にも満たない。それも大きな転機があってからだ。

　1983年2月16日、その後アッシュ・ウェンズデー(灰の水曜日)と名付けれた大きな山火事によって、130年以上の歴史を持ったこの建物を始め、この一帯が瞬く間に燃え尽きてしまった。僅かに残ったものといえば、石造りの外壁と煙突だけ。この惨状を知ったアデレードの建築家ロス・サンズは、歴史的建造物であるこの建物を何とか再生させようと、自らが買取り、ホテルとして新たに蘇生することを考えた。彼は英国にあるカントリー・ハウスのイメージを、細部に渡るまで忠実に再現することに心血を注いだ。それは、建築家とオーナーが一体となっていたからこそ、なしえたことのように思える。火災から丁度3年後の1986年2月15日のアッシュ・ウェンズデーに、たった8室の小さなホテルとして、マウント・ロフティ・ハウスは誕生した。

　当然のことながら、このホテルの存在は話題となり、多くの人たちの支持を得ることとなり、1988年10月「サミット・ウイング」を増築して、客室29室、レストランが2つ、それにコンファレンス・ルームを備えた、現在の形に発展していった。

　しかしながら、元のカントリー・ハウスのイメージも、そしてその雰囲気もきちんと守られ、訪れたものに他では得られない、やすらぎを与えてくれる。目を奪うような眺望や施設はないけれど、都会で傷ついた「鳥」たちを暫し休ませ、また大空にそっと戻してくれるような、そんな味わいのホテルだ。こういったホテルが存在できるのも、アデレードという街と、そこに住む人々の「豊かさ」に起因しているような気がしてならない。

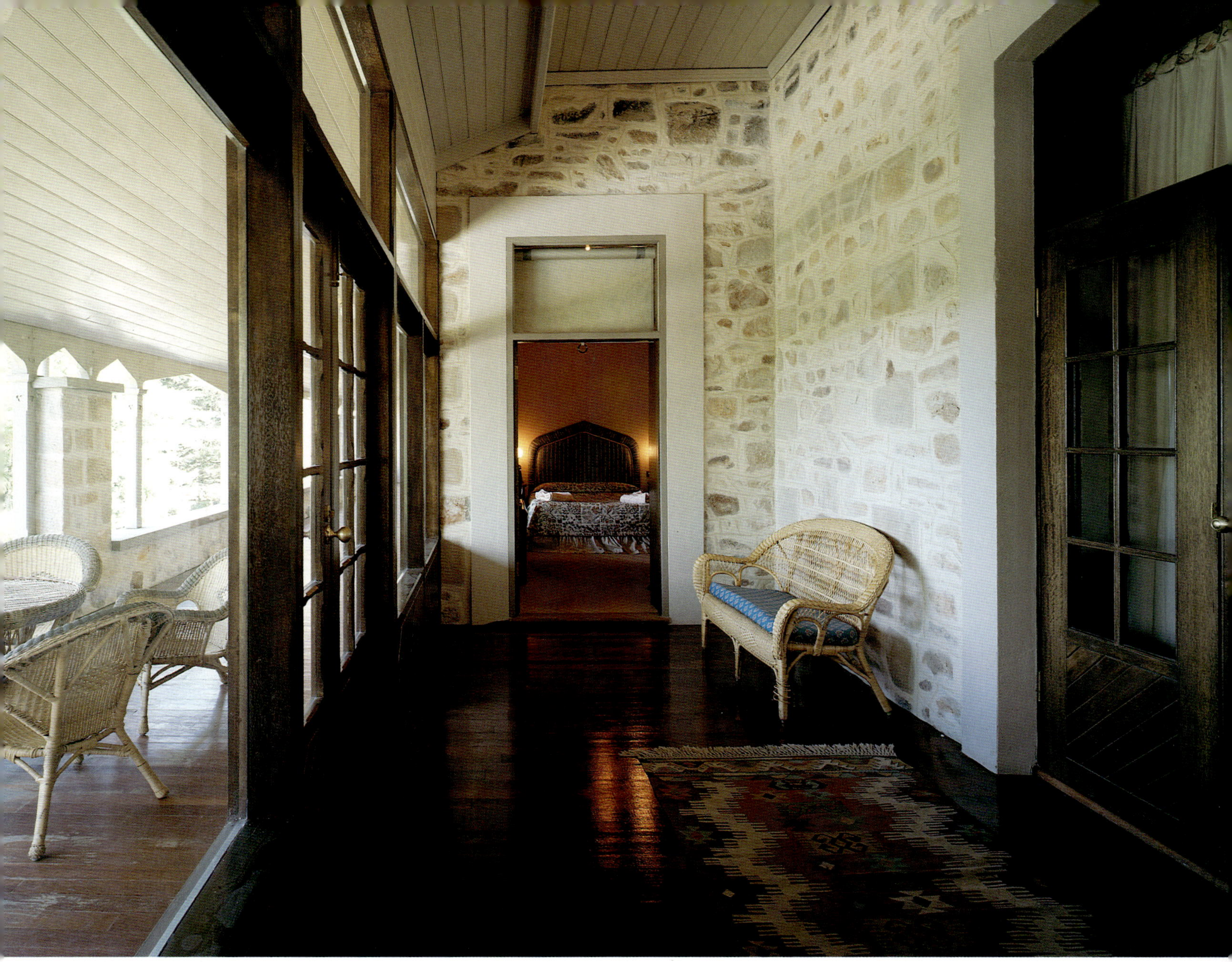

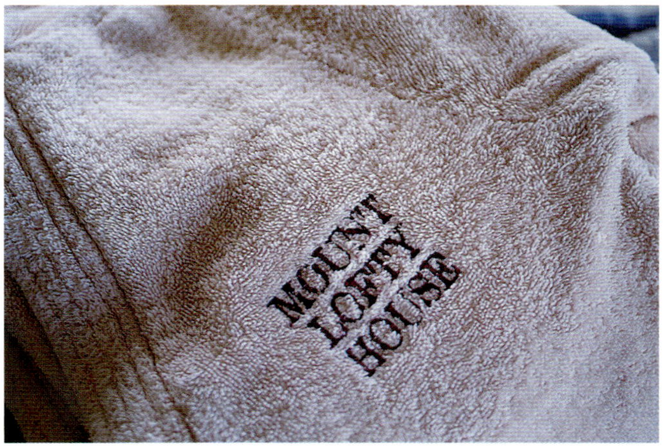
MOUNT
LOFTY
HOUSE

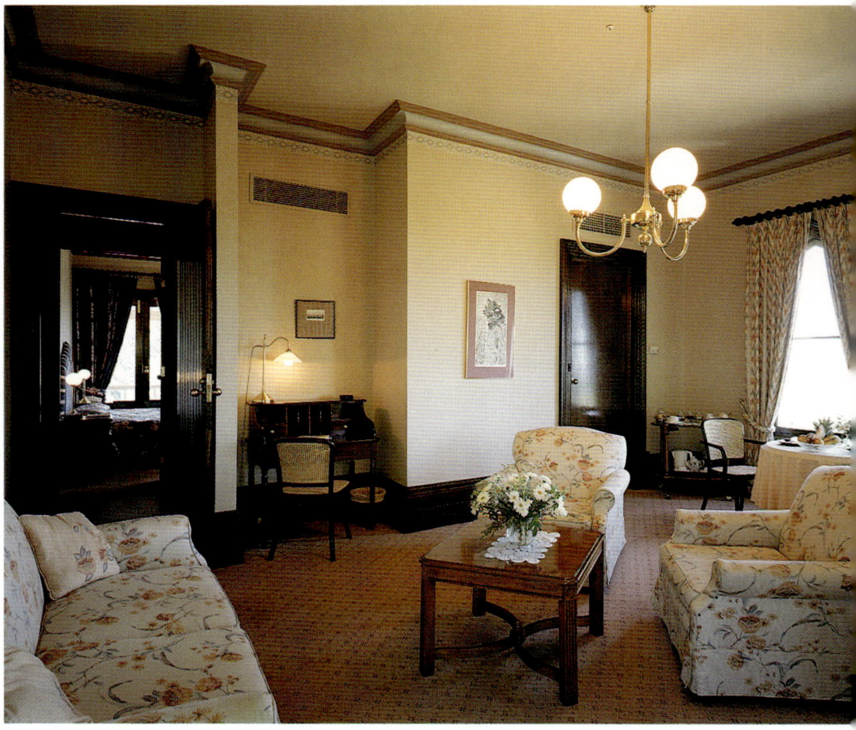

Page 170 Reception
Page 171 <Top> View from Original House, <Bottom> Tree burnt in the bush fire
Page 172 <Top> Terrace connecting rooms, <Bottom left> Bathrobe embraidered with name of the hotel, <Bottom right> Living room of Piccadilly Suite

Page 173 <Top> View of Piccadilly Valley from Original House, <Center> Balcony of Original House
Page 174 <Top> Guests are free to have tea at anytime in Tears Lounge, <Bottom> Arthur Waterhouse Lounge
Page 175 Big tree in the courtyard

P. 170 レセプション
P. 171 上 「オリジナル・ハウス」からの景観、下 山火事の痕跡を残す樹木
P. 172 上 部屋をつなぐテラス、下左 バスローブ、下右 「ピカデリー・スイート」のリビングルーム
P. 173 上 「オリジナル・ハウス」からピカデリー谷の眺望、中 同ハウスのバルコニー
P. 174 上 いつでも自由にお茶を楽しめる「ティアーズ・ラウンジ」、下 「アーサー・ウォーターハウス・ラウンジ」
P. 175 中庭の大木

Deluxe Room

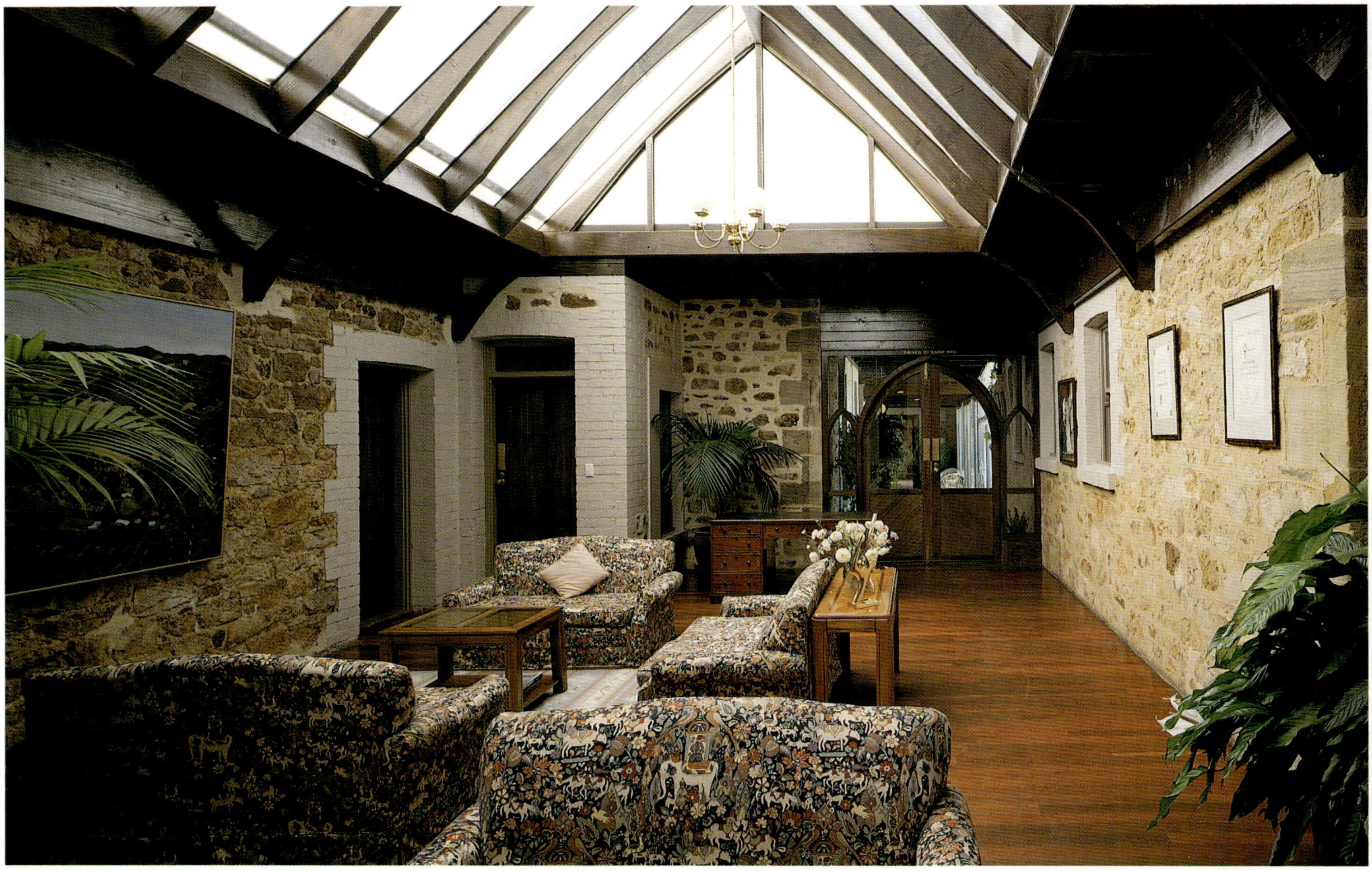

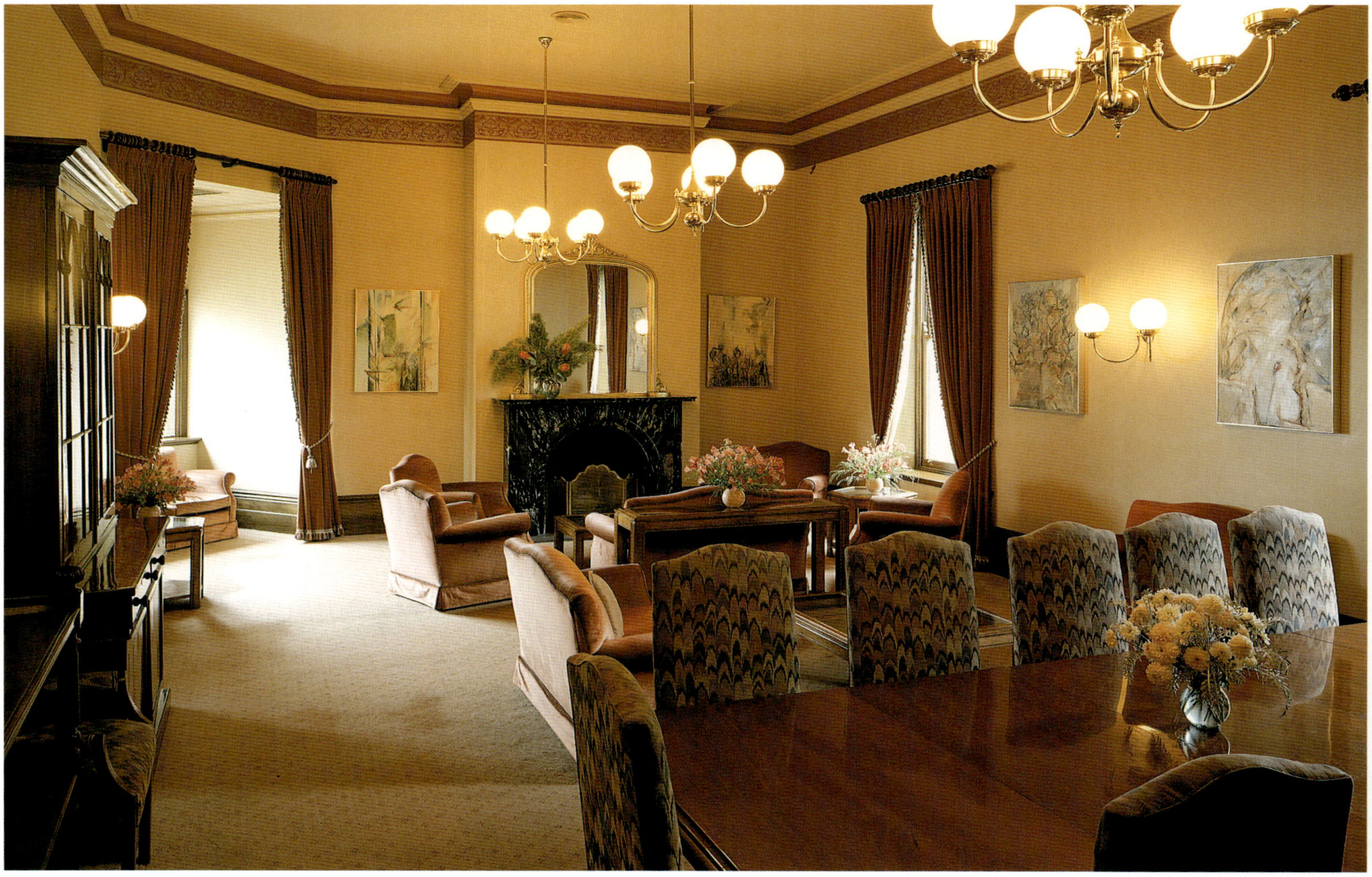

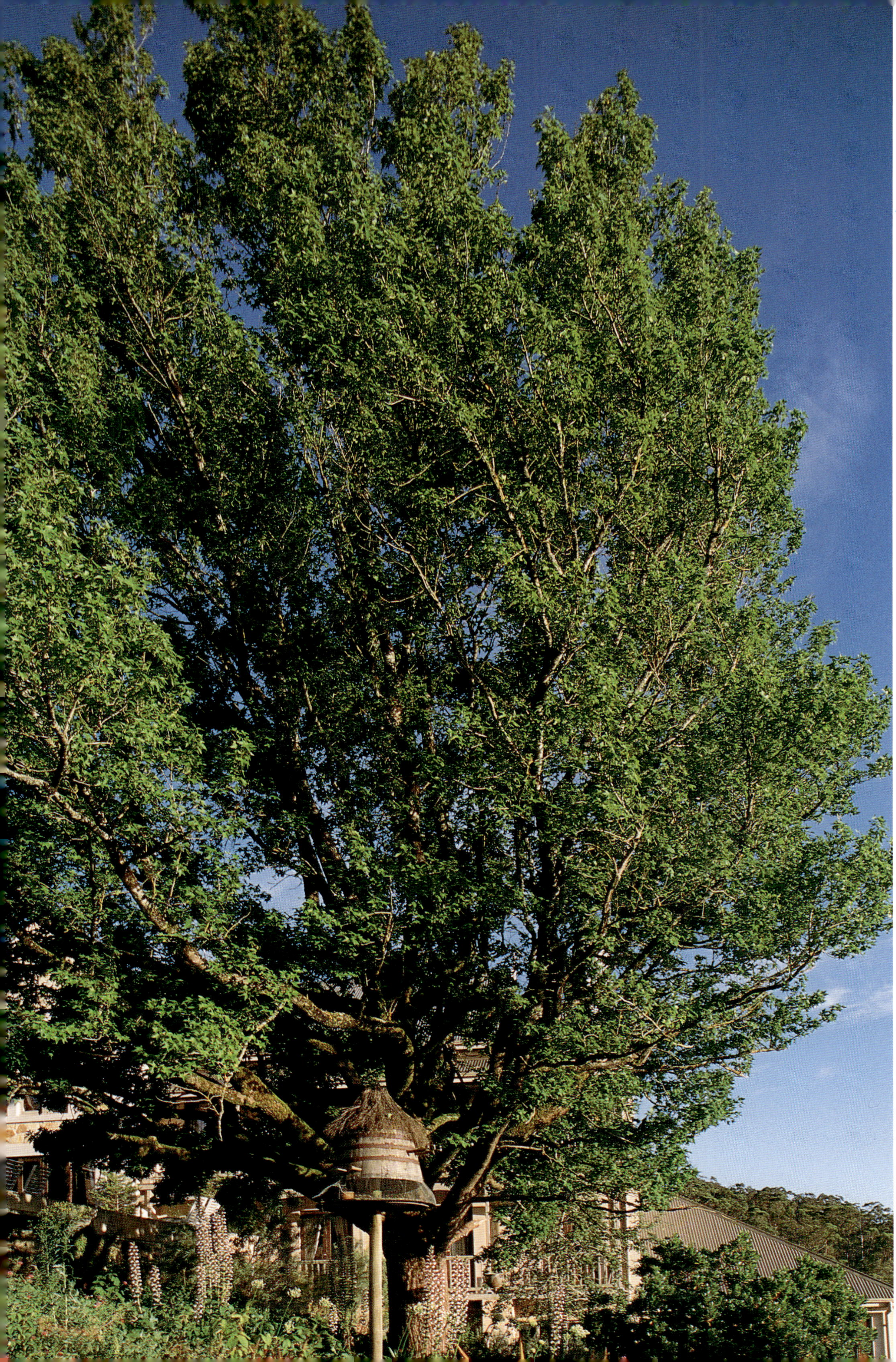

General Manager Mr. Kerry Bielik

総支配人　ケリー・ビエリック

*Page 176 <Center> Hotel entrance, <Bottom> Terrace links Original House to Summit Wing
Page 177 <Top> Piccadilly Dining Room in the morning, <Bottom left> Cereals for breakfast, <Bottom center> Views of Adelaide*

P.176　中　ホテル・エントランス、下　「オリジナル・ハウス」と「サミット・ウイング」をつなぐテラス
P.177　上　朝の「ピカデリー・ダイニングルーム」、下左　朝食用のシリアル、下中　丘の上からアデレードの街を見る

Mount Lofty House

Page 178 A number of photographs imbeddied in a wall of the lobby
Page 179 Corner of Encore restaurant

P. 178　ロビーの壁に飾られたスターの写真の数々
P. 179　レストラン「エンコア」の一角

シーベル・タウン・ハウス／シドニー

Sebel Town House

Sydney, Australia

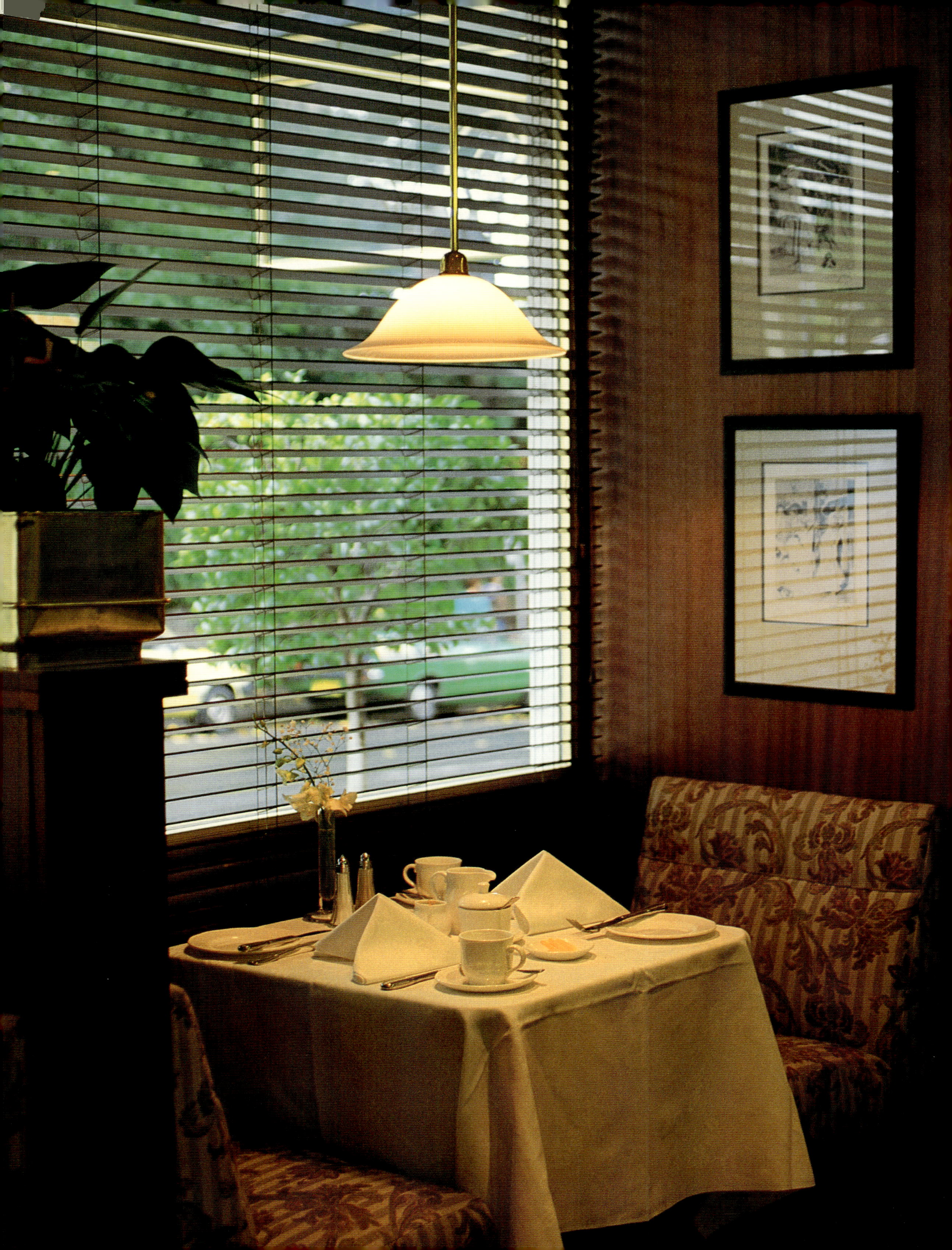

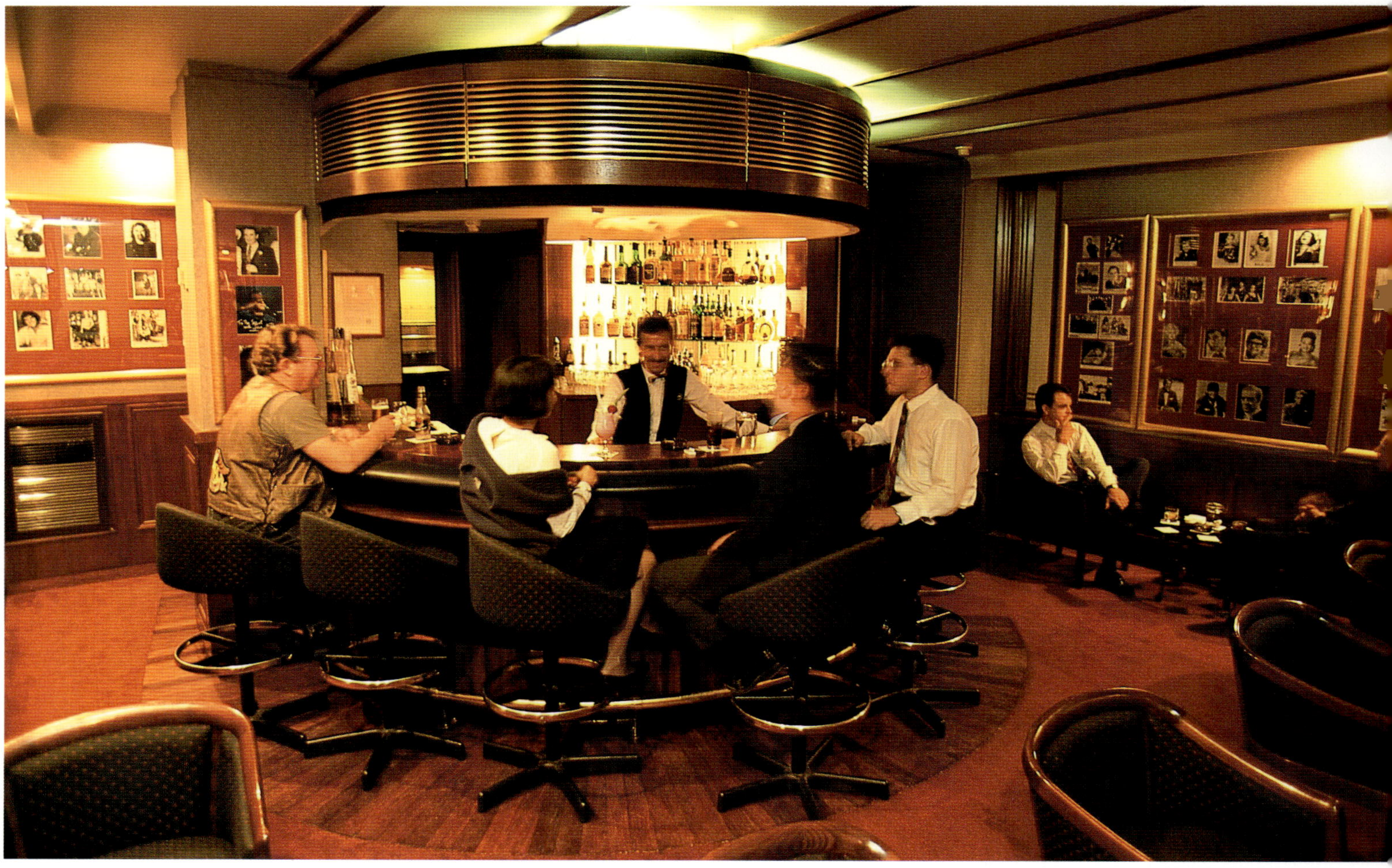

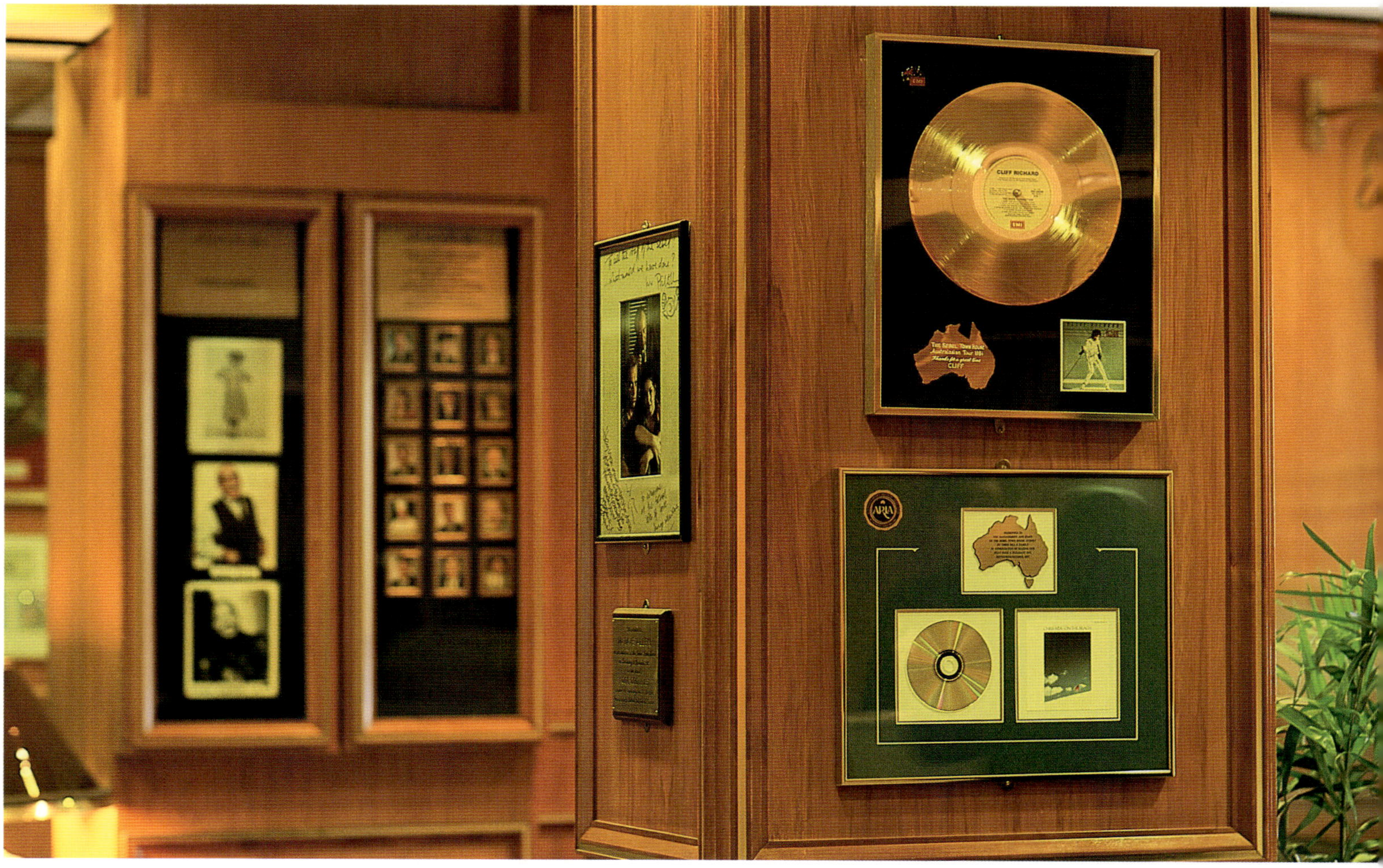

Urban Star Dock

スターが翼を休める都会の宿

Sebel Town House, which was awarded the 1991 Australian Music Industry prize for the best hotel, is unique among the numerous small and luxury hotels in Australia. It stands quietly in contrast with the neighborhood relatively near King's Cross, which is the busiest street in the vast Australian city of Sydney. Since it opened 30 years ago, not only has it become the leading hotel in the city but the fact that it is well known to, and much loved by entertainers from all over the world, distinguishes it from all the others.

Proof of this is to be found all around the hotel. For instance, compact discs decorate the lobby and a number of signed photographs have been imbedded in the wall of fame in the bar. This colorful collection includes such stars as Shirley McClane, Rod Stewart, Michael Jackson and Tom Cruise. Paul Hogan of Crocodile Dandy fame is of course a patron and all the big names in the entertainment world, be they film stars, musicians or producers are there. Some of the suites are named after the people who always stay in them and yet it is odd that there is none of the vulgar glitter that is commonly associated with the stars. This obviously is because the hotel was not built expressly for them. Instead, it was created with the basic idea of providing really relaxed spaces without worrying about the surroundings; a small hotel where guests would be able to experience what it is like to stay in a club.

A typical example of this is the bar, which has no official closing time and closes only when the last guest has gone home. This means that the bartender is sometimes still working, when the rest of the staff arrives for work in the morning. The secret of the hotel's long popularity most probably lies in this warm hospitality.

The 167 guest rooms have been renovated over the years so it is difficult to believe that it has been open for so long. Moreover, because changes have been made after consulting the opinion of regular guests, there is a rich variety of new taste. Perhaps it would be possible to refer to it as a 'Boutique Hotel' in the true sense of the word. The basics have certainly been preserved and in pursuing a continual freshness, the hotel has managed to faithfully maintain its club-like atmosphere. It really is an indispensable hotel especially in such a large city as Sidney.

The secret of its popularity over the last 30 years is surely none other than the constant effort by the management to maintain the atmosphere of the hotel. But it is the guests themselves who know best.

1991年度オーストラリア音楽産業が選んだ「ザ・ベスト・ホテル」。シーベル・タウン・ハウスは、数あるスモール＆ラグジュアリー・ホテルの中にあっても極めてユニークな存在といえるだろう。オーストラリア一の大都市シドニー。その中でも一番の繁華街、キングス・クロスに程近い場所に、付近とは対照的に静かに佇む。オープン以来既に30年、常にシドニーの第一線のホテルとしてだけではなく、世界のエンターティナーたちに愛され、親しまれてきたことは、このホテルを特徴付けるにあまりあることだろう。

その証拠は、ホテルのあちこちで見ることができる。ロビーに飾られたコンパクト・ディスク、バー"セレブリティーズ(名士達)"の壁面を埋め尽くすサイン入り写真の数々。シャーリー・マクレーンからロッド・スチュアート、マイケル・ジャクソン、トム・クルーズに至るまで、実に多彩。勿論「クロコダイル・ダンディ」のポール・ホーガンも御愛用。映画スター、ミュージシャン、プロデューサー等、エンターティナーのオンパレード。スイート・ルームのいくつかにも、定宿としている人々の名前がついたところがある。それでいて、ありがちなギラギラした、いやらしさがないのが不思議なことだ。それは当然といえば当然のことながら、彼らのためにホテルがつくられたからではないからだ。

小さくて、クラブのような感じを味わえるホテル。周りを気にせずに、本当に寛げるスペースが用意されているホテル、そういったことを基につくられた。典型的な例がある。ここのバーは閉店時間が決まっていない。最後のお客が帰ったときが、その時だという。だから朝、他のスタッフが出勤してもまだバーテンが働いていることがあるという。そんな細かなもてなし心が、長年人気の秘密かも知れない。

167室ある客室は、常にどこかでリノベーションをしており、30年という歳月を微塵も感じさせない。その上、リピーターたちの意見を参考にしながら変更を加えているので、新しいテイストで、バリエーションも豊富に揃えられている。本当の意味での、ブティック・ホテルといえるだろう。基本が適確に守られ、常に新しさを追及し、なおかつクラブの雰囲気をきちんと維持している。そういった当たり前のことが、当たり前にできている。特に、大きな都市のホテルにおいては不可欠なことだ。

30年に亘る人気の秘密は、不断の努力という、いってみればなんでもないところにあった。しかしそれは、お客自身が一番良く知っている。

The Helen Montagu Suite

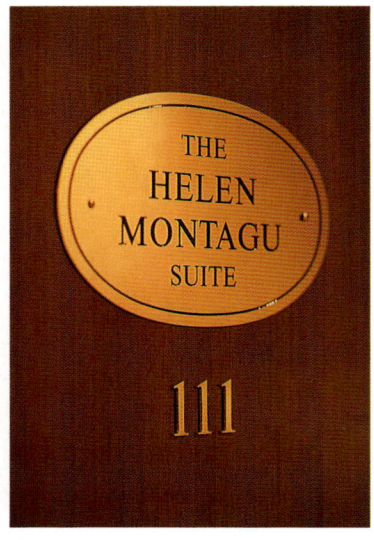

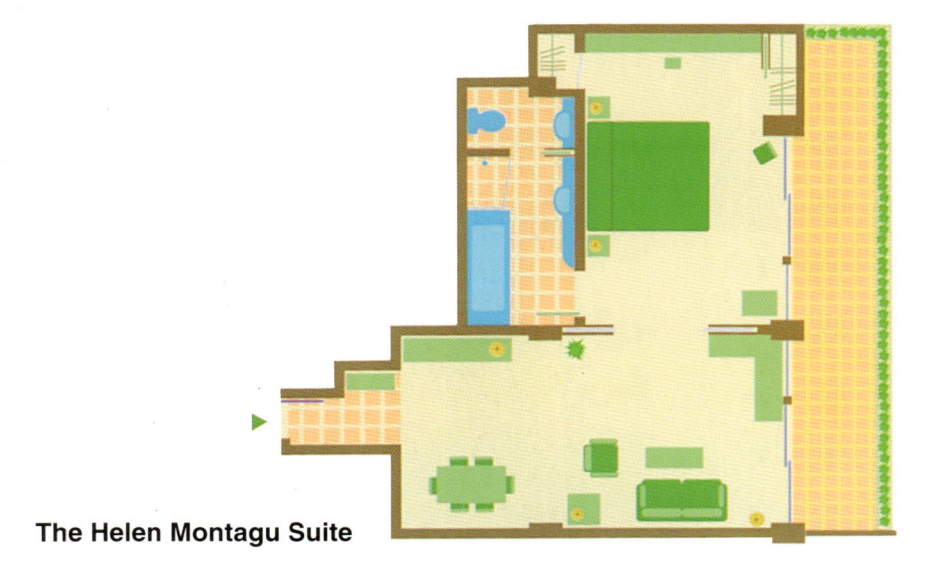

Page 180 <Top> Bar "Celebrities", <Bottom> Mementos left by musicians
Page 182 <Top> Functional and clean bathroom, <Center left> Plate of suite room, <Center right> Looking outside from desk of suite room
Page 183 Interior of suite room

P.180　上　バー「セレブレティーズ」、下　ミュージシャンたちが残していったディスク
P.182　上　機能的で清潔なバスルーム、中左　スイートルームのプレート、中右　スイートの書斎デスクからの眺め
P.183　スイートルームのインテリア

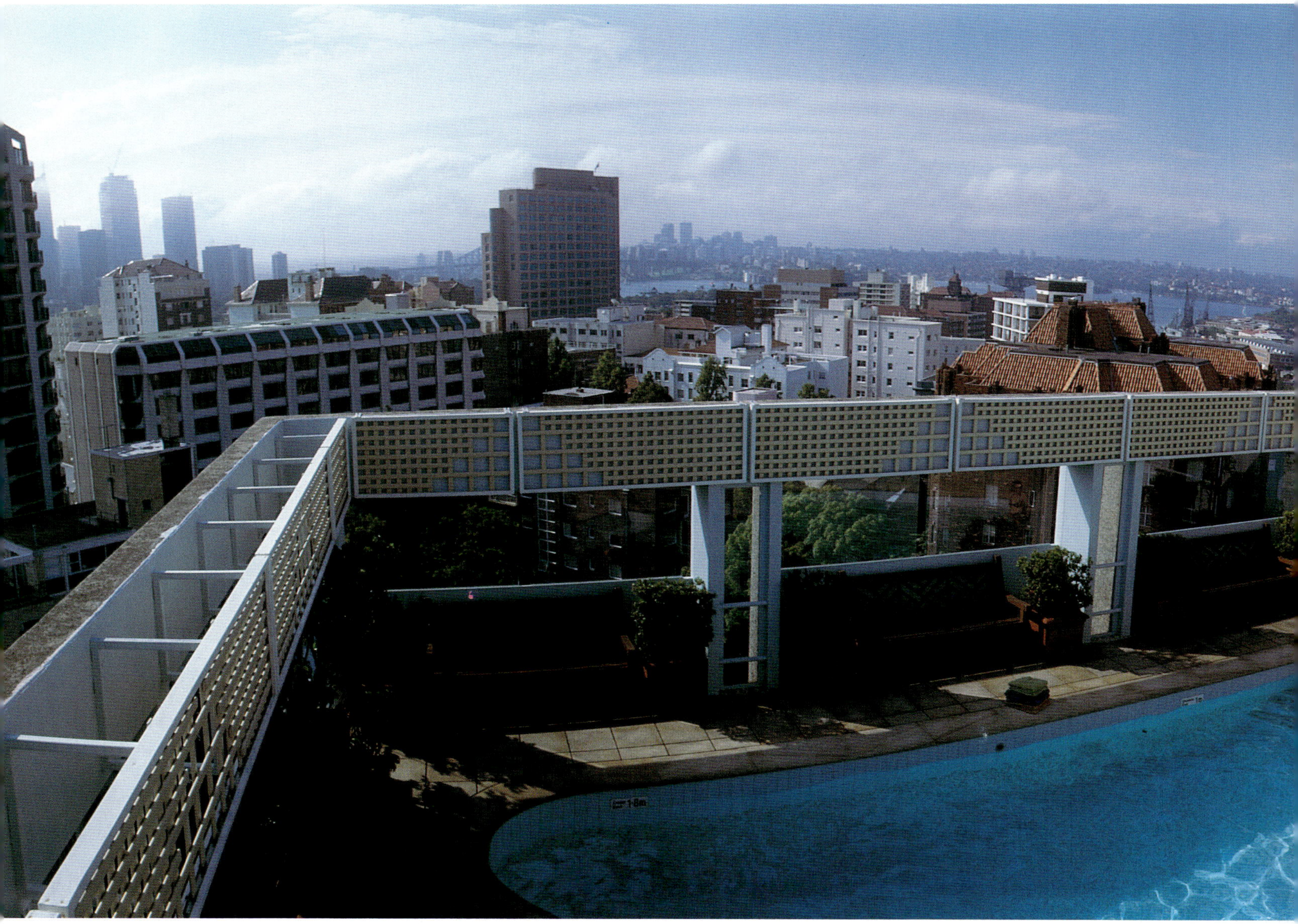

General Manager Mr. Nicholas Truswell
総支配人　ニコラス・トラズウエル

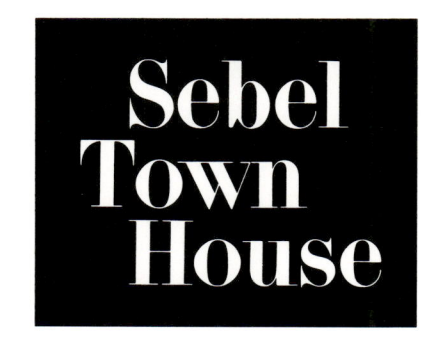

Page 184 View of Sydney Bay from rooftop pool
Page 185 <Center> Entrance of hotel, <Bottom> Lobby

P.184　屋上プールから遠くにシドニー湾を望む
P.185　中　ホテル・エントランス、下　ロビー

Sebel Town House

Huka Lodge

Taupo, New Zealand

フカ・ロッジ／タウポ（ニュージーランド）

Page 186　Cottages nestling amongst the trees
Page 187　<Top> The Dining Room, notorius for its food, <Bottom> Lodge Room tastefully decorated lounge with open hearth

P.186　コテージ外観
P.187　上　定評ある料理が楽しめる「ザ・ダイニングルーム」、下　暖炉のあるラウンジ「ロッジ・ルーム」

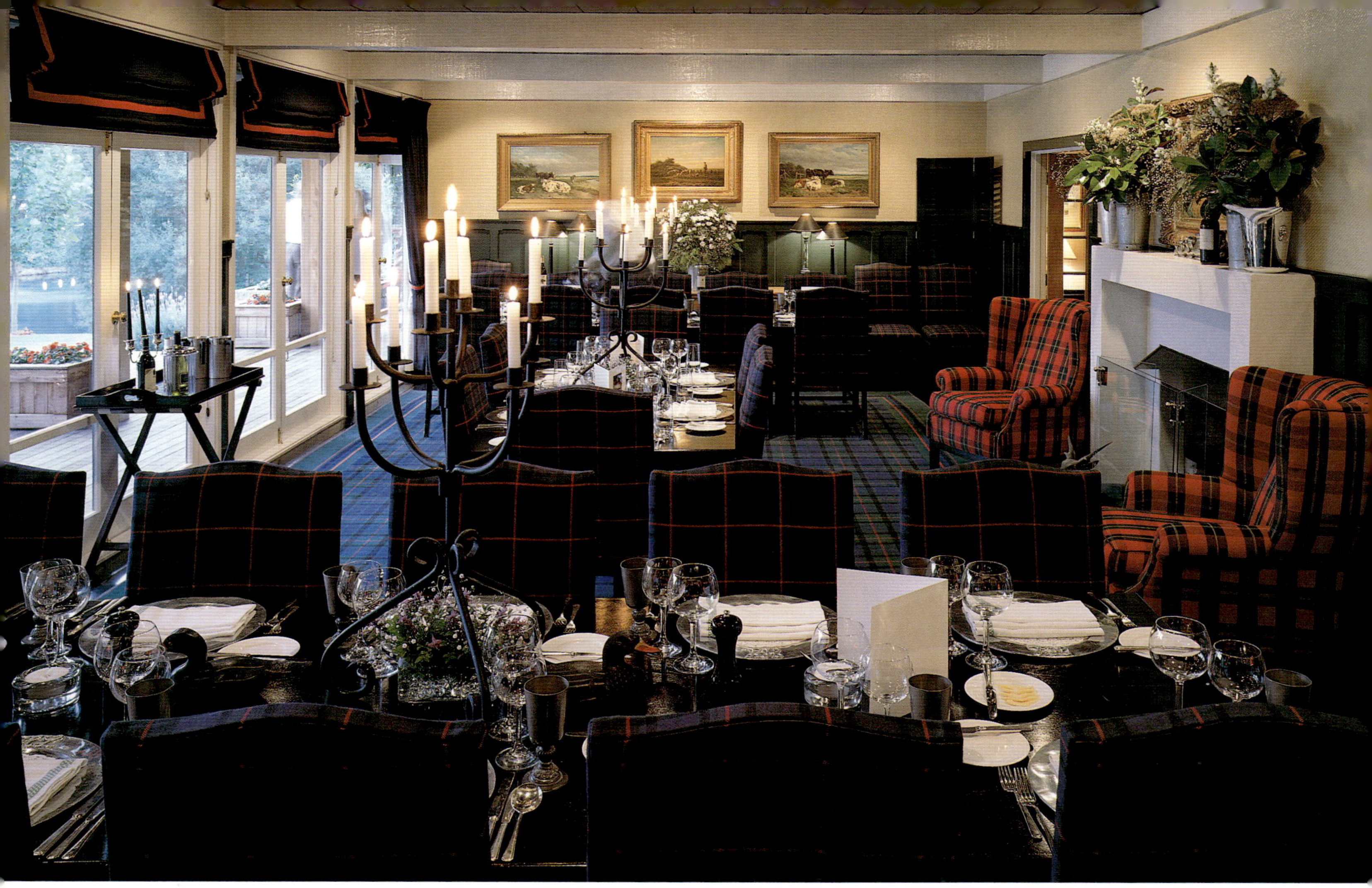

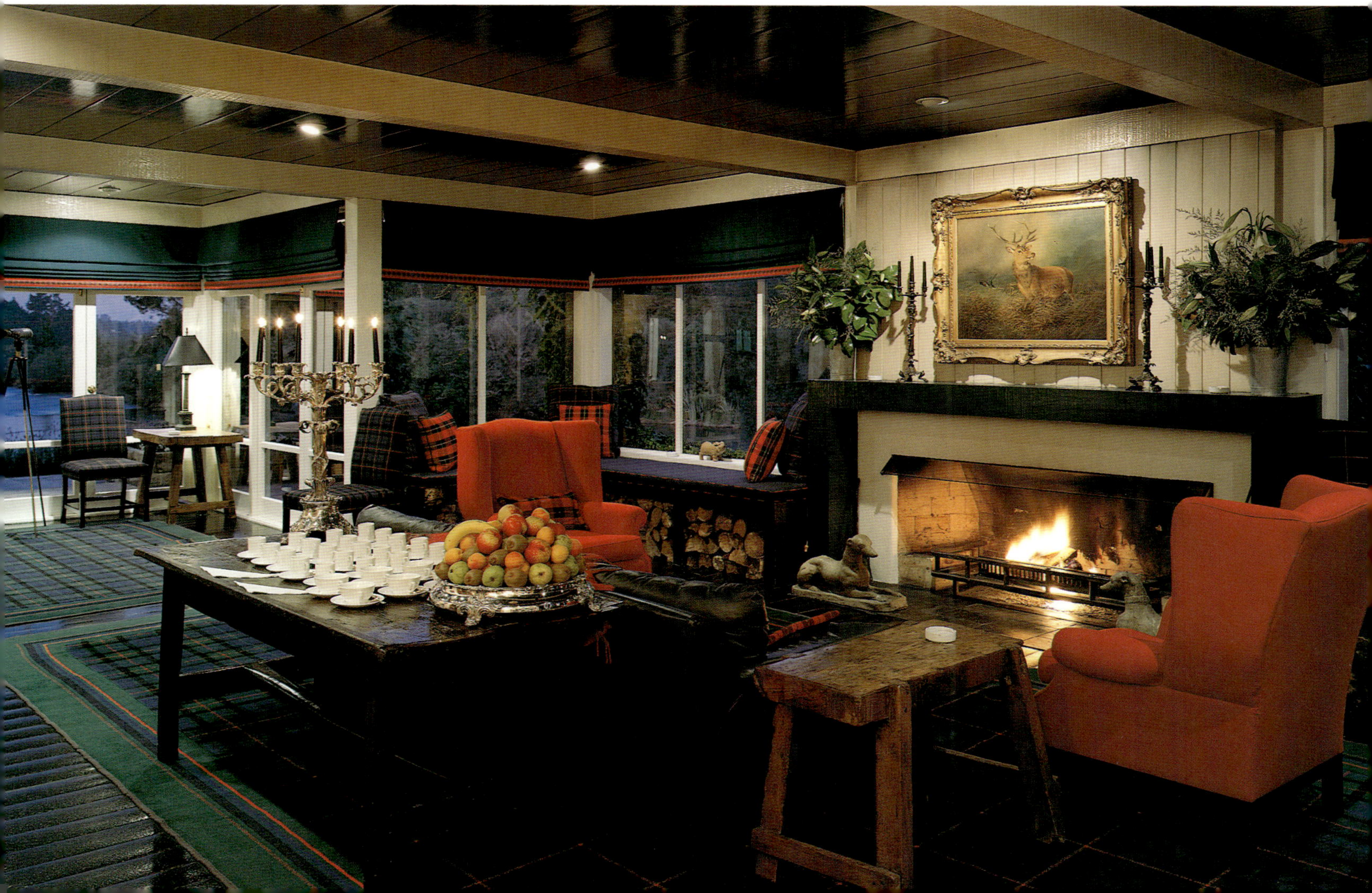

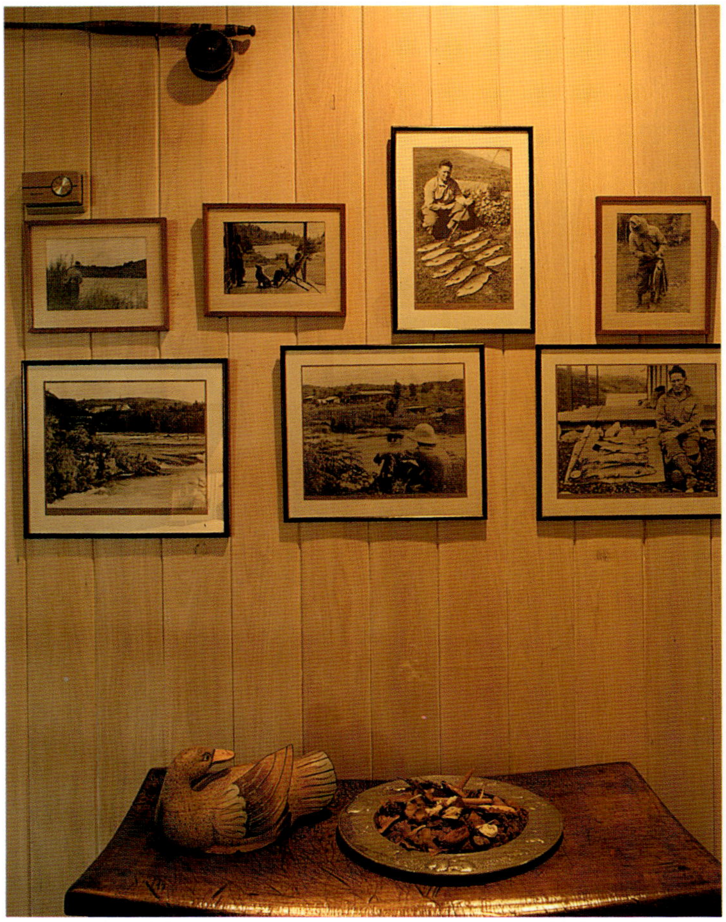

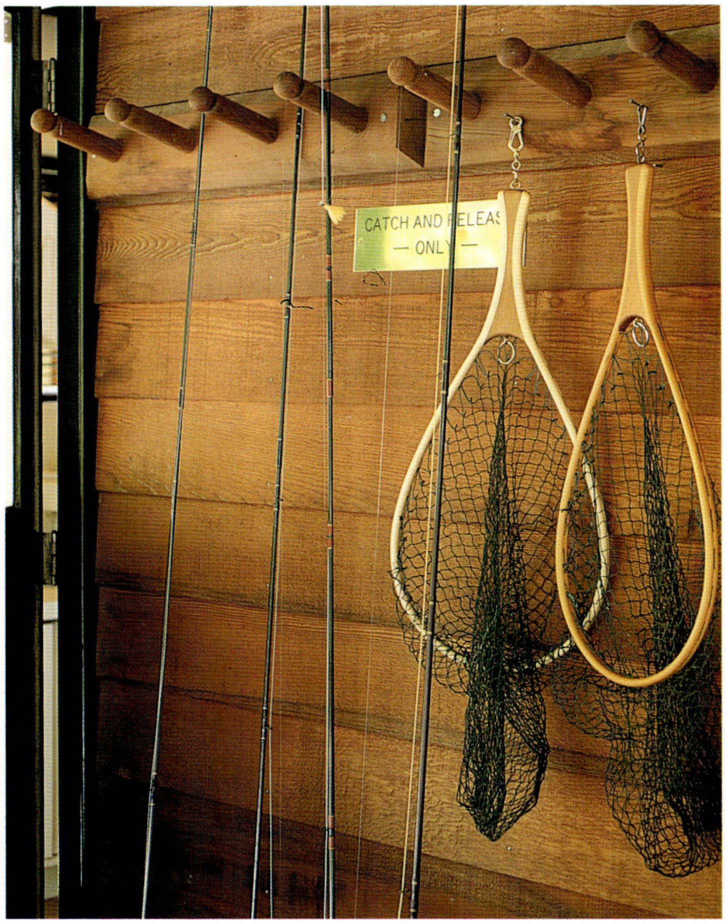
CATCH AND
— ONLY —

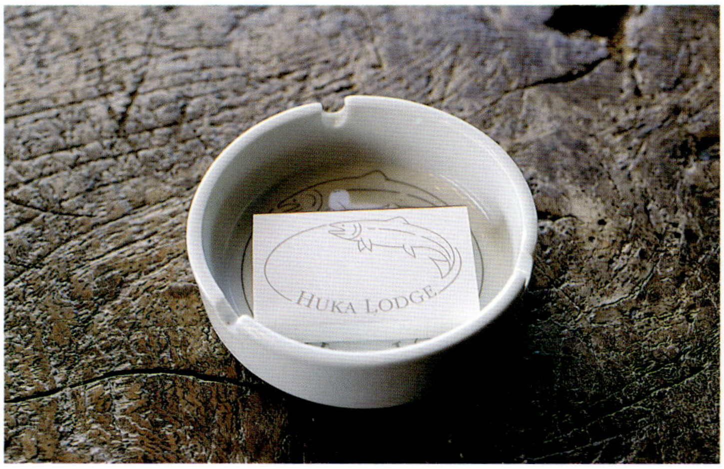
HUKA LODGE

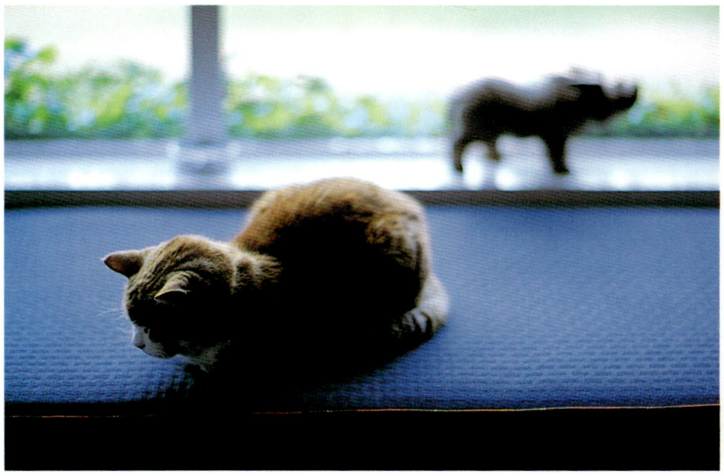

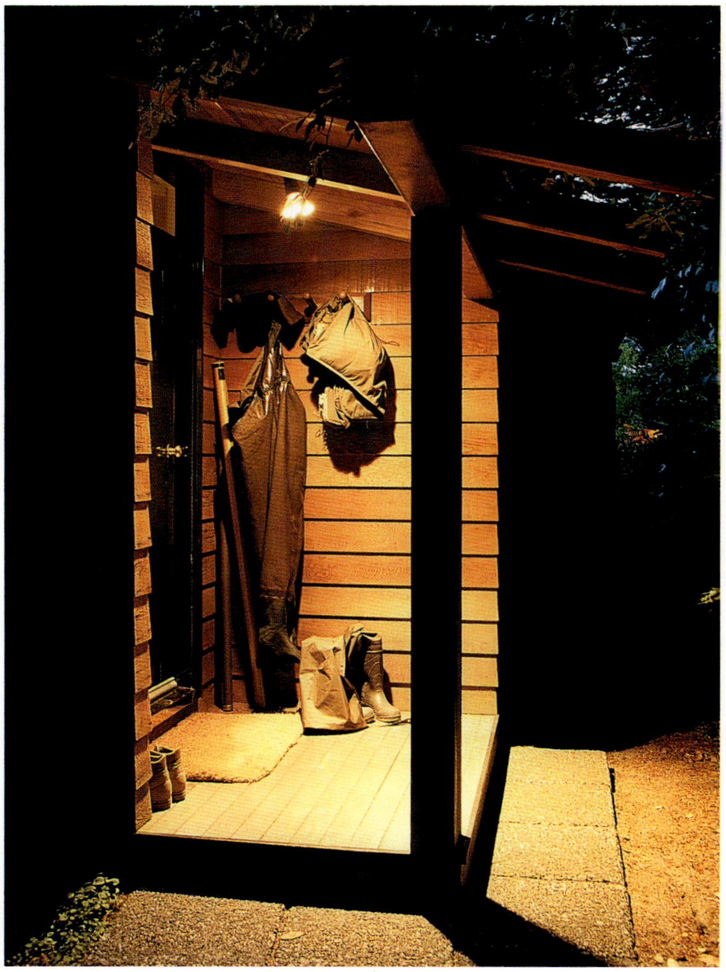

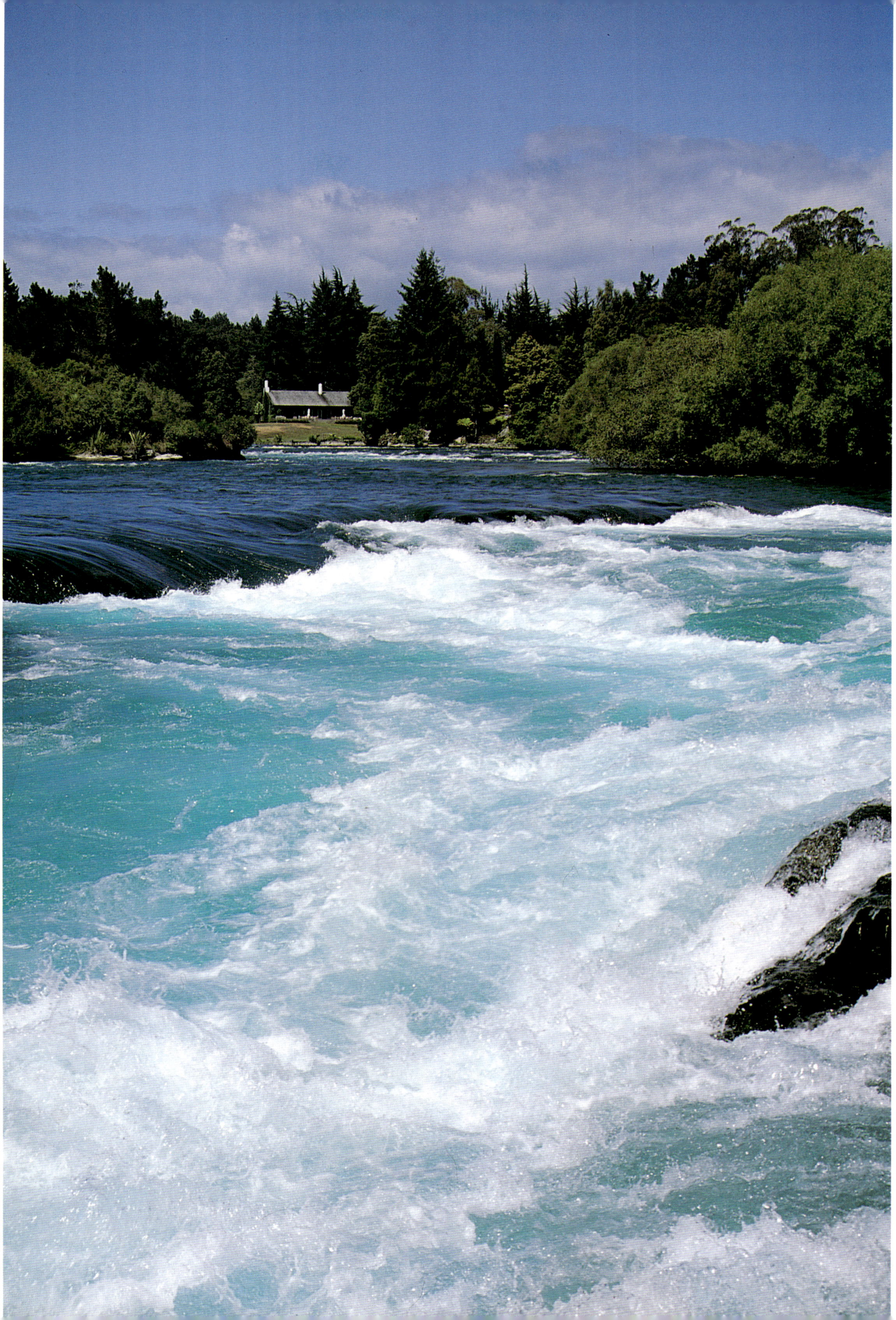

Foaming Water
「泡立つ水」

Huka Lodge is situated 280 km (175 miles) to the south of Auckland on the North Island of New Zealand in a summer resort and recreation area which focuses on Lake Taupo. It really is a wonderful location with the Waikato River flowing right in front of the hotel and the Huka Falls cascading some 300 meter (1,000 feet) beyond. No wonder it is called Huka for it means "Foaming Water" in Maori. In the latter half of the 1920s, an Irishman called Alan Pye chose this site to build himself a house for fishing. However, it seems that it was only ever used as a house. When the fishing bug took hold afterwards, people pitched their tents outside the house and enjoyed life in whatever manner pleased them most. This idea still lives on today.

The present owner, Alex Van Heeren, a Dutch businessman, bought this place in 1984 with a view to turning it into a hotel. The 17 room lodge was completed the following year and opened for business.

One of the reasons why people gather at Huka Lodge is the food. The service too is impeccable as one look at the polished, smearless glasses will confirm. The five course menu is really well planned from day to day and it makes ones mouth water even to look at it. As may be expected from the fact that it is now a sporting lodge, guests come from all over the world, including North and South America, Europe and Asia. Groups of guests enjoy dinner together round a table just like they did in the old days when Huka Lodge was simply a fishing lodge. The food of course is excellent and that is why Huka Lodge is well known throughout the world.

Even though her interior design is brimming over with a sense of luxury, Virginia Fisher has used simple materials and the contrast between the private and public spaces is superb. The main lodge, which houses the dining room, has been coordinated very aptly with a keynote of traditional English tones of rich greens, reds and navy blue as well as tartan check. In contrast to this, each lodge is decorated in white or pastel shades with an emphasis on country taste. The mosquito nets over the beds are very effective and have a soft enveloping effect, which adds to the overall composition of the room. They also help to create a relaxed atmosphere.

A special mention must be made of the bathroom. The skylight or rather the whole ceiling is covered in glass and the whiteness which increases the brilliance further promises a rather fresh start to the day. Nevertheless, it is a masterpiece of design.

Making the most of the environment, Huka Lodge offers a kind of comfort that can only be found there and the staff, of course, positively back this up. Because everything is well polished, just like the water of the Waikato River which flows in front of the hotel, guests can expect a relaxing stay at this wonderful lodge.

ニュージーランドの北島オークランドより、レクリエーション基地として、また避暑地として名高いタウポ湖を目指し、南下すること280km。その湖の少し手前に、フカ・ロッジはある。目の前にはワイカト川が流れ、300m先にはフカ滝という絶好のロケーション。それもそのはずで、フカとは原住民マオリ族のことばで、「泡立つ水」という意味。1920年代後半、アイルランド人のアラン・ペイが、自らの釣りのための家として、この地を選んだ。しかしあくまでも家としてのもので、その後釣りの格好のポイントとして、釣り好きが押し寄せるようになると、家の外にテントを張り、皆思い思いにここでの生活を楽しんでいたという。その思いは、今でもしっかりと受け継がれている。

1984年、現在のオーナーであるオランダ人の実業家、アレックス・ヴァン・ヒーレンがこの場所を買い取り、ホテルとしての計画が進められた。翌年、今ある17室のロッジが完成して、正式に営業が開始された。

フカ・ロッジに人が集まる大きな理由のひとつは、その料理にある。それは、一点の曇りなく磨き込まれたグラスたちを見ただけでも、窺い知ることができる。スープに始まり、デザートに至るまでの5つのコースメニューには、毎日それぞれに指向が凝らされており、見るだけでもワクワクしてくる。ニュージーランド一のスポーティング・ロッジというよりは、今や世界に名だたるスモール＆ラグジュアリー・ホテルだけあって、そのゲストは北米、南米、欧州、アジアなど世界各地から集まっている。それらの人々が一堂に会して、テーブルを囲みディナーを楽しむ。正しく、その昔のフィッシュ・ロッジの時のスタイルが、今も生き続けている。勿論その味も秀逸で、フカ・ロッジが世界に知られたフカ・ロッジたる所以である。

ヴァージニア・フィッシャーの手によるインテリアデザインは、シンプルな素材を使いながらも高級感に溢れ、なおかつパブリックとプライベート空間の対比を見事に演出している。ダイニング・ルームなどのあるメインロッジは、グリーン、レッ

ド、紺そしてタータンチェックなど、濃厚な色を基調としたトラディショナルな英国調でカッチリとまとめられている。それとは対照的に各ロッジは、白をベースとした淡い色使いで、カントリー・テイストを強調。リラックスした感覚を充分味わせてくれる。ベッドの上のモスキートネットも効果的で、部屋全体をより一層柔らかく包み込んでいる。特筆すべきはバスルームで、トップライト、というよりは天井全体がガラスで覆われていて、一段と輝きを増した白さが、新鮮な朝の目覚めを約束してくれる。それにしてもここのバスルームは、絶品だ。

　環境を最大限に生かし、ここでしか得ることのできない快適さを提供し、またそれらを適確にサポートするスタッフたち。ここでの滞在は、目の前を流れるワイカト川の水のように、すべてに研ぎ澄まされていて心地良い。

Page 188 <Top left> Various images of the old Huka Lodge, <Top right> Fishing tackle, <Center left> Ashtray, <Bottom left> Mitton, the Lodge cat and mascot, <Bottom right> Entrance of cottage

Page 189 View of main lodge from Huka Falls
Page 191 <Bottom left> Hotel register and picture of Queen Elizabeth II, <Top right> Bright bathroom

P.188　上左　昔のフカ・ロッジを伝える写真の数々、上右　釣り宿としての装備は万全、中左　フィッシュ・ロッジらしい灰皿、下左　ロッジのマスコット、猫の「ミトン」、下右　コテージの玄関

P.189　フカ滝からホテル・メインロッジ棟を望む

P.191　左下　宿泊名簿と傍らのエリザベス女王の写真、右上　明るく清潔なバスルーム

Page 192 Light floods the kitchen through the skylight
Page 193 <Top> Main lodge at night, <Center> A quiet chat on the terrace before dinner, <Bottom> A sumptuous breakfast laid out in the Dining Room
Page 194 Living corner of cottage
Page 195 <Top> Mosquite net draped bed adds to the overall atmosphere of the room, <Center> Waikato River can be seen beyond terrace
Page 196 Bathroom
Page 197 Terrace of main lodge

P. 192　トップライトで明るいキッチン
P. 193　上　夜のメインロッジ、中　テラスでディナーを待つひととき、下　ダイニングルームでの朝食

P. 194　コテージのリビングコーナー
P. 195　上　モスキート・ネットが印象的なベッド、中　テラス越しにワイカト川を見る

P. 196　バスルーム
P. 197　メインロッジのテラス

193

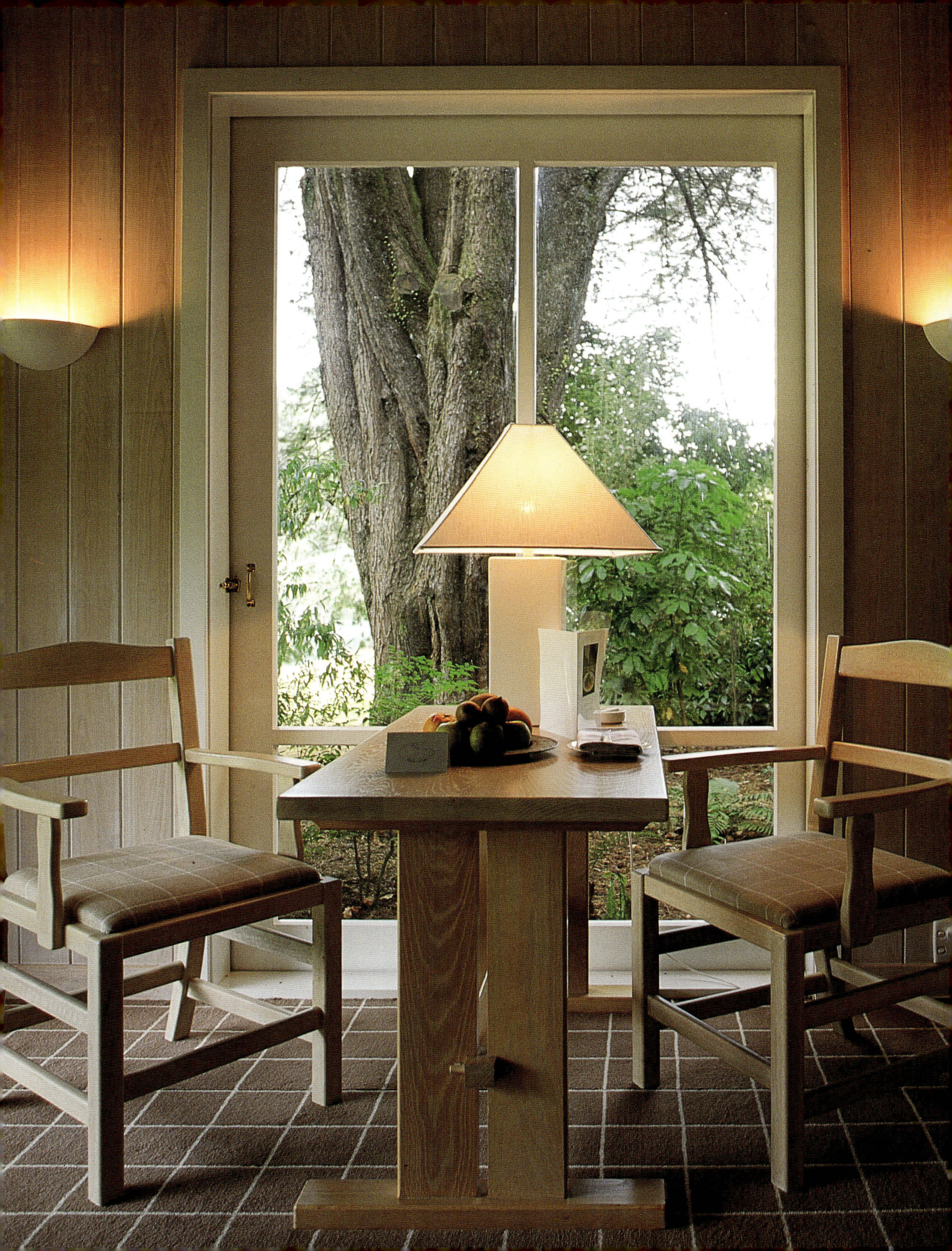

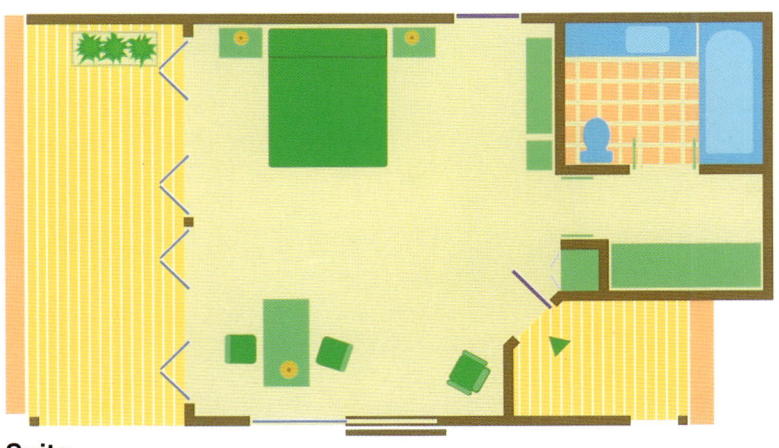

Suite

195

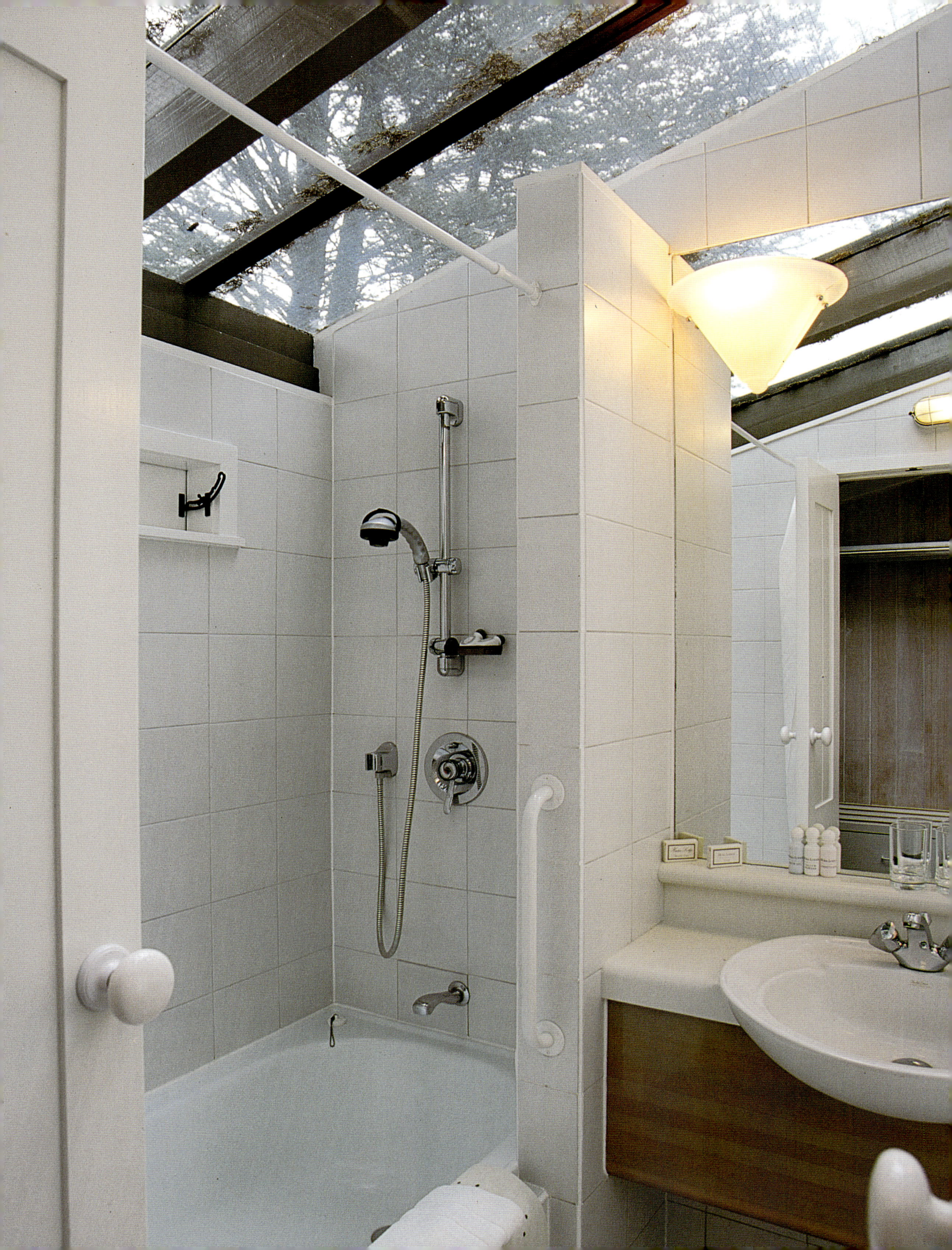

Huka Lodge

Interview

Huka Lodge
Lodge Manager: Mr. Christiaan Palsenberg
フカ・ロッジ
ロッジ支配人　クリスチャン・パルゼンバーグ

What are the special features of the hotel?
I think it is probably the fact that it started as a private fishing lodge in 1920. The present owner maintained the fishing lodge atmosphere, when he built the new hotel from scratch in 1984 and guests still enjoy dinner together in a homely way even though the service is of an international standard. Also, there are so many things to do here. With the river and lake nearby, fishing and rafting are very popular but other sports such as golf and riding can also be enjoyed.

What type of guests come to stay?
About 40% of our guests are from home and 60% from abroad. This is one of the few and may be the only lodge which can be run primarily on New Zealand guests. From the very beginning, we decided to market for New Zealanders and in this way, we are able to operate with comparatively little seasonal or economic climatic change in bed occupancy. A large proportion of the guests from overseas are people over 50 years old with a large expendable income. Their children have grown up so they can afford a two or three week holiday alone. Most of the young people are honeymoon couples. New Zealanders are mainly in their 30s or 40s and come here for a weekend or to celebrate some anniversary or other.

What are the advantages of doing business in Taupo?
First of all, the location is, of course, unique with the river, falls and lake in a very secluded setting. It is a very attractive area with so many things to do. The climate too is wonderful. Finally, being situated as it is in the dead center of the North Island, it is accessible from everywhere and there is an airport too.

What points do you particularly pay attention to usually?
As the location, buildings and decor cannot be faulted, we try to concentrate on details. Staff training is very important here because we don't want to create a typical hotel atmosphere and want to offer a more personal service. However, it is very difficult to teach the staff where to draw the line between becoming too familiar and still being professional.

How can you make a profit from so few rooms?
There are 2 types of lodges in New Zealand. The first type are owner operated with between 4-6 rooms. However, in order to be able to offer a more professional service, it would be very difficult to operate a lodge with less than 15 rooms. Furthermore, it is necessary to be very cost conscious. We are flexible

with our staff, 50-60% working full time and the rest on a casual basis. The general manager must be well versed in everything, I myself can do the cooking or act as a porter besides being the manager.

As I said before, because we cater for the New Zealand market, bed occupancy does not fall dramatically in winter. It is usually necessary to have a 35-40% bed occupancy all the year round in order to break even. That means that you need 60-65% to make it worth while. However, we have an 85% occupancy throughout the year. We do close for between 7 and 10 days in the winter in order to renovate or upgrade the buildings.

What do think is important in order to manage a small and luxury hotel?
You have to be close to your staff so it is a really 'hands on management'. It is very important to work together with the staff and not just sit behind a desk.

We try very hard to adapt our approach to suit our guests so that they can enjoy their stay, And as our guests vary from a local farmer to the Queen of England, it is important to have good social graces.

Do you have any plans for the future?
We do not intend to increase the number of rooms but I hope that Huka Lodge will continue to mature and become more mellow in the future. We also would like to compete on an international level while still maintaining our position as a trendsetter for lodges in New Zealand. We would like to try this concept elsewhere and are considering building a similar lodge in the South Island of New Zealand, Fiji or in Zimbabwe at the moment. However, wherever we decide to build must have a perfectly suitable environment.

Lastly, if you were to open your own hotel?
I would like to build an up-market hotel with between 15-20 rooms based on the same concept as we have here in South Africa where I lived for about two years. I would want to be able to offer a professional service even if I were not there. I don't thing that luxury is important but, of course, relaxed social conditions would be the premise here. I think guests would probably be prepared to pay for that kind of experience. Wherever you go, you can, I think, find a kind of comfort special to that place.

——ここの特徴を教えて下さい。
1920年代にフィッシュ・ロッジとして、個人の家からスタートしたことだと思います。フィッシュ・ロッジのスタイルを守り、皆で食事をする習慣が、1984年に現在のオーナーになりホテルとなってからも、ゲストがインターナショナルにはなったものの、今でも続いています。それと、スポーツ、特に「水」にまつわるアクティビティが豊富なこと。釣り、ラフティング、ゴルフ、乗馬などです。
——ゲストの特徴を教えて下さい。
国内からのお客様が40％、残り60％が外国のお客様。ニュージーランドのこの手のロッジにあって、これだけローカルに支えられているところは少ないと思います。それは初めに、ニュージーランドのマーケティングをしっかり行なったことにあります。季節変動や景気に比較的左右されることなく、ビジネスができます。

ゲストの特徴としては、海外からの場合は50歳以上の高収入で、子供が大きくなって2〜3週間の個人旅行ができる人たち。若い人は新婚旅行が中心です。国内では30〜40代で、週末や何かの記念日に利用される方が多いです。
——タウポでビジネスをすることは、どんなことが恵まれていると思いますか？
まず、ロケーションがユニークなことです。川や湖、滝などがあります。その上プライベートな感じが味わえます。次に、アトラクティブなエリアで楽しみも多く、気候も穏やかで、2〜3日過ごすのに最適なことです。最後に、北島の中心でどこに行くのにも、どこに帰るのにも便利で、その上空港もあります。
——普段から気を付けていることは？
スタッフがフレキシブルに、それでいてTPOを弁えたサービスができるよう、普段から教育しています。同時にゲストとの距離感を縮める努力もしています。
——小さい部屋数を確かなビジネスに結び付けるには、何が必要だと思いますか？
まず、ニュージーランドには2つのタイプのロッジがあります。ひとつは完全な個人（家族）経営で、この場合多くても4〜6室。本当のプロのサービスが可能になるには、最低でも15室以上の部屋がないと経営は難しいでしょう。その上で、コスト意識が必要です。ここでは常時30〜40人の人が働いていますが、正社員は半分です。それに、支配人がすべてのことに精通していないといけません。私は、経理も料理も、そしてポーターもすべてできます。

前にも申した通り、初めにニュージーランドのマーケティングをしっかり行なっていたために、冬場になっても稼動率は落ちません。通常採算分岐点は35〜40％、収益が上がるのは60％以上で、私たちの場合は、年間を通して85％をキープしています。

それから、毎年冬場に7〜10日間クローズして、全館のオーバー・ホールを行ないます。
——スモール＆ラグジュアリー・ホテルでは、何が大切だと思いますか？
スタッフとの密接な関係を、自分自らが動くことによって作っていくこと。つまり一緒に働き、手本を見せることです。

それからお客様のタイプに合わせ、それぞれ楽しんでもらえるように努力もします。ここには、近郊の農家の人からエリザベス女王まで、さまざまな人がお客様としていらっしゃるからです。
——将来計画がありましたら教えて下さい。
これ以上部屋を増やすようなことはしません。成熟してメロウな感じがよりでることを望んでいます。ニュージーランド一のロッジであることを保ち、今後は海外でのポジションを着実に確保したいと思っています。

このコンセプトを他で試したいと思っています。構想では、ニュージーランド南島、フィジー、ジンバブエ（アフリカ）などで考えています。どこでやるとしても、常に環境にジャストフィットした完璧さを持っていたい、と思います。
——もしあなたが新しいホテルを創るとしたら？
昔2年ほど暮したことのある南アフリカで、同じようなコンセプトの、15〜20室のアップ・マーケットをターゲットにしたホテルを創りたい。勿論社会情勢が落ち着いたことが前提ですが。その時は、私がいなくとも、プロのサービスが提供できるようにしたいと思います。お客様はその「経験」に対してお金を払ってくれるでしょうから。

どこに行っても、そこにしかない快適さは、それぞれあると思います。

© Larry Dale Gordon

The Wakaya Club

Wakaya Island, Fiji

ザ・ワカヤ・クラブ／フィジー

A Glimpse

一片の写真

I have seen very little of the world but there are some things which I shall never be able to forget. However small that thing might be, it somehow swallows you up and I can only think that it is because a mysterious charm lies hidden there. It was like that when I caught a glimpse of a small aerial photograph of the Wakaya Club in a foreign magazine. Cottages lay scattered along the coast half hidden by palm trees. Of course, it was impossible to distinguish either the merits or demerits of a place from a photograph but the image of this club will always be indelibly imprinted on my mind.

世の中にはほんの少し見ただけで、忘れられなくなってしまうものがある。例えそれがどんなに小さくとも。何かに吸い込まれていってしまうような、不思議な魔力が、そこに潜んでいるとしか思いようがない。このワカヤ・クラブの時がそれだ。外国の雑誌に載っていた、名刺の半分位の大きさの空から撮った写真には、海岸沿いのコテージが椰子の木に見え隠れしながら点在していた。写真からはその善し悪しは判断できるはずもなかったが、いつまでも頭の片隅に焼きついて離れなかった。

Page 200 Aerial view of the Wakaya Club
Page 201 <Top> People of Wakaya Island <Bottom> Traditional style mbure nestling amongst palms

P. 200　空からのワカヤ・クラブ全景
P. 201　上　ワカヤ島の人々、下　コテージ「ブレ」と周辺環境

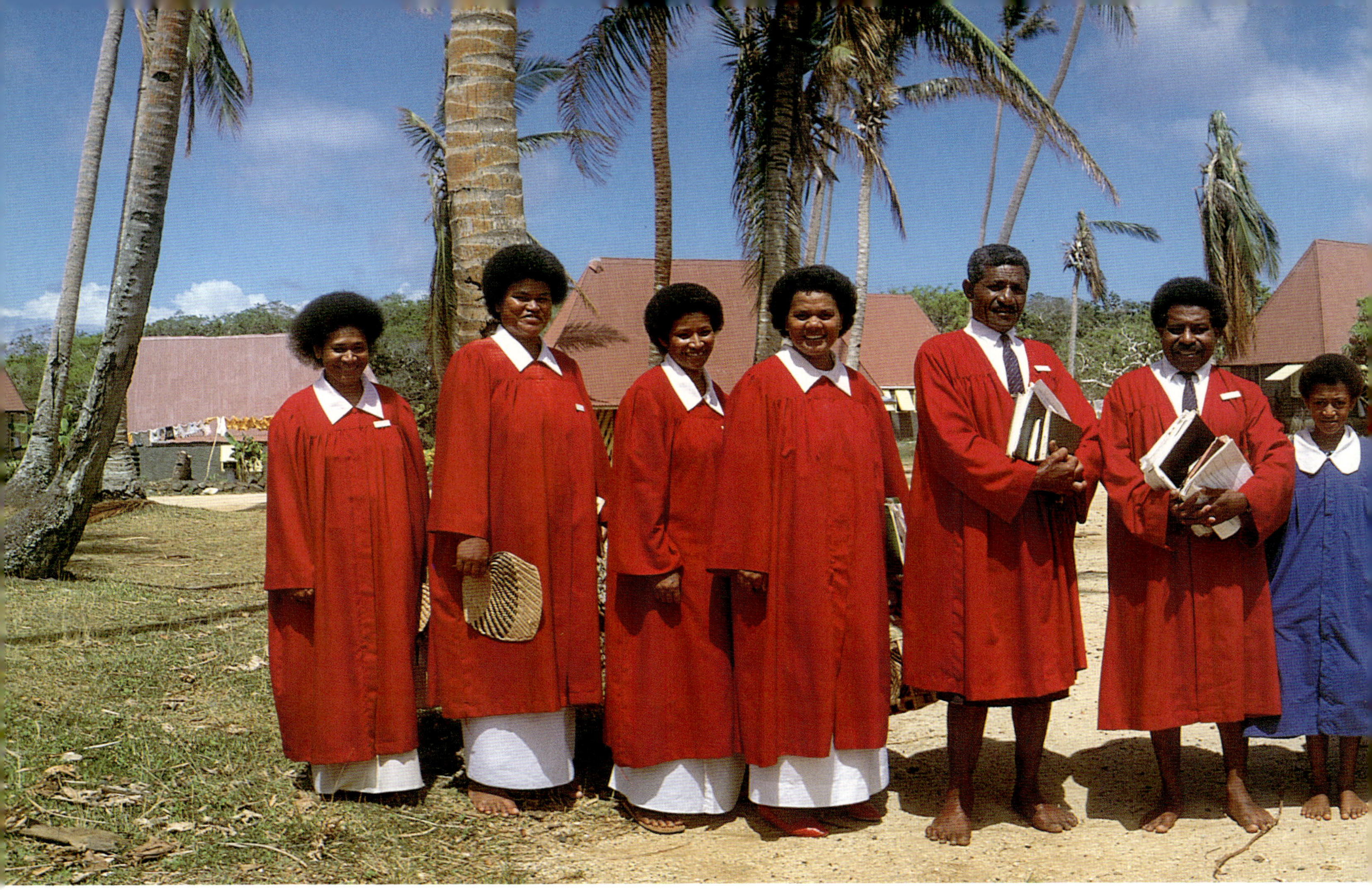

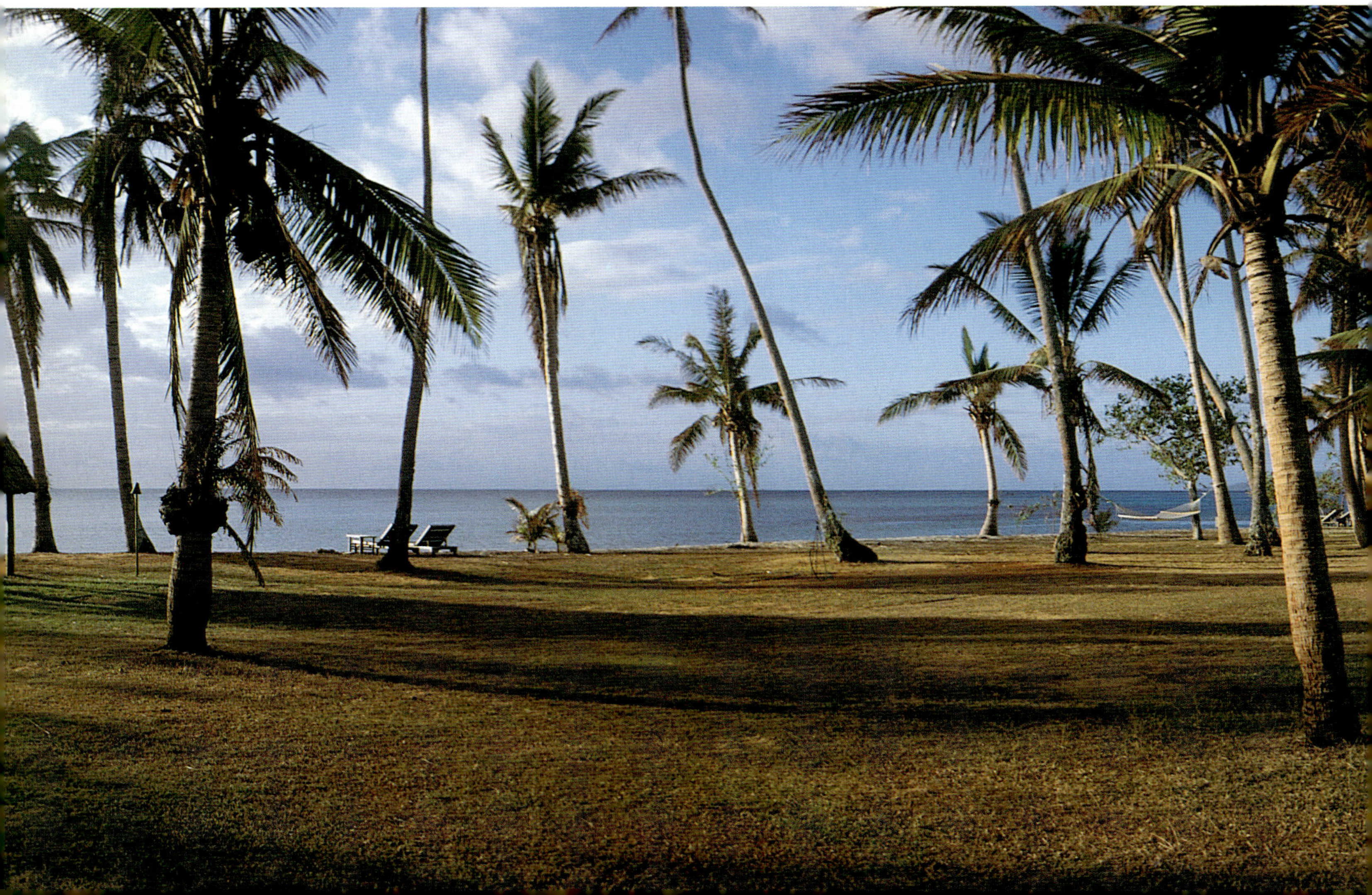

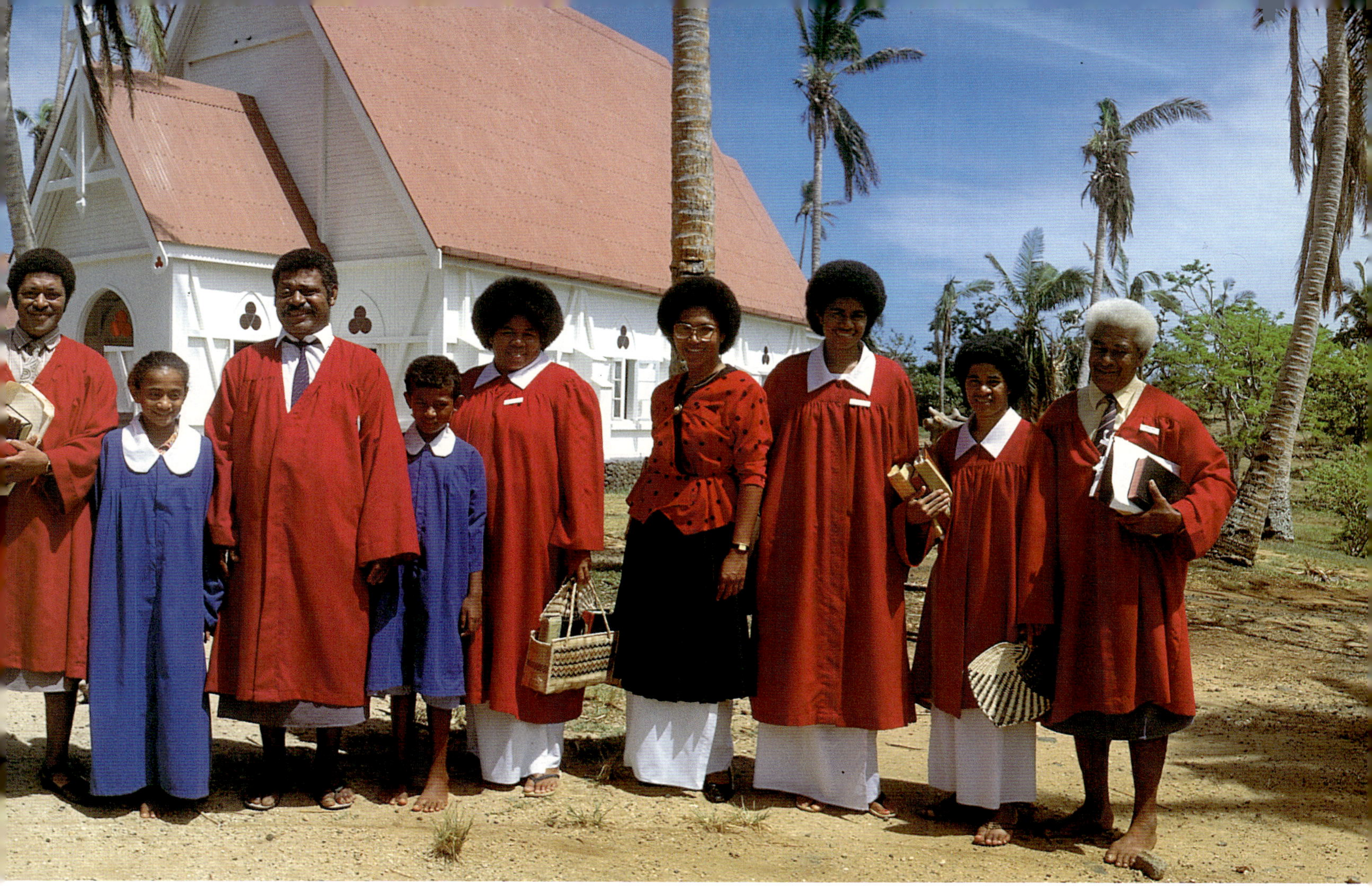

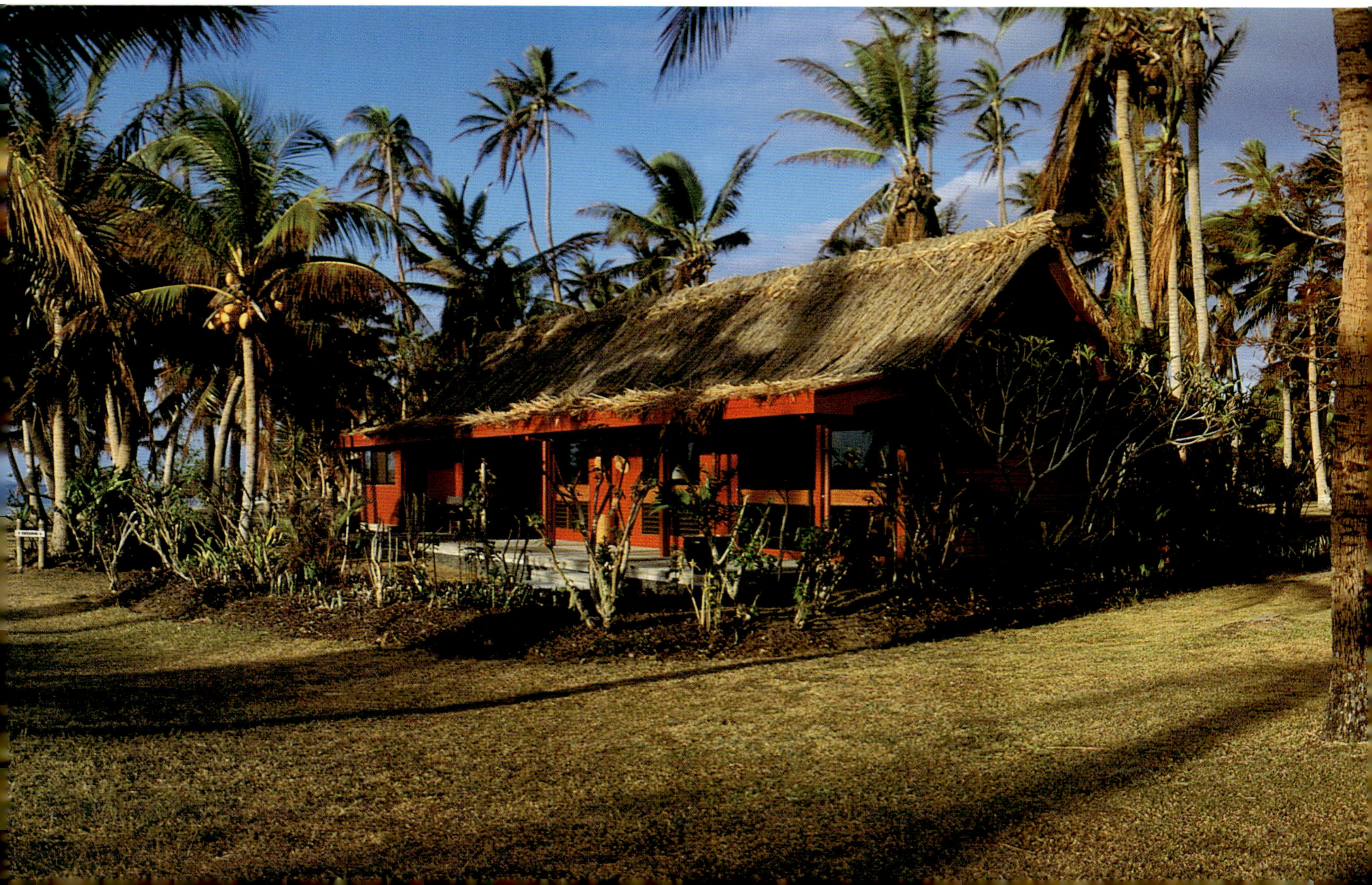

Wakaya Island is a small 81 ha (200 acres) island lying in the South Pacific some 45 minutes by light aircraft of Air Wakaya, an exclusive airline for the club, from Nadi, the gateway to the Fiji group of islands. It is a completely private island owned by David Gilmour, who says that when he first saw the island in 1971, his life completely changed. Together with his partners, he managed to buy the island and started to slowly create his own world by building roads, boring wells, creating electricity and building an airport. He bought his partners out in 1987 and is now the sole owner of the island. In the course of development, he was careful to consider the indigenous plants and animals such as the wild boar that had existed there before his arrival. At the same time, he built houses for the 200 inhabitants, together with a church and primary school and also a hotel with a view to providing employment.

The Wakaya Club consists of just eight traditional Fuji cottages called *mbure*, which can accommodate a maximum of 16 guests, all of whom must be over 16 years of age. These typical buildings, which consist of a living room and bedroom connected by a terrace, have all been created by the local people as have the interiors. There is nothing flashy but a truly wonderful and relaxing space has been created with the woven bamboo walls and wisteria sofas. As might be expected, each building is a perfect size with an area of 135 sqm (1,500 sqft).

Below the windows of the *mbure* are slits, which can be opened or closed to allow the cool breeze to blow through at night. These together with the fan on the ceiling help to create comfort in an island where there is only a 3° centigrade difference in temperature throughout the year.

None of the mbure has a key and it is only the bathroom which can be locked from the inside. Important things can be deposited in the special safety deposit box set aside for each cottage and it follows then that it is only these boxes that have keys. These sole keys are labelled with a letter between A-H to coincide with the initial of the eight *mbure*. Each cottage is named after a flower.

There is a very simple system at the Wakaya Club. Before setting out for the island, guests pay the return fare of US$780 for two and hotel expenses of US$875 per night for two so that they do not need any cash while they are in the hotel. Everything from meals, drinks and sporting activities down to launry is included in this price. If guests want to have a picnic lunch, the staff will prepare a perfect meal, barbecuing and serving fish caught on the spot at one of the 32 beaches on the island. There is no extra charge even if the picnics become a daily occurrence. Everything is done here. As the majority of things necessary while staying at the club are provided, all that is needed is a swimming costume, a few clothes, some favorite CDs to play on the player provided, and a book or two, to relax and do nothing. After all, there are 32 private beaches alone.

The person who took that original photo which caught my fancy, was a Californian called Larry Dale Gordon. He too was enchanted by this place and built a house on the island, where he spends the greater part of the year.

フィジー諸島のゲートウェイ、ナンディからクラブ専用の航空会社エア・ワカヤの小型飛行機にて45分、南太平洋に浮かぶ80ha（24万坪）の小島、ワカヤ島。この島は完全なるプライベート・アイランドである。所有者である、カナダ人の実業家デイヴィット・ギルモーは、「1971年に初めてこの島を見た時に、私の人生が変わった」といっている。早速パートナーたちと共にこの島を手にいれ、道を切り拓き、井戸を掘り電気をおこし、飛行場をつくり、少しずつ自分の世界を実現させていった。1987年にはパートナーたちの分も引き受け、完全な個人所有となった。勿論開発に当たっては、以前からこの地に生息する野生の鹿やイノシシなど動物、植物の生態に細心の注意が払われた。同時に200人の住民に対しては、家を建て、教会、小学校をつくり、そしてホテルなどでの雇用を図るなど、切っても切れない関係ができあがっている。

ワカヤ・クラブには、「ブレ」と呼ばれるコテージタイプの部屋が、僅かに8棟。そして定員は16人（16歳以上の大人のみ）、それですべてだ。リビング・ルームとベッド・ルームが外のテラスによってのみ繋がるという、フィジー・スタイルに則った建物は、インテリアも含めすべてローカルの人々の手による。派手さこそないが、竹で編んだ壁、籐製のソファなどがしっくりとした居心地の良い空間をつくり出している。それもそのはずで、一棟当り約42坪という申し分のない広さだ。ブレの窓の下は、開閉可能なスリットになっていて、夜になると気持の良い風が通り抜ける。天井に設けられたファンと共に、年間の温度差が

3度しかないこの島ならではの、快適な設備だ。

　もうひとつ、各ブレには鍵がない。(バスルームだけは内側から鍵ができる)大切なものは、各自のセイフティ・デポジットにしまうことができるが、鍵があるとすればこれだけ。またすべてのブレには、それぞれ花の名前が付けられていて、唯一のこの鍵には、そのA～Hまで8つのブレの頭文字が付いている。

　ワカヤ・クラブのシステムは、至って簡単。出掛ける前に、エア・ワカヤの往復の航空運賃(2人分780米ドル)と1日当たり875米ドル(2人分)の滞在費を払い込んでおけば、滞在中に現金やサインが一々必要ないことだ。食事、飲み物、スポーツ・アクティビティ、そしてクリーニング(ドライはない)まですべてが料金の中に含まれている。例えば、ピクニック・ランチに行きたければ、スタッフが完璧にお膳立をしてくれて、島内に32あるビーチのどこかで、獲れたての魚をその場で焼いてサービスしてくれる。これを毎日続けようも、一切チャージされることはない。ここではすべてが万事この調子。滞在に必要なものはほとんど用意されているので、小さなバッグに、水着とほんの少しの着替え、それに好きなCD(デッキは用意されている)と本を詰め込んで、1週間ボーッとするのが、ここでのお薦めの過ごし方だ。なにしろ、プライベート・ビーチだけでも32もあるのだから。

　さて、あの空からの写真を撮った張本人、カリフォルニアの写真家ラリー・ゴードンもこの地に魅せられ、今この島に家を建て1年の大半をここで暮らしている。

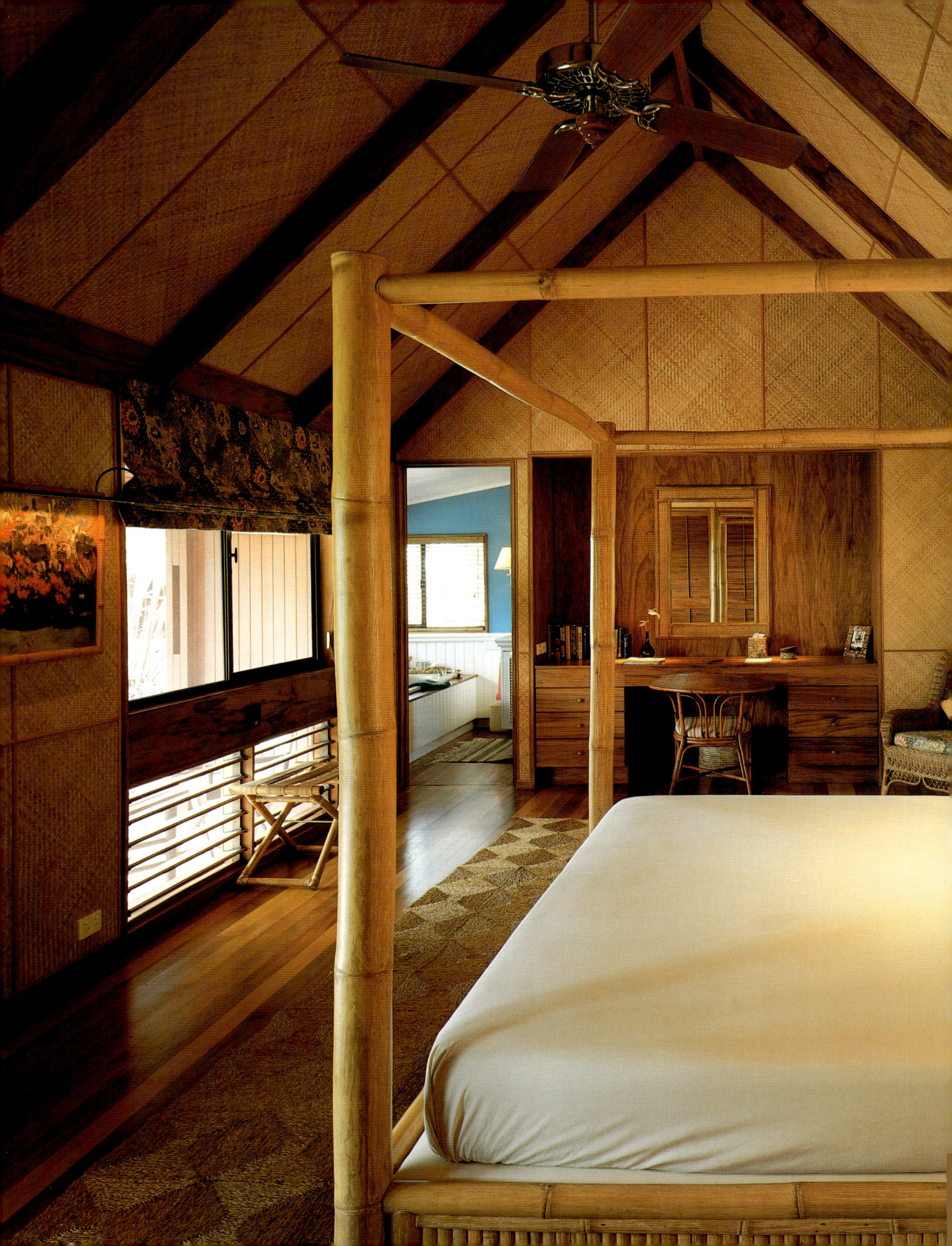

Bure

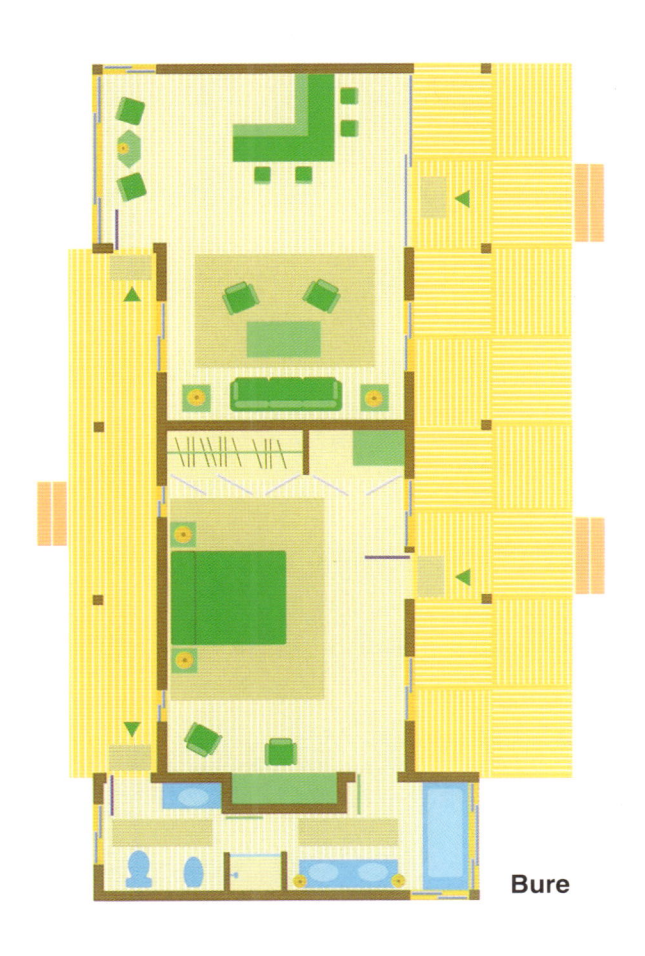

207

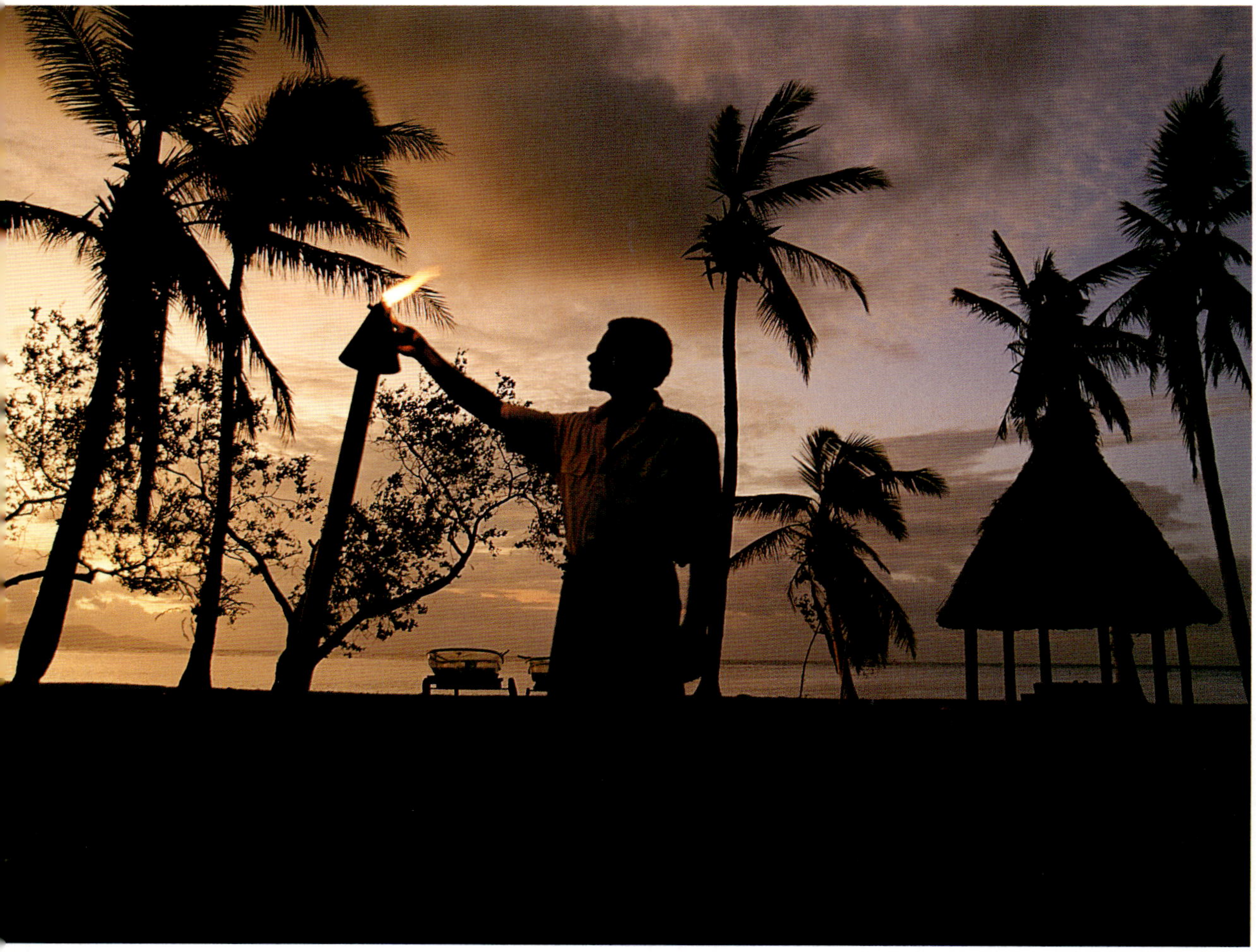
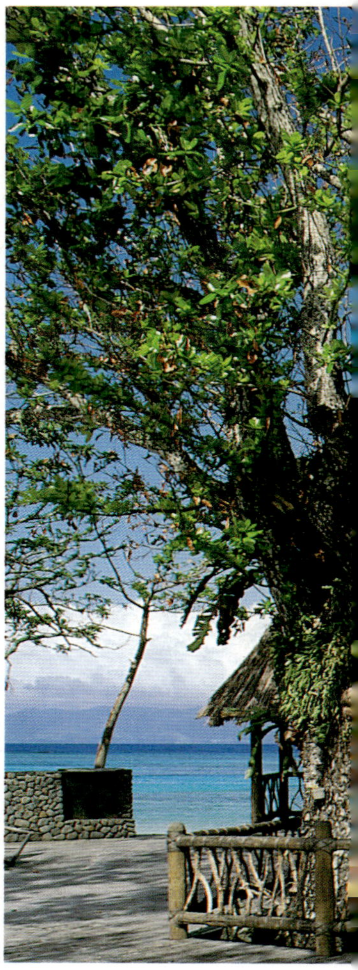
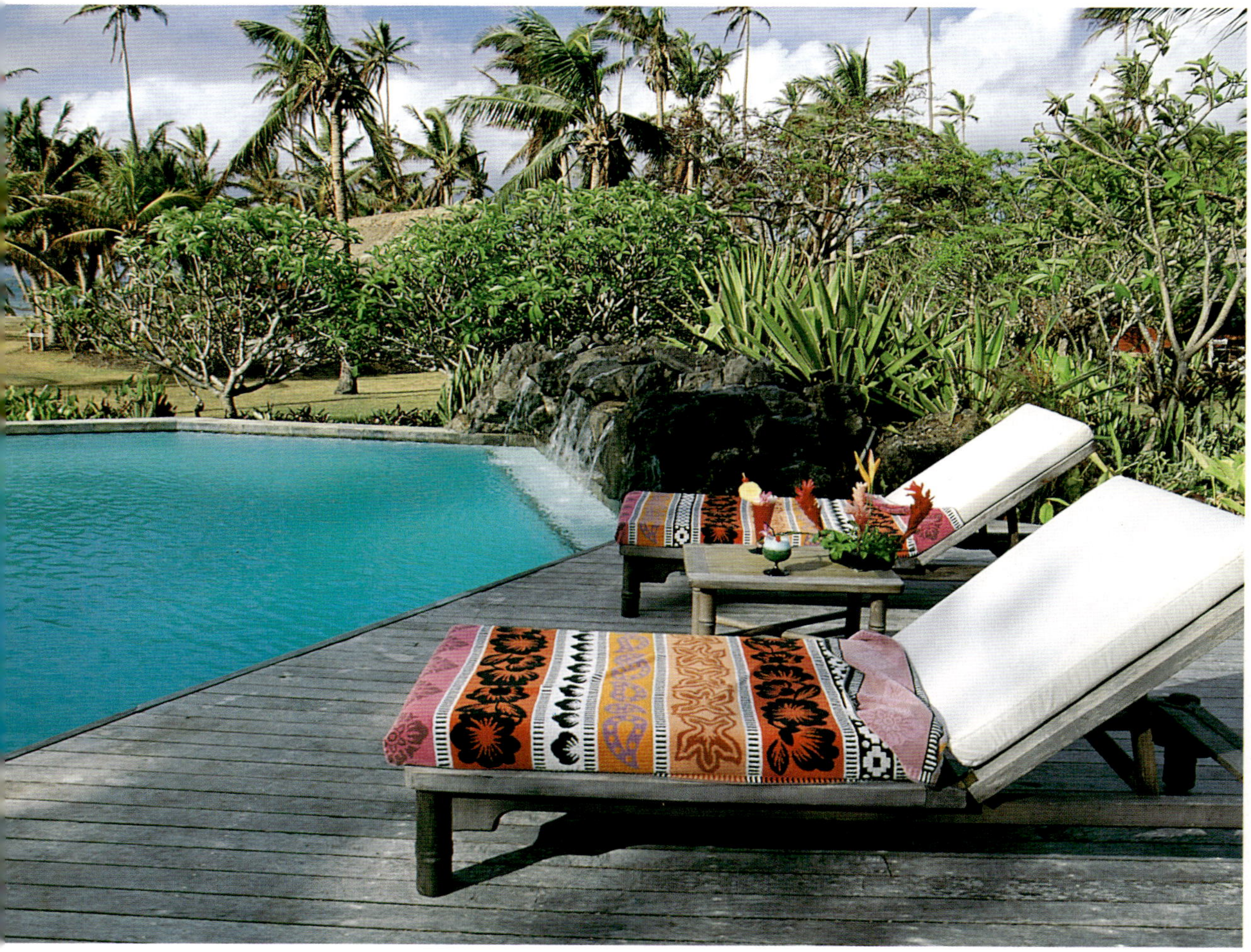
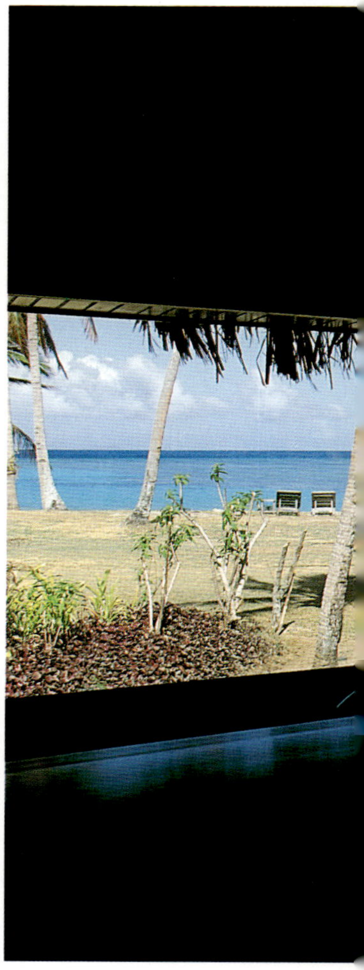

Page 204 Entrance of mbure
Page 205 <Top> Lunch on the terrace, <Center> The Palm Grove restaurant
Page 206 Bedroom with a glimpse of the bathroom in the upper left
Page 207 <Top> Separate living room, <Center> Bathroom
Page 208 <Top> Torches are lit at dusk at Wakaya, <Bottom> Poolside deckchairs, Page 209 <Top> View of the South Pacific from terrace, <Bottom> A glimpse of the sea from inside a mbure

P. 204　「ブレ」の入口
P. 205　上　テラスでのランチ、中　レストラン「ザ・パーム・グローブ」
P. 206　ベッドルーム、左奥にバスルームが見える
P. 207　上　独立したリビングルーム、中　バスルーム
P. 208　上　トーチに火が灯され、ワカヤの夜が始まる、下　プールサイドのデッキチェア
P. 209　上　テラスから南太平洋を見る、下　「ブレ」の中から海を見る

210

Managing Director Mr. Robert Miller

取締役社長　ロバート・ミラー

Page 210 <Top six pictures> Happy smiles from the staff of the Wakaya Club, <Bottom left> Entrance of mbure <Bottom center> Added local color even on the roof supports, <Bottom right> Robo, traditional island fare
Page 211 <Center> Air Wakaya connects Nadi to the Wakaya Club

P.210　上、中段　ワカヤ・クラブのスタッフたち、下左　「ブレ」の入口、下中　レストランの吹き抜け、下右　地元料理「ロボ」
P.211　中　ナンディとクラブを結ぶ自家用機

The Wakaya Club

Information

N. B. The data here was correct at the time of writing on March 1st 1993 but there may be changes in prices and other things in the future.

注：ここで使われているデータは、1993年 3 月 1 日現在のものです。料金その他につきましては変更されている場合があります。

Hote Hana Maui

General Manager
Mr. Frederick J. Orr

*Address
Hana, Maui, Hawaii 96713-0008

*Phone
808-248-8211

*Toll Free
800-334-8484

*Fax
808-248-7202

*Chain Affiliation
ITT Sheraton Hotels & Resorts

*Total Number of Rooms and Suites
96

*Rate
Standard Double from $305   Suite from $525

*Distance from
Hana Airport from 5km (3.1 miles)

*Credit Cards
All Major

*Main Restaurant Name
The Dining Room

type cuisine
Hawaiian/Continental

*Other Restaurants & Bar Name
Paniolo Bar
Hamoa Beach Restaurant

*Other Faciliteis and Services
Private Beaches and Pools
2 Tennis Courts
3 Holes Golf Course
Wellness Center
Horseback Riding
Boutique
Library

HOTEL
Hana-Maui
AT HANA RANCH

Maui
Kahului A/P
Hana A/P
Hotel Hana Maui

[Reservation]
ITT Sheraton USA (toll free)   1-800-325-3535
シェラトン・ホテルズ日本支社 (フリーダイヤル)   0120-00-3535

Checkers Hotel Kempinski

General Manager
Mr. Volker Ulrich

*Address
535 South Grand Avenue, Los Angeles, California 90071

*Phone
213-624-0000

*Toll Free
800-426-3135

*Fax
213-629-9906

*Chain Affiliation
Kempinski Hotels International

*Total Number of Rooms and Suites
188

*Rate
Standard Double from $180 to $190   Suite from $350 to $1,000

*Distance from
LA International Airport from 32km (20 miles)

*Credit Cards
All Major

*Main Restaurant Name
Checkers Restaurant

type cuisine
American

*Other Restaurants & Bar Name
Checkers Lounge

*Other Facilities and Services
Satellite Cable Television
Health Club
Sauna and Jacuzzi
Outdoor Pool

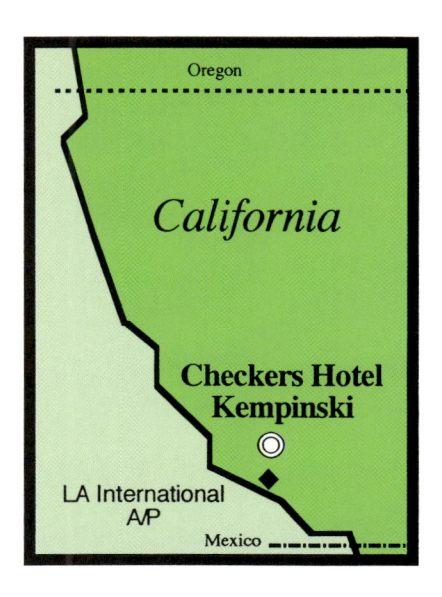

CHECKERS HOTEL
Kempinski Los Angeles

[Reservation]
Kempinski Hotels USA (toll free)   1-800-426-3135
ケンピンスキー・ホテルズ東京事務所   03-3437-0781

San Ysidro Ranch

General Manager
Ms. Janis Clapoff

*Address
900 San Ysidro Lane, Montecito, California 93108

*Phone
805-969-5046

*Toll Free
800-368-6788

*Fax
805-565-1995

*Chain Affiliation
Relais & Chateaux

*Total Number of Rooms and Suites
44

*Rate
Standard Double from $195 to $375   Suite from $425 to $695

*Distance from
Santa Barbara Airport from 22.4km (14 miles)

*Credit Cards
American Express, Visa, Master Card

*Main Restaurant Name
The Stonehouse

type cuisine
American

*Other Restaurants & Bar Name
Plow & Angel Bar

*Other Facilities and Services
Pool
Two Tennis Courts
Hiking Trails
Horseback Riding

All cottages have a fire place and private patio or terrace.

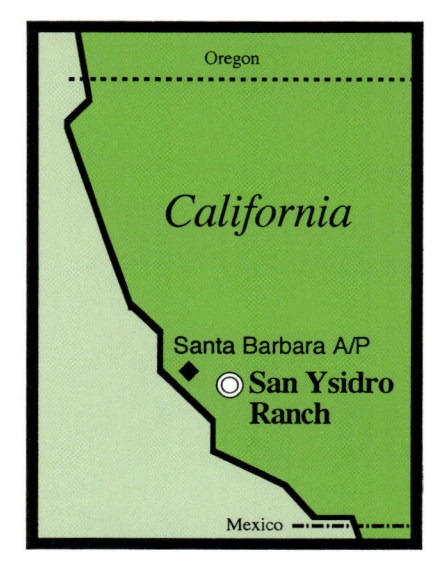

[Reservation]
Relais & Chateaux USA (toll free)   1-800-677-3524
ルレ・エ・シャトー東京事務所   03-3407-8858

Campton Place Hotel

General Manager
Mr. Peter Koehler

*Address
340 Stockton Street, San Francisco, California 94108

*Phone
415-781-5555

*Toll Free
800-647-4007

*Fax
415-955-8536

*Chain Affiliation
Kempinski Hotels International

*Total Number of Rooms and Suites
126

*Rate
Standard Double from $185 to $320   Suite from $395 to $800

*Distance from
San Francisco International Airport from 24km (15 miles)

*Credit Cards
All Major

*Main Restaurant Name
Campton Place Restaurant

type cuisine
American

*Other Restaurants & Bar Name
Campton Place Bar

*Other Facilities and Services
Complimentary limousine service Monday through Friday to the Financial District

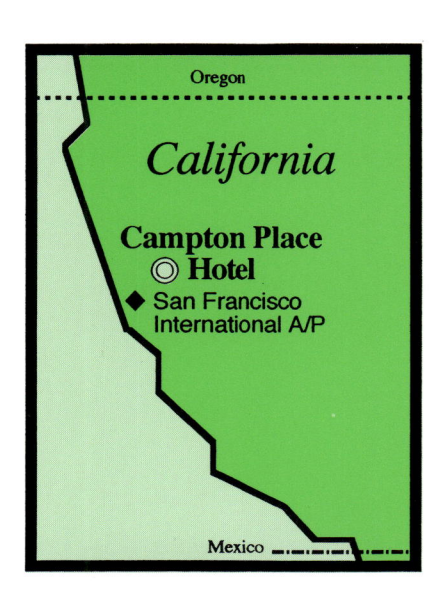

CAMPTON PLACE
HOTEL

[Reservation]
Kempinski Hotels USA (toll free)   1-800-426-3135
ケンピンスキー・ホテルズ東京事務所   03-3437-0781

Post Ranch Inn

General Manager
Ms. Janis Donald

*Address
P.O.Box 219 Highway 1, Big Sur, California 93940

*Phone
408-667-2200

*Toll Free
800-527-2200

*Fax
408-667-2824

*Chain Affiliation
Small Luxury Hotels

*Total Number of Rooms and Suites
30

*Rate
Standard Double from $245 to $ 450   Suite from $385

*Distance from
Monterey Airport from 56km (35 miles)

*Credit Cards
American Express, Visa, Master Card

*Main Restaurant Name
Sierra Mar

type cuisine
California Regional

*Other Facilities and Services
In Room Massage
Pools

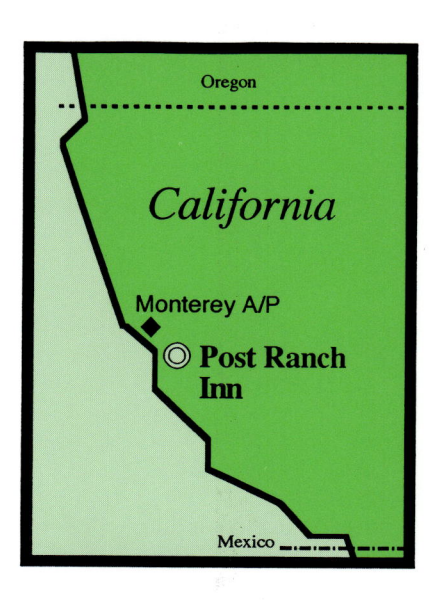

Post Ranch Inn

[Reservation]
Small Luxury Hotels USA (toll free)   1-800-525-4800
スモール・ラクシャリー・ホテルズ東京事務所   03-3431-6524

The Alexis

General Manager
Mr. David Morgan

*Address
1007 First Avenue at Madison, Seattle, Washington 98104

*Phone
206-624-4844

*Toll Free
800-426-7033

*Fax
206-621-9009

*Chain Affiliation
none

*Total Number of Rooms and Suites
54

*Rate
Standard Double from $165   Suite from $205

*Distance from
Seattle/Tacoma International Airport from 24km (15 miles)

*Credit Cards
All Major

*Main Restaurant Name
The Painted Table

type cuisine
Pacific Northwest

*Other Restaurants & Bar Name
The Bookstore
The Volcano Cafe

*Other Facilities and Services
Meeting Rooms
Private Steamroom
Shops

Complimentary Guest Services
-Continental Breakfast
-Choice of Morning Newspaper
-Evening Shoe Shine

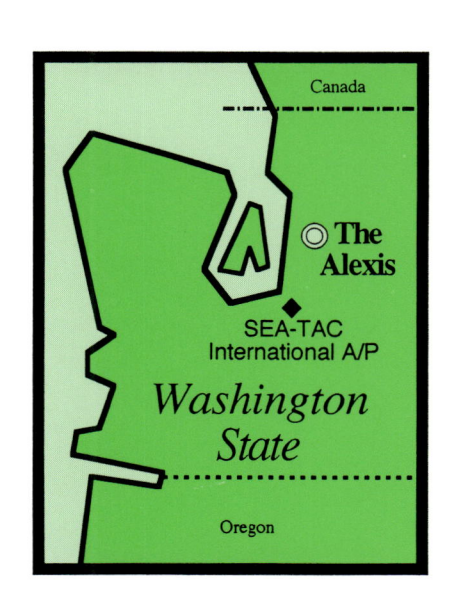

Tawaraya Inn

Proprietress
Ms. Toshi Okazaki Sato

*Address
Fuyacho, Anekoji, Nakagyo-ku, Kyoto 604 Japan

*Phone
81-75-211-5566

*Toll Free

*Fax
81-75-211-2204

*Chain Affiliation
none

*Total Number of Rooms and Suites
18

*Rate
Standard Double from ¥43,000 to ¥90,000 (RC)

*Distance from
Osaka International Airport from 50km (32 miles)
Shinkansen Kyoto Station 5km (3 miles)

*Credit Cards
American Express, Diners, Visa, JCB

*Main Restaurant Name
(each room)

type cuisine
Japanese

俵屋旅館

京都市中京区麩屋町姉小路上ル　〒604
JR京都駅より車にて10分

電話 075-211-5566　　Fax 075-211-2204

部屋数　18室

宿泊料金（一人当たり）　35,000～60,000円（1泊2食、1室2名）

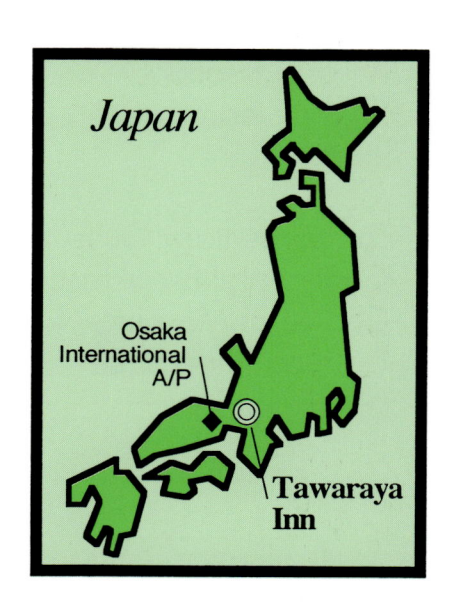

Hotel Bela Vista

General Manager
Mr. Brian E. Williams

*Address
8 Rua do Comendador Kou Ho Neug, Macau

*Phone
853-965333

*Toll Free

*Fax
853-965588

*Chain Affiliation
Mandarin Oriental Hotel Group

*Total Number of Suites
8

*Rate
Suite from PTC/HK$1,700 to $4,000

*Distance from
Macau Ferry Terminal from 8km (5 miles)

*Credit Cards
All Major

*Main Restaurant Name
The Dining Room

type cuisine
Continental

*Other Restaurants & Bar Name
The Verandah Restaurant
The Bar

*Other Facilities and Services
Guests can use facilities of the Mandarin Oriental Hotel Macau

HOTEL BELA VISTA
MACAU

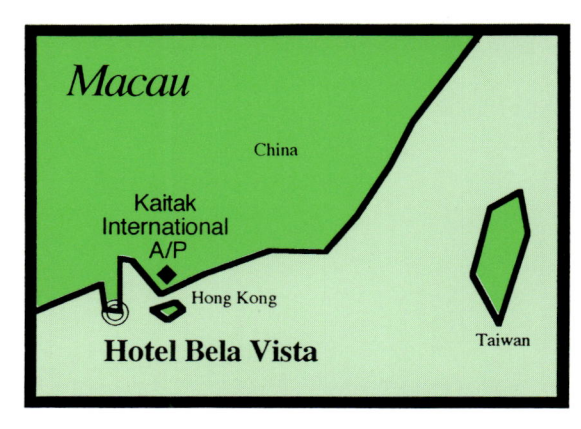

[Reservation]
Mandarin Oriental Hotel Group USA (toll free)   1-800-526-6566
マンダリン・オリエンタル・ホテル東京事務所   03-3433-3388

The Duxton

Director
Mrs. Margaret Wong

*Address
83 Duxton Road, Singapore 0208

*Phone
65-227-7678

*Toll Free

*Fax
65-227-1232

*Chain Affiliation
none

*Total Number of Rooms and Suites
49

*Rate
Standard Double from S$260 to $305   Suite from S$350 to $400

*Distance from
Changi International Airport from 10km (6 miles)

*Credit Cards
All Major

*Main Restaurant Name
L'aigle D'or Restaurant

type cuisine
French

*Other Restaurants & Bar Name
Duxton Bar Lounge

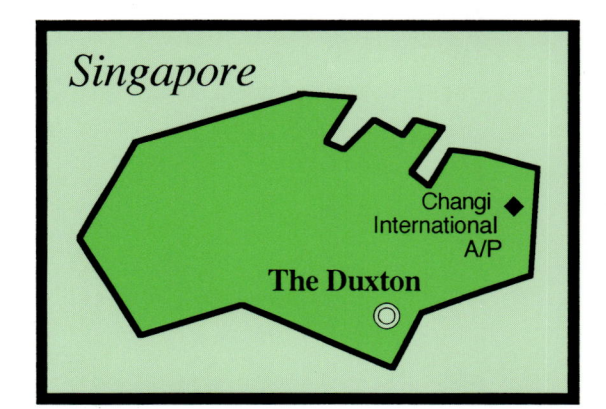

THE DUXTON

[Reservation]
The Duxton USA (toll free)   1-800-272-2480

Carcosa Seri Negara

General Managers
Mr. & Mrs. Shaun & Beverly Matthews

*Address
Taman Tasik Perdana 50480 Kuala Lumpur, Malaysia

*Phone
60-3-282-1888

*Toll Free

*Fax
60-3-282-7888

*Chain Affiliation
Amanresorts

*Total Number of Suites
13

*Rate
Suite from US$317 to $933

*Distance from
Suban International Airport from 18km (11 miles)

*Credit Cards
All Major

*Main Restaurant Name
Mahsuri

type cuisine
Continental

*Other Restaurants & Bar Name
Veranday Tea Lounge
Titiwansa Bar Lounge

*Other Facilities and Services
2 Tennis Courts
Health Club
Swimming Pool
Meeting Rooms

CARCOSA SERI NEGARA

[Reservation]
Amanresorts USA (toll free)   1-800-223-1588
プリマ・ホテルズ東京事務所   03-5210-2050

Amandari

General Managers
Mr. & Mrs. Henry & Char Gray

*Address
Kedawatan, Ubud, Bali, Indonesia

*Phone
62-361-95333

*Toll Free

*Fax
62-361-95335

*Chain Affiliation
Amanresorts

*Total Number of Suites
29

*Rate
Suite from US$300 to $700

*Distance from
Ngurah Rai International Airport from 55km (35 miles)

*Credit Cards
All Major

*Main Restaurant Name
The Restaurant

type cuisine
Indonesian/European

*Other Restaurants & Bar Name
The Bar

*Other Facilities and Services
Tennis Courts
Swimming Pool
Library

Complimentary round trip airport transfers

amandari

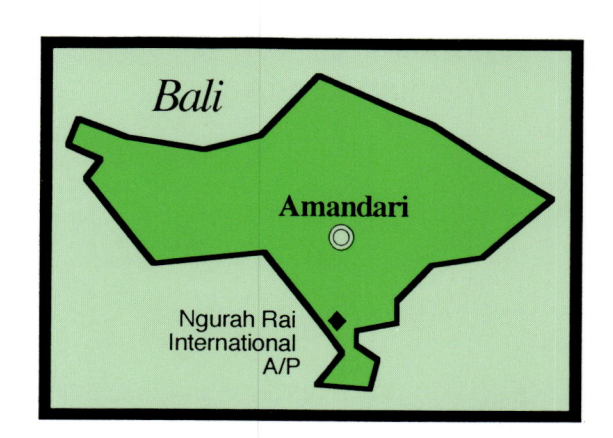

[Reservation]
Amanresorts USA (toll free) 1-800-223-1588
プリマ・ホテルズ東京事務所 03-5210-2050

Tandjungn Sari

Managing Director
Mr. Agustiwan Wawo-runtu

*Address
P.O.Box 25 Denpasar Sanur, Bali, Indonesia

*Phone
62-361-88441

*Toll Free

*Fax
62-361-87930

*Chain Affiliation
none

*Total Number of Rooms and Suites
28

*Rate
Standard Double from US$195 to $210   Suite from US$250 to $380

*Distance from
Ngurah Rai International Airport from 10km (6 miles)

*Credit Cards
All Major

*Main Restaurant Name
The Restaurant

type cuisine
International

*Other Restaurants & Bar Name
The Beach Bar

*Other Facilities and Services
Beach
Swimming Pool
Library

Balinese dances is performed in the courtyard every Saturday at 8:00 pm.

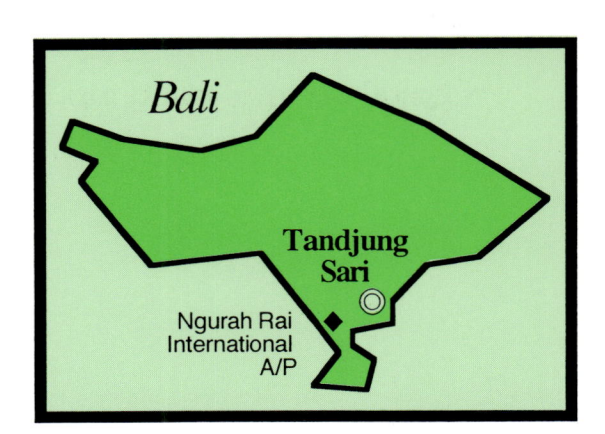

tandjung sari
cape of flowers

Amankila

General Manager
Mr. Alistair Anderson

*Address
P.O.Box 133 Klungkung 80701 Bali, Indonesia

*Phone
62-366-21993

*Toll Free

*Fax
62-366-21995

*Chain Affiliation
Amanresorts

*Total Number of Suites
35

*Rate
Suite from US$300 to $1,100

*Distance from
Ngurah Rai International Airport from 80km (50 miles)

*Credit Cards
All Major

*Main Restaurant Name
The Terrace & The Restaurant

type cuisine
Indonesian/European

*Other Restaurants & Bar Name
The Bar
Beach Club

*Other Facilities and Services
Swimming Pool
Library

Complimentary round trip airport transfers

amankila

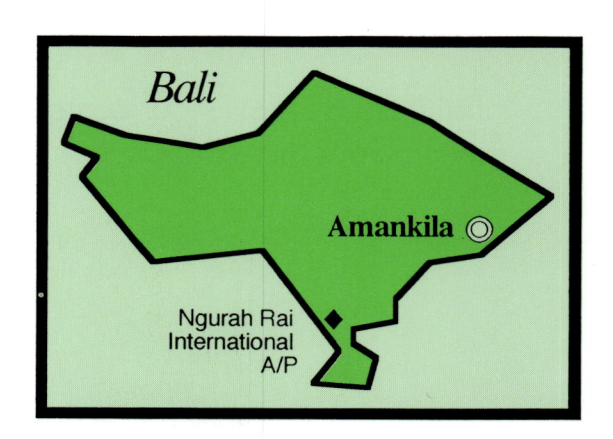

[Reservation]
Amanresorts USA (toll free)   1-800-223-1588
プリマ・ホテルズ東京事務所   03-5210-2050

The Oberoi Bali

General Manager
Mr. Kamal K. Kaul

*Address
Legian Beach, P.O.Box 351, Denpasar 80001 Bali, Indonesia

*Phone
62-361-51061

*Toll Free

*Fax
62-361-52791

*Chain Affiliation
Oberoi Hotels
The Leading Hotels of the World

*Total Number of Rooms and Suites
75

*Rate
Standard Double from US$160 to $265   Suite from US$295 to $800

*Distance from
Ngurah Rai International Airport from 10km (6 miles)

*Credit Cards
All Major

*Main Restaurant Name
The Kura Kura

type cuisine
Indonesian/Continental

*Other Restaurants & Bar Name
Frangipani Cafe
Kayu Bar
Kul Kul Pool Deck

*Other Facilities and Services
Beach
Tennis Court
Swimming Pool
Health Club
Shopping Arcade
Travel Agency

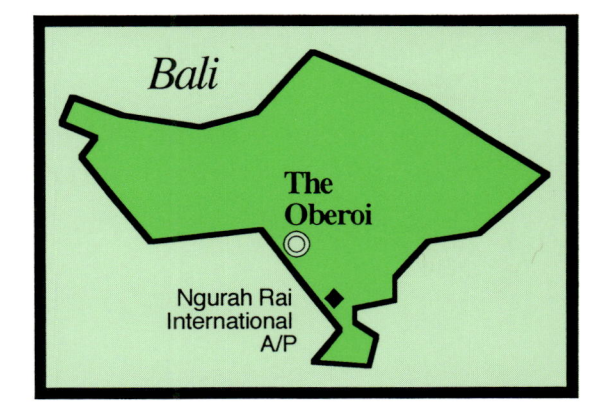

[Reservation]
Oberoi Hotels USA (toll free)   1-800-223-6800
オベロイ・ホテルズ東京事務所 03-5210-5135

Mount Lofty House

General Manager
Mr. Kerry Bielik

*Address
74 Summit Road, Crafers, S.A. 5152 Australia

*Phone
61-8-339-6777

*Toll Free

*Fax
61-8-339-5656

*Chain Affiliation
Relais & Chateaux

*Total Number of Rooms and Suites
29

*Rate
Standard Double from A$245 to $280   Suite from A$360 to $495

*Distance from
Adelaide Airport from 28km (18 miles)

*Credit Cards
All Major

*Main Restaurant Name
Hardys Dining Room

type cuisine
Austraian Regional

*Other Restaurants & Bar Name
Piccadilly Dining Room
Tiers Cocktail Bar

*Other Faciliteis and Services
Outdoor Heated Pools
Extensive Gardens
Conference Facilities

Spring water through all water outlets
Guest lounge with tea and coffee

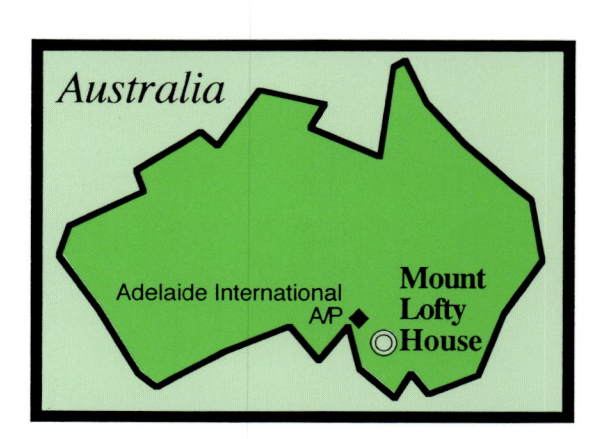

[Reservation]
Relais & Chateaux USA (toll free)   1-800-677-3524
ルレ・エ・シャトー東京事務所   03-3407-8858

Sebel Town House

General Manager
Mr. Nicholas Truswell

*Address
23 Elizabeth Bay Road, Sydney, N.S.W. 2011   Australia

*Phone
61-2-358-3244

*Toll Free

*Fax
61-2-357-1926

*Chain Affiliation
Mirvac Hotels
The Leading Hotels of the World

*Total Number of Rooms and Suites
167

*Rate
Standard Double from A$265 to $280   Suite from A$450 to $1,200

*Distance from
Mascot International Airport from 10km (6 miles)

*Credit Cards
All Major

*Main Restaurant Name
Encore

type cuisine
International

*Other Restaurants & Bar Name
Celebrities Bar

*Other Facilities and Services
Health Club
Outdoor Pool
Complimentary Parking

[Reservation]
The Leading Hotels of the World USA (toll free)   1-800-223-6800
ザ・リーディング・ホテルズ東京事務所   03-5210-5131

Huka Lodge

Lodge Manager
Mr. Christiaan Palsenberg

*Address
Huka Falls Road, P.O.Box 95 Taupo, New Zealand

*Phone   *Toll Free   *Fax
64-7-378-5791   64-7-378-0427

*Chain Affiliation
Relais & Chateaux
Select Hotels & Resorts International

*Total Number of Rooms and Suites
17

*Rate
Standard Double from NZ$850 to $1,000   Suite from NZ$1,360 to $1,575
(includes full breakfast & dinner)

*Distance from
Taupo Airport from 8km (5 miles)

*Credit Cards
All Major

*Main Restaurant Name   type cuisine
The Dining Room   French

*Other Restaurants & Bar Name
The Breakfast Bar

*Other Faciliteis and Services
Helipad
All Weather Tennis Court
Outdoor Hot Pools
Conference Facilities
Complimentary Taupo A/P transfers

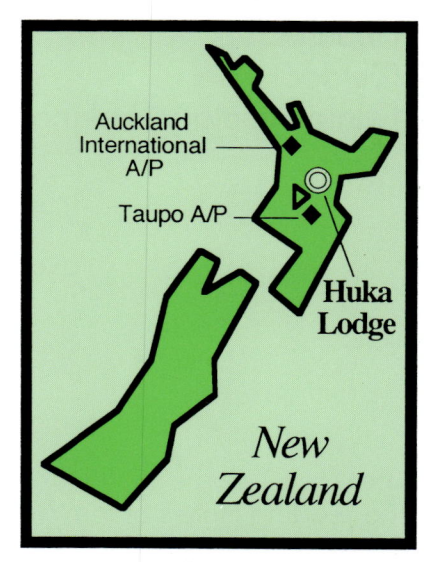

[Reservation]
Relais & Chateaux USA (toll free)   1-800-677-3524
ルレ・エ・シャトー東京事務所 03-3407-8858

The Wakaya Club

Managing Director
Mr. Robert Miller

*Address
P.O.Box 15424 Suva, Fiji Islands

*Phone
679-440-128

*Toll Free

*Fax
679-302-714

*Chain Affiliation
none

*Total Number of Suites
8

*Rate
Suite US$875 (all inclusive)

*Distance from
Nadi International Airport from 45 minutes by Air Wakaya

*Credit Cards
All Major

*Main Restaurant Name
The Palm Grove

type cuisine
Continental

*Other Facilities and Services
32 Private Beaches
Outdoor Pool
Tennis with Lights
9 Hole Golf Course
Croquet
Scuba Diving
Nature Walks

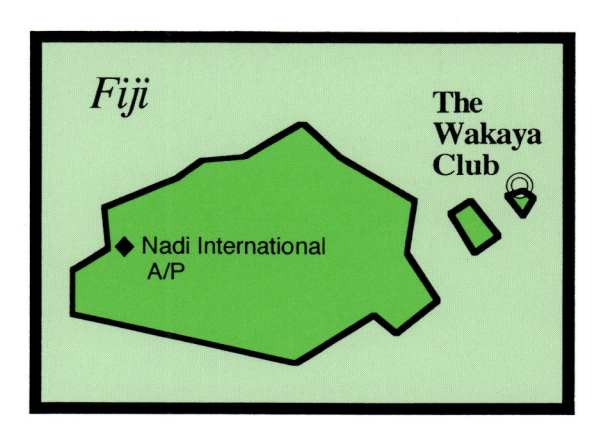

[Reservation]
The Wakaya Club USA (toll free)   1-800-828- 3454

Acknowledgments
あとがき

This book attempts to rediscover community development and architecture which people carefully tend during their day to day life against a background of the various cultures and traditions indigenous to each part of the globe.

Individuals today are living more personal lives than ever before but they are joined by a magnanimous cultural sympathy in spite of being more personalized. This disparity is also a cultural binder. New culture grows from there, and there is a maturity which has its feet planted firmly on the ground and is not grafted. This book is not a hotel guide for it contains only 18 hotels, the smallest of which has no more than 8 rooms and the largest 188 rooms. Consequently, I should like to ask your forgiveness, if more suitable examples do exist and hope that you will accept this selection.

I have troubled many people in compiling this book and I am deeply grateful especially to Bunji Murotani of Process Architecture, Teruhisa Koida for planning and compiling the book, Sigeru Oki for his wonderful photography, Tomoko Yasuda the coordinator and Chris A. Carlson. Finally and by no means least, I should like to thank all the hoteliers without whose co-operation, this publication would never have been possible.

本書は、地球上のさまざまな文化、伝統を背景に、人々の生活が大切に育んだ建築、街づくりを再発見する試みでもある。

現代は、個人がこれまでよりもさらに個性的な暮らしを生き、より個別化する方向にありながら、ゆるやかな文化的共感によって結ばれている。こうした「差異」こそ文化の紐帯である。そこに新しい文化が芽生え、接ぎ木ではない、地に足をつけた成熟がある。本書はいわゆる「ホテルガイド」ではなく、最少で8室、最大でも188室の、わずか18のホテルを取り上げたにすぎない。したがって、もっと適切な例があったとしても、ひとつの選択として、ご容赦いただきたい。

出版にあたって多くの方々の手を煩わせた。とくに、プロセスアーキテクチュア社の室谷文治氏、企画・構成の小井田光久氏、写真家の大木茂氏、コーディネイトの安田智子、C.カールソン両氏、さらにご協力いただいた各ホテルの皆さんに深く感謝します。

1993年6月吉日　著者